International Yearbook of Oral History and Life Stories

VOLUME II

1993

International Yearbook of Oral History
and Life Stories

VOLUME II

Between
Generations

Family Models, Myths,
and Memories

Editors

DANIEL BERTAUX

and

PAUL THOMPSON

OXFORD UNIVERSITY PRESS

1993

Oxford University Press, Walton Street, Oxford OX2 6DP
Oxford New York Toronto
Delhi Bombay Calcutta Madras Karachi
Kuala Lumpur Singapore Hong Kong Tokyo
Nairobi Dar es Salaam Cape Town
Melbourne Auckland Madrid
and associated companies in
Berlin Ibadan

Oxford is a trade mark of Oxford University Press

Published in the United States
by Oxford University Press Inc., New York

British Library Cataloguing in Publication Data
Data available

Library of Congress Cataloging in Publication Data
Data available
ISBN 0–19–820249–0

1 3 5 7 9 10 8 6 4 2

Typeset by Cambrian Typesetters
Frimley, Surrey
Printed in Great Britain
on acid-free paper by
Bookcraft (Bath) Ltd.
Midsomer Norton, Avon

Preface

This second volume of the *Yearbook* follows the first, edited by Luisa Passerini, on *Memory and Totalitarianism*. The tragic relevance of the struggle for new national identities drawing on the past has become painfully evident since that volume went to press: a history which we hoped that Europe would never allow to be repeated has indeed returned to haunt us all.

The question which we confront in *Between Generations* again concerns powerful memories which still shape the present, but this time it is truly international: what is it that parents pass down to their children? It is a simple question which turns out to be unexpectedly complicated, and answering it has suggested how a life-story approach can provide a new key to research both on the dynamics of the family and on social change.

The third *Yearbook* is to be on international migration and the sustaining or abandoning of memory and identity as people move between fundamentally different cultures. The special editors for that volume are North American. We intend the fourth *Yearbook* to focus on the theme of gender in public and private memory; and the fifth on the interpretation of life stories in terms of genre and narrative. For all these volumes ahead we welcome contributions from every part of the world.

Paul Thompson
November 1992

Contents

Contents

Contents

List of Contributors

LUZ GABRIELA ARANGO is a professor of sociology in the Universidad de los Andes and the Universidad Externado de Colombia, Bogotá.

DANIEL BERTAUX is directeur de recherche at the Centre d'Étude des Mouvements Sociaux in Paris.

ISABELLE BERTAUX-WIAME is a researcher in sociology at Travail et Mobilités, University of Paris X.

NATASHA BURCHARDT is a child and adolescent psychiatrist in National Health Service practice in Oxfordshire, England.

WEIYAN FARMER was a family law lecturer in Nanjing and is now a research student at the University of Essex, England.

ELENA GEORGIOU is an English-Cypriot currently working at the Hunter College Family Policy Institute in New York.

LENA INOWLOCKI is a sociologist researching on three-generation families at the University of Kassel, Germany.

MARIA DE LOURDES MONACO JANOTTI and ZITA DE PAULA ROSA are professors of history in the Pontifícia Universidade Católica de São Paulo, Brazil.

KLIMIS NAVRIDIS is a professor of Communications and Mass Media at the University of Athens.

ALESSANDRO PORTELLI is a professor of American Studies at the University of Rome, La Sapienza.

REINHARD SIEDER is profesor of history at the Institüt für Wirtschafts- und Sozialgeschichte in Vienna.

VALENTINA STOEV is a researcher at the Institute of Sociology of the Bulgarian Academy of Sciences, Sofia.

PAUL THOMPSON is research professor at the University of Essex and director of the National Life Story Collection, British Library Sound Archive, London.

Book reviews: Roswitha Breckner, Technische Universität Berlin; John J. Fox, Salem State College, Massachusetts; Birgitta Frykman, University of Göteborg; Francisca Koch, Istituto Romano per la Storia d'Italia dal Facismo alla Resistenza, Rome; Anne Muxel, Centre d'Étude de la Vie Politique Française, Paris; Freddy Raphaël, University of Strasbourg; Kim Lacy Rogers, Dickinson College, Pennsylvania; Simonetta Picone Stella, Istituto Universitario Orientale, Naples; Elizabeth Tonkin, Queen's University, Belfast.

I

Introduction

DANIEL BERTAUX and PAUL THOMPSON

Transmission between generations is as old as humanity itself. It arises from the fundamental human condition. Our lives are a fusion of nature and culture; but nature and culture are in contradiction. Because culture is the essence of what makes individual humans into a group, the core of human social identity, its continuity is vital. Certainly cultures are always changing; but only in part. And the ability of languages, religions, and cultural habits such as those concerning food to survive in the most adverse conditions can be astonishing. But in contrast to the claims of culture to represent tradition over centuries, even eternal truths, stands the sheer brevity of individual human life. Hence the universal necessity for transmission between generations.

The role of family in this intergenerational transmission goes back equally far. On the other hand, it has never held a monopoly of it. A second basic channel, with quite different rhythms, has been the peer group, which has had a particularly crucial role in the transmission of models of femininity and masculinity, sexual and social relationships, fighting and parenting. There have also been, throughout known history, more specific social institutions for transmission: apprenticeship to work skills, shamans or medical schools, apostolic successions of sacred knowledge.

It is, however, the role of the family in transmission on which this book is focused. And it is important to emphasize at the start that it is a very broad role. We may not bring up our children today to worship the shrines of family ancestors as was the practice in many European and Asian societies in the distant past. Nevertheless the family remains the main channel for the transmission of language, names, land and housing, local social standing, and religion; and beyond that also of social values and aspirations, fears, world views, domestic skills, taken-for-granted ways of behaving, attitudes to the body, models of parenting and marriage—resulting in the condensation of experiences characterizing particular class groups, which Tocqueville called 'les habitudes du cœur', the habits of the heart, and Bourdieu chose to characterize with the old word 'habitus'.[1]

Families are not, however, neat collective units. Even the word itself has many different meanings. The sense in which we refer to 'family' here is as a network of individuals related by kinship and including two or more generations. In terms of transmission, the wider family is likely to be as important as the simple family household in which most children are reared in contemporary western Europe. But while a household normally has clear boundaries, a family in our sense is less easy to pin down. This is because it is a collectivity constituted from an individual standpoint. Every person has a unique position in a family, and as a result defines relationships differently—so that my niece may be your mother-in-law; and for the same reasons, includes or excludes different members in defining the network. 'Family' is a cultural image constructed out of real individuals, and also, sometimes, mythical ancestry.

This same double-faceted character applies to transmission. Culture is social, but it is carried and realized by individuals. Most parents seek to transmit only the aspects of their family culture which they approve. Quite often, indeed, they deliberately attempt to hand down a different model, even a mirror image, in certain crucial respects. Thus the 'family strategies' of which historians and social scientists write are not so much collective strategies as selections from the culture which the family offers. Equally, one of the fundamental dynamics behind transmission is the search for individual self-perpetuation. Physically, a child is of one's own flesh: and often evidently so, witnessed through the same eyelashes, the same smile, or less luckily, the same big feet. In the same way, parents hope to see many of their own social characteristics continued through their children. More than that, they may be handing down through their ambitions for their children their own unrealized projects: to become a famous artist, or a scholar, to be comfortable, to have a loving marriage, or to be an independent woman. But again, individuality shapes not only what the family offers, but also what is taken up. Thus parents may offer their own unrealized dreams to their children, but the children on their side must either turn them down or make them their own. Transmission is at the same time individual and collective; and it takes place through a two-way relationship.

Family transmission between generations is thus an intrinsically complex process which also, because of the existence of other channels, lacks a monopoly of what may be handed down. It has in fact been frequently argued that the long-term development of more complex societies, and particularly of industrialized or 'modernized' societies, has resulted in a diminution of the role of the family in cultural transmission and the socialization of children. The trend in this direction was particularly dramatic under the totalitarian regimes of the mid-twentieth century, when specialized organizations such as the Hitler Youth or the Red Guards were used to remould young people's values away from the orbit of their families. But the idea goes back further:

if one values the existence of society . . . education must make sure that its citizens hold a sufficient community of ideas and feelings without which no society is possible; and for such an outcome, education cannot be abandoned to the arbitrariness of individuals. Since education is an essentially social function, the state cannot turn its back on it. On the contrary, everything that pertains to education must somehow be submitted to its determination. . . . The role of educator can only be fulfilled by those who possess specific qualifications, of which only the state can judge.[2]

This strong statement does not come, as one might guess, from the worlds of Stalin or of Mao, but from Émile Durkheim, founding father of sociology and a profound influence in the shaping of the French educational system. It would be difficult to put more strongly the 'modern' tendency to undervalue, and even delegitimize, family as a channel of transmission.

There are also plenty of indisputable instances of encroachments on family territories besides the impact of the growth of formal education. Economists have shown, for example, how an increasing proportion of the transfers of financial resources between generations takes place outside the family, through taxation, welfare, and pensions. Even the direction of these currents has been changing—although partly also for demographic reasons—so that it is no longer predominantly from older to younger, but from the middle adult generation to both the young and the elderly. Many social-mobility studies also suggest an evolution from 'ascription', in which the crucial determination of occupation was your father's, to a 'meritocratic' competition for jobs in an open labour market, with education as the crucial factor in reaching a high social standing. Although the narrow basis of these studies makes such inferences doubtful, they echo the wider climate of opinion of the welfare-state era.

It seems possible that a similar, less noticed process has also been happening in the sphere of cultural memory. On the one hand the last hundred years have seen a proliferation of public monuments, such as war memorials in western Europe, or giant statues of Mao and Lenin in communist countries, which create 'lieux de mémoire' for collective remembering.[3] But in the cities at least, and in England more generally, cemeteries are no longer the regularly visited shrines of family memory that they once were: how else could the City of Westminster have sold off all its cemeteries to private enterprise for a pittance? The Protestant families of southern France who take their children to the mountain refuges where their ancestors fought the armies of Louis XIV and held secret religious open-air assemblies in the woods two hundred years ago are not at all typical: they are an instance of a minority, struggling against the odds to maintain its identity.[4] With the increasingly comfortable majorities the accepted occasions on which family history and memories could be transmitted have been shrinking. Funerals and mourning in particular were radically reduced, almost as if the final pain of death would disappear if mention of it was silenced. And at the same time specialists on ageing argued that 'reminiscing' by the elderly was in itself a sign of mental and social deterioration, of an inability to adapt to the present.[5] One can indeed see how the development of oral history itself, the popularity of family genealogical research, or the media success of *Roots*,[6] have offered many people more legitimate ways of seeking the transmission of their family memory. We would also suggest that the scant attention paid by researchers to the forms of transmission which certainly continue through the family is again a reflection of its conventional devaluation.

Durkheim was not the only social scientist who assumed the shrinking of the family sphere to be one of the hallmarks of historical progress. The same assumptions underlie the thinking of Talcott Parsons in post-war America and his 'functional' division of social life between the masculine 'instrumental' world of work and the feminine 'affective' sphere of the home. The return of married women to paid work has ended that male dream-world. Nor is he the only grand theorist of family and socialization dwarfed by subsequent history. Margaret Mead in her widely read book on the youth movements of the 1960s,[7] drew on a full life's work in anthropology to set out a three-stage development of human societies in terms of intergenerational relationships. In the earliest, pre-literate societies, which she calls 'post-figurative', grandparents are the dominant holders both of social knowledge and of moral authority, and they therefore are the socializers of the children. In the second stage, as the pace of change quickens, the practical experience and skills of the grandparents become obsolete, and parents become the transmitters in this sphere; but the older generation still tell the young what is right and wrong. In the third stage, with change still faster, and also with the increase in long-distance migration, the parents too find their life experiences and skills and even their moral views redundant. The children are left on their own to pick up and teach each other—and often their parents too—new skills, new values, new ways of living. Only the young are nimble enough to look forward, to anticipate the future course of their societies; hence Mead called them 'prefigurative'. She saw the rebellion of young Americans as heralding the advent of this new stage.

The 1970s showed that she was mistaken. The older generation remained in economic power and political control, while the young sought jobs rather than to change the system. Mead's misunderstanding came from her failure to distinguish the coexistence of many different channels of transmission. The challenges to parental authority in the 1960s were certainly important and reflected fundamental changes, particularly in the separation of sexuality from family-building; and the resulting tremors also temporarily shook the educational systems. But in Western countries transmission in political and economic spheres was little affected. Significantly, it was only in China, where the youth rebellion was deliberately instigated by the ageing Mao for his own political purposes, that it penetrated the whole social system. And equally significantly, the outcome was not the revolutionary progress for which he had hoped, but a collapse of civic society and politics into anarchical violence and bitter individualistic cruelty.[8]

The early 1990s offer us, however, another viewpoint as a result of the collapse of the Communist societies which Stalin and Mao had built. A century earlier, Durkheim's optimistic faith in progress and rationalization had been wholly in tune with the thinking of his time; as also Max Weber's analyses of historical development through bureaucratization. But by a curious twist of history, their utopian visions were realized in nightmares, of which the most sustained was the reign of Stalin. His centralized system aimed to have all under its gaze, responsive to its iron will. It is notable that two of the centres of resistance which the totalitarian system repeatedly sought to destroy were the family and memory. Family properties were seized and family enterprises suppressed. Not only having been a capitalist, or a political opponent, but even being descended from one became a pretext for social exclusion or imprisonment. Public statues were replaced, streets and towns renamed. Whole peoples were uprooted from where they lived and forcibly resettled; and some of them too were renamed. Children were forced to denounce their parents. More fortunate families kept their past a secret and, if need be, changed to safer names before being exposed.

The collapse of these totalitarian societies has had a double consequence. The first is that a vital part of their struggle to transform themselves into democratic societies has been to recover the histories of family and everyday life that had been suppressed for two or in the Russian case three or four generations. Living testimonies constitute a crucial part of this huge effort. They were already the inspiration of its anticipation in Solzhenitzyn's *Gulag Archipelago*.[9] This is why in the major Russian cities the Memorial associations documenting the victims of Stalin have not only attracted thousands of members, but can be seen with their banners among the leading democratic pressure groups in political demonstrations.

The second consequence is a new salience of the experience of grandparents, and especially of grandmothers. They have always played a crucial role in Russian families, very often raising children for working mothers, so that the emotional bonds across the generations remained stronger than in western Europe. They were also the last generation to have an extensive knowledge of religious practices. Not surprisingly, they have proved an invaluable resource in the turning back to religion which many Russians have sought in the moral vacuum following the collapse of the Communist world view. But more surprisingly, there is also evidence that their earlier practical life experience can be equally significant. Their generation survived even harsher periods of social disorder, economic collapse, and famine in the years immediately following the 1917 Communist revolution. Many of them suffered extreme hardship and only survived through drastic adaptations. In the present context, it is above all those among the young people who were brought up by grandmothers such as these who are now able to follow them as models and seize their chances in the new market system.[10]

As we have already hinted, the topic of this book, although fundamental to human society both past and present, is not one which has so far been much studied, particularly at a general level. The most ambitious attempt has been in Pierre Legendre's series of volumes. His final conclusion, 'that the object of transmission, is to transmit',[11] may seem at first glance merely tautological; but it is indeed important that for most transmissions between generations the significance of the particular content is, for the participants, much less than the fact that transmission to children in itself constitutes a relationship transcending the limitations of human mortality. It is probably more accurate, however, to say that the objective content, whether a piece of land, a genealogical tree, or a style of flirting, is loaded with psychological meanings: with projections and identifications, love and anger, symbols and desires. In so far as human psychology reaches beyond cultural differences it touches upon human universals: and there does indeed appear to be a universality in the desire to transmit.

It has been proposed by Erick Erikson that in the life cycle of human psychological development the desire to transmit normally arises at a specific point.[12] Provided that identity has been firmly established during adolescence and intimacy subsequently achieved in early adulthood, men and women then feel a growing wish to create new lives and hand on all that they can give to a younger generation. This desire for 'generativity', as Erikson termed it, is directly linked to each individual's personal experience of childhood. Those who were brought up with sufficient affection and love, and taught the basis of how to live by significant parental or quasi-parental figures, feel a growing urge to *give back*, as if a hitherto secret feeling of debt built into their psyche, like a mole, had waited for the right moment to emerge into the light. Fulfilment of this desire for 'generativity' can also be found in teaching and caring relationships for other children than one's own, but is, of course, most often realized directly within the family. Oral historians and gerontologists would rightly criticize Erikson's exclusive focus on such an early phase in adulthood, especially given the well-recognized wish to transmit which character-izes the 'life review' phase typical in later life after transitions and losses such as widowhood and retirement.[13] Conversely, oral historians themselves need to recognize how early transmission can begin.

Nevertheless such suggestions, however interesting, do not take us much closer to the understanding of transmission in practice. In this respect we have found considerably more helpful the 'family systems' approach, which has been developed by therapists working with two or more generations of families whose problems appear to have been transmitted within the family.[14] Although the cases on which the family systems interpretation has been developed are of families with a significant degree of distress, or even, like Holocaust survivors, have suffered exceptionally traumatic experiences, the approach has much more general implications. A family system is defined as an interpersonal unit of two or more persons with a continuous contractual relationship, and the structure of the system is examined in terms of the relationships and the assumptions which underlie them. Writers on family systems and therapy emphasize especially the need for families to develop clear rules and order in their interpersonal relationships, and in particular to establish boundaries and differentiation between generations. They suggest that where pathologies appear to have transgenerational sources, this may be because the older generations are unable to distinguish clearly enough between themselves and their children, and the children have failed to establish their independence. Consequently parents transmit unresolved tensions, frustrations, and hostilities in their own lives and relationships to their children. When they project such problems with sufficient power, they can pin down their life paths to the demands of 'ghosts', or push children into becoming anxious 'parental figures' more concerned with appeasing their parents' unmet pains than with taking hold of their own lives. Intergenerational transmissions of such a negative kind are often discovered by therapists treating children suffering from anorexia nervosa or depression. These observations mesh closely with our own understanding developed through interviewing families from the general population—with one qualification, that family therapists have perhaps underestimated the normality of the transmission processes which they describe.

The systems approach has also led to a useful specification of some of the roles commonly observed in families in relation to transmission. Therapists have noted how often one member of a family may be assigned or take on the role of peacemaker, or the family conscience, or symbol of the older generation. In particular one family member, usually but not always a woman, often takes on the role of the one who tells family stories, and others, when seeking information about the past, will turn first to her. John Byng-Hall has written particularly eloquently about the role of the family story itself in creating a 'script' which successive generations may appear compelled to follow.[15] We return to this point in more detail later (see Thompson). These observations have been generated by clinical interviews which typically bring together more than two family members, for relatively short sessions, and are focused on present problems. But they are confirmed by life-story interviews which, it should be added, provide a much fuller and more complex account of the development of inter-generational relations in a family through coherent, extended state-ments from the perspective of individual family members. In clinical sessions the approach is thematic rather than historical, there is no space for extended individual narrative, and vital information about some family members may often be missed.[16]

In principle, it might be expected that research by anthropologists and historians would also throw considerable light on the issues which concern us. Indeed, both anthropologists and (mostly oral) historians came together in an earlier volume on *The Myths We Live By*; but the only articles focusing on the transmission of myths within families were in fact from two practising family therapists.[17] Anthropologists seem to have examined systematically only the specialized genres of long-term intergenerational transmission of 'oral tradition', and that too most typically at a communal rather than familial level. The recent work of Elizabeth Tonkin, in calling for a new focus on the often informal processes of *Narrating our Pasts* in everyday life, is an important and encouraging new development which very much needs to be followed up. Nor, if an Africanist concerned with 'traditional' societies needs to take a new stand of this kind, is it so surprising that the transmission of memory within families has been even less studied in Western societies. As Anne Muxel indicates in her review article here, the gleanings are surprisingly thin even in France, where the understanding of memory as a social phenomenon goes back to the pioneering work of Maurice Halbwachs in the 1920s. Nor in the United States is there any serious parallel to the entertaining popular investigation offered by Elizabeth Stone in *Black Sheep and Kissing Cousins*.[18]

There are certainly a number of studies by historians and social scientists which concern specific aspects of more material transmission. Some political scientists have tried to measure the extent to which children take their political attitudes from their parents.[19] Studies of the difficulties of immigrants in adapting and integrating into their 'host societies' can be reread in terms of their maintenance or abandonment of cultural transmission. Accounts by linguists of the attenuation, spread, or fusion of languages have similar implications. Both historians and economists have examined general patterns in the transfer of wealth and property.[20] Sociologists, and a few historians, have made statistical analyses of the transmission of occupational status between generations, usually from fathers to sons.[21] All this research seems, however, surprisingly compartmentalized—so that, for example, social-mobility studies are rarely concerned with the inheritance of capital—and therefore contributes much less than it could do to the understanding of the overall phenomenon of transmission.

We have indeed arrived at the overall question ourselves as one consequence of an empirical research project on 'Families and Social Mobility' which we began ten years ago and are still pursuing.[22] In conceiving this Anglo-French project we took a crucial leap in bringing together the previously unrelated research fields combined in the project's title. Our intention was also to combine the strengths of qualitative and quantitative research by using a random-sample basis for our choice of families. In each family our aim was to interview at least two generations. The result has been an immersion in extraordinarily rich life-story material which demonstrates irrefutably how the social, economic, and psychological dimensions of transmission are inextricably mixed. We hope that through this issue of the *Yearbook* many other researchers will be able to grasp the opportunities which this new perspective opens.

Since the first two articles which follow, by Thompson and Bertaux-Wiame, spring directly from this project and spell out in much greater detail the thinking which has developed from it, neither of them requires further introduction. A second group of articles looks at situations in which abrupt external changes have been imposed on the family, interrupting previous patterns of the transmission of values. Arango shows how a succession of sharply different ideologies of work changed the family roles which were open to women in a Colombian factory town, and so also transformed the character of intergenerational relationships. Navridis examines how in a northern Greek village which survived depopulation through agricultural development, new attitudes to money and its inheritance again reshaped family relationships. Farmer argues that the dramatic politically imposed transformation of Chinese views on marriage and love has broken earlier patterns of transmission between mothers and daughters and even in some instances reversed its direction.

The third group of articles (and also a double review article) focuses on the period of National Socialism and its aftermath. Sieder's account of the socialization of an Austrian Nazi based on a very extended narrative interview shows not only the complex interweaving of family and wider social and political influences, but also how his tortuous relationship with his father made him open to reinterpretations of family influence as well as to particular choices from the attitudes pressed on him through his peer group and community. Burchardt and Inowlocki look at the other side of the Nazi legacy: how the families of Holocaust survivors have sought both to convey the cultural continuity of their Jewishness, and also to avoid conveying aspects of their family histories which are too painful either to tell or to hear.

The last three articles concern the transmission of family memory itself, each in a context of radical social change. Janotti and Rosa show the means through which black Brazilian families in São Paulo continue to pass down their own family memories and myths of slavery times, which can still shape their sense of social identity and their demands for social change now. Georgiou describes how for a migrant Greek Cypriot family oral history itself provided an opportunity for a granddaughter to record a grandmother's life story: but a truncated story in which certain well-known family 'secrets' were conspicuously missing. Finally Stoev's autobiographical family story shows how it was precisely the family secrets about an alternative world view which were not only transmitted throughout the Communist epoch in eastern Europe, but now provide a crucial psychic inspiration for men and women who, like herself, are today struggling to construct a different society amidst its rubble.

Notes

1. Alexis de Tocqueville, *Democracy in America*, trans. George Lawrence, ed. J. P. Mayer, New York, 1969, 287; Pierre Bourdieu, *Distinction: A Social Critique of the Judgement of Taste* (Cambridge, Mass., 1984), and *Esquisse d'une théorie de la pratique* (Geneva, 1972).
2. Émile Durkheim, *Éducation et sociologie* (Paris (1922) 1989), 59.
3. Pierre Nora, *Les lieux de mémoire* (Paris, 1984); Gerard Namer, *Mémoire et société* (Paris, 1987); Jacques Le Goff, *Histoire et mémoire* (Paris, 1988); Alain Brossat *et al.* (eds.), *A l'est la mémoire retrouvée* (Paris, 1990).
4. Françoise Zonabend, *La mémoire longue* (Paris, 1980); Philippe Joutard, *La légende des Camisards* (Paris, 1977); Pierre Gaudin and Claire Reverchon, 'Le sens du tragique dans la mémoire historique: Un exemple dans la Drôme', *IVme Colloque International d'Histoire Orale* (Aix-en-Provence, 1982), 89–98.
5. Paul Thompson, *The Voice of the Past* (Oxford, 1988), 160–4.
6. Alex Haley, *Roots* (New York, 1976); Tamara Hareven, 'The Search for Generational Memory', *Daedalus*, 106 (Fall 1978), 137–49.
7. Margaret Mead, *Culture and Commitment: A Study of the Generation Gap* (New York, 1970).
8. One of the most powerful descriptions of the Cultural Revolution in China is in the

transgenerational story of a grandmother, mother, and daughter, fusing oral testimony and autobiography: Jung Chang, *Wild Swans: Three Daughters of China* (London, 1991). This also reveals how much personal and family experience contributed to making Jung Chang's parents dedicated Communists, as well as to her own rejection of Communism.

9. Alexander Solzhenitzyn, *The Gulag Archipelago* (London, 1974).

10. Victoria Semenova, 'The Situation of a Socioeconomic Crisis in the Life Experience of Families: History and the Present', paper, Latky, 1992.

11. Pierre Legendre, *L'inestimable Objet de la transmission: Études sur le principe généalogique en Occident* (Paris, 1985).

12. Erik Erikson, *Identity and the Life Cycle* (New York, 1959).

13. Thompson, *Voice of the Past*, 113–17.

14. Murray Bowen, 'The Use of Family Theory in Clinical Practice', *Comprehensive Psychiatry*, 7 (1966), 345–74; G. Spark, 'Grandparents and Intergenerational Family Process', *Family Process*, 13 (1974), 225; Karl Menninger, *Love against Hate* (New York, 1958); Carl Whitaker, *Marital and Family Therapy* (Chicago, 1970); I. Boszormenyi-Nagy and G. Spark, *Invisible Loyalties* (New York, 1973).

15. John Byng-Hall, 'Family Legends: Their Significance for the Family Therapist', in A. Bentovim, G. Gorell Barnes, and A. Cooklin (eds.), *Family Therapy: Complementary Frameworks of Theory and Practice* (London, 1982), 213–28.

16. These comments are based in particular on the pilot work for a continuing project, 'Growing Up in Stepfamilies: A Long-term Study', by Gill Gorell Barnes, Natasha Burchardt, Gwyn Daniel, and Paul Thompson, for which an experiment was made in carrying out subsequent life-story interviews with some members of families whose earlier therapy sessions had been recorded.

17. 'The Power of Family Myths': John Byng-Hall interviewed by Paul Thompson, and Natasha Burchardt, 'Stepchildren's Memories: Myth, Understanding and Forgiveness', in Raphael Samuel and Paul Thompson (eds.), *The Myths We Live By* (London, 1990), 216–24 and 239–51.

18. Elizabeth Tonkin, *Narrating our Pasts: The Social Construction of Oral History* (Cambridge, 1992); Elizabeth Stone, *Black Sheep and Kissing Cousins: How Family Stories Shape Us* (New York, 1988).

19. David Butler and Donald Stokes, *Political Change in Britain* (London, 1969); Anne Muxel and Annick Percheron, 'Histoires politiques de famille: Premières illustrations', *Life Stories/Récits de vie*, 4 (1988), 59–72.

20. A. B. Atkinson, *The Economics of Inequality* (Oxford, 1983); Jack Goody, Joan Thirsk, and E. P. Thompson (eds.), *Family and Inheritance: Rural Society in Western Europe, 1200–1800* (Cambridge, 1976); Leonore Davidoff and Catherine Hall, *Family Fortunes: Men and Women of the English Middle Class, 1780–1850* (London, 1987); Paul Thompson, Catherine Itzin, and Michele Abendstern, *I Don't Feel Old: The Experience of Later Life* (Oxford, 1990), 24–30.

21. Robert Erikson and John Goldthorpe (eds.), *The Constant Flux: A Study of Class Mobility in Industrial Societies* (Oxford, 1992).

22. Daniel Bertaux, 'Familles et mobilité sociale: La méthode de généalogies sociales comparées', in Ana Nunes de Almeida, Maria las Dores Guerreiro, Anália Torres, and Karin Wall (eds.), *Famílles et contextes sociaux* (Lisbon, 1992), 315 ff.; and 'Social Genealogies Commented and Compared: An Instrument for the Observation of Social Mobility Processes in the "Longue Durée" ', *Current Sociology*, forthcoming.

2

Family Myth, Models, and Denials in the Shaping of Individual Life Paths

PAUL THOMPSON

For most of us it is a commonplace that who we are, who we have become both socially and personally, is rooted in our families and yet also—for some much more decisively, for some much less—distinct from them. Telling one's own life story requires not only recounting directly remembered experience, but also drawing on information and stories transmitted across the generations, both about the years too early in childhood to remember, and also further back in time beyond one's own birth. Life stories are thus, in themselves, a form of transmission; but at the same time they often indicate in a broader sense what is passed down in families. My purpose here is to ask what they can tell us in both ways about the process and the scope of intergenerational transmission.

When Ben Bradgate, English North-country ex-miner, by then in his mid-seventies and living in poverty, was asked when he was born, he replied:

That's a story in itself! I was the youngest to be born in the family. I had, there was nine of us . . . and the story goes that when I were born—I suppose me mum would be getting on like, and probably be almost beyond child-bearing, really—when I was born they said I was so very small, they never expected me to live. I was born in 1912, and that's famous for another thing, isn't it, the *Titanic* went down didn't it? And so I was born a Catholic, a Roman Catholic, and they always a tendency, they still have, of getting the children christened as soon as humanly possible: so when they saw me, I believe the weight was 2 lb. 1 oz., and after two days they wrapped me up in cotton wool, pushed me off to the church . . . this is only what they've told me . . . then I was wrapped in cotton wool, and when the priest saw me, he said, 'Sure 'n' all', he said, 'this is the smallest baby I ever did christen.'

And so anyhow they looked after me, and kept me warm in cotton wool, and then I got through the initial stages, and apparently I was just about getting to crawling, about ten or eleven months, and the priest had a habit of calling on the parishioners for his cash, you see, monthly . . . and mother invited him in, and I was crawling under the old table that we had, and he said, 'Is that the small baby I christened, Mrs Bradgate?' 'Yes, father.' 'And sure 'n' all, he'll be the main support yet!'[1]

The intermingling of a family and personal story, and even some sense of a more public history beyond them, can be found in innumerable personal accounts. But Ben was a more artful narrator than most—after decades of evenings in the pub, where he also performed as an amateur singer at the piano—and he has also managed to slip into this story of his birth two of the principal themes of his entire life. These were religion and work. Both themes were embedded in his family tradition, yet also a rejection of that tradition: like his infant survival, against the odds. He abandoned religious practice of any kind after the family bitterness which ensued when he chose to make a love-marriage to a Protestant—although one of his sons has reconverted to Catholicism, again on marriage. And he worked a full fifty years, over thirty in the pits, indeed supporting his parents, his wife, and his four children; but here too he both took up his family tradition and turned against it.

There was never much doubt that Ben was destined to become a miner. His parents had 'come to the conclusion, like, long before I was going to school, there's only one thing for us all, pit'. His father's sister's husband's family were pit bosses:

and, you see, that story that led to us all going and working in that pit, you see, because when they [his parents] married and went to Bidley, it came out that [aunt] Maggie's husband's brother was the under-manager, the boss underground, his other brother, the elder one, Bill Dainton, was the general manager. So what would you do if you're a family with a lot of kids and they want a job? Found me dad a job, to start off with: he said, 'Come to the pit and we'll find you a job, a nice job', he said, 'it'll be night turn but you'll have nothing to do, just knocking about the pit, watching people.' Well, he took us all, eventually.

Ben was almost 50 before he worked above ground, as a school caretaker. But he was absolutely certain that he did not want his own sons to follow him as a miner, nor did they:

before either of them left school, I said, 'I can't rule you, but my advice to you is to try and keep away from pit work, colliery work. I can't make you, it's up to you, but I don't advise it.' Cos I'd done my life in it.[2]

A life story of this kind is at once the raw material of social history and of the interpretation of social mobility. It is at the same time both a personal self-analysis, and an example of oral literature. It can be equally read as true or as mythical. It brings together direct personal testimony with collective memory to build up an individual auto-biography and identity. And nothing could sum up better the complexity of the transmission of family influences across the generations. It shows both the strength of transgenerational family culture, and how within that framework individuals can choose not only to accept but also to reject their transgenerational inheritance.

Yet life stories are surprisingly rarely read for the understanding which they can give of intergenerational transmission. We could learn much from examining just how they are told, how they fuse the personal with the familial, the material with the symbolic: but the literary specialists of genre have focused almost entirely on 'oral literature' of a more formal kind found in still predominantly oral cultures beyond the developed Western world.[3] Historians are trained to search for evidence of the past as it was, rather than the past in the present. Still worse if tampered with in the transmission: family stories seem the most trivial—if therefore professionally the least discomfort-ing—of *The Myths We live By*.[4] Social scientists have taken life stories more seriously, and anthropologists especially are at ease with myth, although principally outside the West; but again, the very sociologists for whom transmission between generations must be a central issue, those who research into social mobility, have proved peculiarly blind to their potential value.[5]

This blindness would seem to rest not in theory but on a methodological narrowness which in turn constrains conceptual development. Thus despite a general recognition of the importance of parental influence and other familial factors both in achievement and in the definition of social status, investigations of social mobility have been almost exclusively focused on statistical studies of *individual* occupational mobility—and a mobility evaluated, because of the broken careers typical of women, primarily through the occupations of men.[6] This characteristic strategy, individualistic, work-centred, and based on standardized questionnaires rather than in-depth interview-ing, has effectively prevented consideration not only of the role of the family in social mobility, but even of the social mobility of women as individuals.

This article began with the analysis of an Anglo-French comparative study, carried out with Daniel Bertaux and Isabelle Bertaux-Wiame, whose objective has been to link the normally separate fields of study, social mobility and the family. For this, in Britain interviews were carried out with a hundred families, selected on the basis of a random representative sample, and where possible two or three generations were interviewed within each family.[7] Here I have also drawn on a second set of life-story interviews, again taken from a random sample, this time with adults who grew up as stepchildren.[8]

It became quickly apparent that introducing a family dimension could throw a different light even on the occupational mobility of individuals between generations. There are striking differences, for instance, on the impact of family commitments on men and women. Thus with the middle generation, born between 1930 and 1955, most men move upward through their working lives to reach their highest occupation during middle age. Women by contrast typically peak early, by the age of 30, and then, with the combined effect of marriage and child-bearing, plunge downward. Only a few recover their position; still fewer their momentum. Social-mobility studies, through their concentration on male occupations, give very misleading impressions of the impact of marriage on women. On the contrary, almost half the women who did succeed in rising occupationally above the level of their parents had been divorced. Men who rose were almost all backed by their wives; women usually rose despite marriage, or after putting it behind them.

The freedom to fly of those who broke with a marriage did, however, also apply to men: and both men and women were as likely to fall as to rise. Risers and fallers were each more than three times as likely as occupational stayers to be divorced.

There is a parallel interweaving of socio-economic and familial factors in terms of geographical mobility. Half of the stayers and nearly half of the fallers were rooted by local networks of kin and friends, having lived close by for three or more generations. Not one of the risers was similarly embedded. There was undoubtedly a heavy loss to face in leaving a neighbourhood 'like a family in itself', however obvious it might be that there was little chance of self-importance in a declining industrial area. As a steelworker put it of his brother,

He wants to get out of it really, he wants to finish. He's had enough really. Long time. Well we are like that down here. Once we have a job, we stick to it. But there's no choice, see. It's always been the same down here. We have the mines, tinworks, or whatever's going: or if they go to university they go further.

Another Welshman, who had moved to the South-East with his family as a teenager, saw the same choice from the other side. At the time of decision, both grandfathers had lost a leg in pit accidents, and four of his five uncles were chronically sick:

one of the reasons why me father moved up here was because he didn't want his children working in the pit. . . . The place is still the same, if not worse, it's getting run down. There's no work there or nothing, do you know what I mean? It looks worse than when we came away from there. Everywhere's shut, all the shops are shut, all boarded up. It depresses you going back. Nothing's changed. It's still the same, still very slow. But the community down there is a lot closer than it is up here . . . in and out of people's houses all the time . . .— you'd just walk in. . . . I was heartbroken when me father said we was coming here to live, I couldn't take it at first. . . . Oh yes. We found it very hard settling up here.[9]

Typically, the decision was made as much in family as in individual terms. The process of migration was very often through family help too; and in particular, those who did not settle permanently, but became return migrants, did so for family reasons. Migrants, like the divorced, were also free to fly, but the effects were more diverse. Some found their families torn apart by too frequent moves; others resettled into other working-class neighbourhoods. Some never quite recovered from a long-distance flight to avoid disaster; while yet others, on the contrary, were able to seize on the new opportunities which they found. These include not only immigrants from other cultures, bringing with them peasant or family-business entrepreneurial skills, but also long-distance British working-class migrants, cut off from their traditional contexts, who positively encouraged their children to better themselves through education, and most often specifically to become teachers. Some of these upwardly mobile internal migrants had moved as children with their families, while others left their communities to pursue their own education and careers.

These paths of social mobility are of course well known and have been described in many classic social studies of immigration and education. We were surprised, however, to find them almost exclusively among long-distance migrants. Neither minor entrepreneurial activity nor—with one exception—the conscious use of the education system as a mobility path appear at all among our locally embedded urban British working-class families. The comparison with France is helpful here. In France a much higher proportion of families are of peasant, small shopkeeper, or artisan origin, so that the first type of migrant is much more common. It seems likely that the most typical relationships between the presence or absence of social mobility and the strength of British family culture reflect the earlier establishment and deeper rooting of an urban and industrial working class in Britain and the relatively slow pace of change up to the late 1970s.

Certainly in Britain, both among middle-class and working-class geographical stayers or short migrants, family culture appears to work much more conservatively and protectively. Well-educated parents ensure that their children are educated too; entrepreneurial families attempt—with mixed success—to maintain their small businesses as builders or specialist craft producers or shopkeepers; working-class children follow their parents into the steelworks or the mill or the car factory. Partly on the basis of earlier findings by our French colleagues in France and Québec, with families we now note to be typically migrants of rural origin (as have also the subjects of most North American studies of immigration), we had anticipated finding instances of family projects of upward social mobility through business or education much more widespread. It began to appear that a cohesive family culture typically becomes dynamic only in response to a sharply changing social and economic context, such as long-distance migration.

I have so far presented our findings in terms of overall patterns of mobility among individual men and women, interpreted through placing them in their family and social context. But it soon became clear from reading the interviews that individual mobility is often generated by a family dynamic over two or three generations. This even shows up statistically. Thus risers tend to have small families and fallers large ones: two as against three children is the median complete family size. The same contrast is repeated with their families of origin, the risers coming from families with a median of two children, the fallers of four. And only children, who appear only once among the fallers, with the risers constituting one-third in terms of both family of origin and family of marriage.

There were other indications which also strongly suggested the mobility needed to be understood as a transgenerational process. We have already noted this in relation to migration: it should be added that there were a few families who seemed to be transgenerational travellers. Divorce was also a transgenerational pattern; and more surprisingly, not only were risers more likely to be divorced themselves, but they were somewhat more likely to have grown up as stepchildren. Yet another sign was the role in some families of an aspiring mother, who had acquired middle-class values either because her own parents had been middle-class and she had married a lower-status husband, or because of working in service or as a teacher or a nurse: a broader version of the 'sunken middle-class' mothers first noted by Jackson and Marsden.[10]

All these patterns challenge conventional assumptions about the positive function of family influence in social mobility. On the contrary, it would seem that in the context of a relatively stable society such as twentieth-century Britain, the effect of family culture and cohesion is essentially conservative and protective rather than dynamic. Furthermore, the larger and more rooted a family, the more this will be. The ties may be loosened in a number of different ways: through migration, through being a small one-child family, or even through family breakdown. We may cite two exceptions which illustrate the rule. One is a transgenerational Coventry family of car workers with a lone sibling riser, 'the clever bod of the family', who had gone to university and on a professional career in engineering design. He turned out to have been brought up outside the family, after suffering from polio as a boy.

Still more remarkable is the story of the son of a laundress, born in a southern railway town with a double handicap: not only illegitimate, but blind. Name apart, 'I don't know anything about my father—at all'. However, he never lived with his railwayman stepfather, stepbrother, or half-sister: from the age of 3 he too was severed from his family, and educated in specialist boarding-schools for the blind. For five years as a child, he never even visited home. Today he is a civil servant.[11] One way or another, it appears that the loosening of family ties may often be an essential prelude to upward social mobility, either backed by family support or through lone determination. Equally, the loosening may be a necessary consequence. But either way, it is typically a long-term transgenerational process.

How could we best make sense of these hints? As the work of interpretation of the interviews has gone forward, we have taken three successive steps in broadening our perspective. The first was intrinsic to the original project: to take advantage of the shift of focus from individual to familial mobility and widen the focus of analysis. Occupation ceased to be the sole indicator of social position: family housing, education, culture, and inheritance could also be taken into account. Women, instead of being largely ignored, gained a central role as child-rearers and as transmitters of family influence and also of their own independent occupational culture (as in the cases of women teachers). Secondly and equally important, rather than simply documenting the mobility which occurs, motivations, relationships, and emotions also become accessible. We began to look for ways in which we could convincingly bring together social and more psychological material at the level of particular cases. Thirdly, we began to look again at what the life stories could tell us about the manner in which family traditions were handed down. We came to see our task, in short, as to identify, through the close analysis of this rich and varied data, the processes of intergenerational transmission.

We have been looking at this question in two ways. The first (influenced by Bourdieu) is to ask what aspects of a family's material and cultural capital can be transmitted, and how this is achieved.[12] Among the English aristocracy the transfer of landed estates and country houses intact to the eldest son has been paramount for centuries, inextricably bound up with the maintenance of genealogical lineage. The middle classes, by contrast, have preferred equal division of their wealth between their children; although among the well-to-do the sharing of a common holiday house in the countryside may again be a powerful symbol of family continuity. One hundred British families, however, included none of this élite: no ancestral home, breathing and changing over the years like Virginia Woolf's living reincarnation in *Orlando*; just one genealogy traced back before the eighteenth century, and very few indeed beyond great-grandparents; and as to money or investments, nothing notable beyond, in more than one family, legendary hints of former wealth that has been lost. One artisan family, for example, spoke of the great-grandfather, a rich silk merchant, who had cut off his daughter for marrying beneath her—'it wasn't a very happy thing that'; another of losing their inheritance from a well-to-do textile designer by being 'done out of their money' by a lawyer.[13]

   There was, on the other hand, a frequent transmission of cultural capital. Among the professional classes, both risers and stayers, education—often linked to the encouragement of reasoning—recurs as a paramount value, in sharp contrast to the lack of emphasis, or even negative values, which characterize both working-class stayers and fallers. One Welsh grandfather, a 'college-educated' man who had become a shopkeeper, would tell his children:

'God gave us a mind and a brain, and eyes and ears, and a mouth,' he said: 'look, listen, see, hear, talk. . . . If you think a thing's wrong, or it doesn't click', he said, 'try and find out about it, try and see if you can get a book and read up . . .'. He said, 'Think about it, and question it. That's the only way you can learn', he said. 'Cos what other people are telling you are their ideas', he said, 'and you have got different ideas.'

In a similar spirit, a three-generational northern family of teachers see even the control of children as a form of learning. As the grandfather put it, 'we both took the attitude that preaching at them and using the heavy hand was a bit stupid—that would be counter-productive'; so the grandmother, a headmaster's daughter and herself a teacher, would 'explain to them why she thought it and that was it: they would listen to her'. And in turn her son says of his own children, when they err, 'usually the more serious, the more discussion involved'.[14]

A different form of transmission, which can occur at any social level, is of social networks. Among small-business, clerical, and working-class families these can often prove the key to work. Ben Bradgate's pit manager kin are an instance; and it was not uncommon for families to colonize a particular firm, not only speaking for relatives and friends to find work, but also marrying workmates and so extending the net. Besides the pits, examples include sweet factories, textile mills, the railways, the post office, and the Gas Board: in the last, for example, one woman secretary worked for the same employer as both her parents, her two aunts, her uncle, and one of her cousins—'I suppose in some ways it was just mapped out that I would get an office job.' For small-business families, however, a network of clients may be as significant: indeed, they could propel the family succession. One Lancashire barber, who had himself started as 'lather boy for me grandad', had later practised from his own home where he 'made the front room into a hairdresser's shop'; and when he died, his son, 'our Ronnie, took over, just at nights—hairdressing, just to keep the customers happy, and to keep me mother happy. "You should have taken this on from your father." '[15]

In a family business, whether or not customers are inherited, there will always be a transmission of work opportunities, and sometimes at the same time of working equipment and specialized skills. The Mullens, a four-generation family of Midlands silversmiths, are a rare classic instance. Sal's grandfather, two great-uncles, father and mother, brother, husband, father-in-law, and two sons have all worked in the trade. 'My father used to work for his father, and his workplace was built at the top of the garden, so when I was old enough to go with my father, he used to take me down to work.' The grandfather who founded the firm is now a legendary example in the family story:

My grandfather kept tight reins on everything until the day he died. He wouldn't even have a telephone put in the factory. He used to say, 'If people want us and want our stuff, they'll come'—and they did. It had a very good name. They made spoons, cutlery . . . only spoon maker in Birmingham. Oh, a very good living, yes. He never paid my father hardly anything—ten shillings a week.[16] He had to work for every penny he got.

Sal's father took a bitter resentment against him, and the trade into which he had been born, to his grave: as he lay dying, he was heard to mutter, 'I never liked spoons.' Her husband felt a similar ambivalence, for he had been drawn back into it against his will when his father's firm had been in crisis. 'He wanted to be an accountant, so he started that, and then his father became very ill, and he was asked to go and help his father. And he went into the family business, and he's never ever liked it.' Yet in just the same way, he took his own son back into the trade: but Steve, by contrast, came gladly. 'He was going through a sticky patch, and at the time he needed me, and I didn't take much pulling away from college.' Steve has tried to introduce new approaches, often against his father's instincts: 'we argue a hell of a lot. . . . I look to the future, and I'm probably a bit more pushy than my father would like.' But he also looks back, for personal inspiration, to the example of his own grandfather:

I go round the factory and I see what that guy did, and I've got a tremendous amount of respect for him. . . . Now he was a really strong character, very determined guy. I think I would have liked him . . . from what people have told me about him, through work, and people round the trade who knew him: he was a very aggressive guy, very fair, pig-headed, and in some ways I'm a bit the same. In work, I know what's right. . . . I'm very meticulous and very thorough, and I've got a reputation. 'If you want a good job done, take it to Mullens.'[17]

Despite all its twists at a personal level, this is the most straightforward instance we have of the transmission of a family business. It seems much more common for small entrepreneurial families to change trades, and quite often to move towns too, from generation to generation: and yet to remain entrepreneurs.[18] In a much less easily defined form they seem nevertheless to pass on a way of living, the knack of trading. The Lancashire barber's children, for instance, did not stick with hairdressing, but one married into a 'corner shop, toffees, pop, potatoes, etc.', while another similarly set up a fish shop with his wife, taking as his family inheritance a speed in learning new skills. His father had been a 'self-taught' barber: 'he were a bit sharp, so he probably practised on me mother for a while till he got things right'. When his elder brother succeeded his father, he simply 'took a few lessons off somebody who didn't know how to cut hair, and he started'. And when he bought a shop himself, it was accidental that it was a fish shop which had come up for sale, and 'very difficult at first because half the time you don't know what you are doing': at the start, he did not even know one fish from another.

But we're learning. I'd say now that we're giving better service than any fish shop in Coketown, and the place that we buy stuff from, well, we know more about the fish than they do that sell it. . . . I did a lot of asking. It's been hard graft. . . . That's me ambition, to make it successful.[19]

Others emphasize, and even mythologize, their skill in dealing. One family from southern England have been in and out of joinery and building businesses and shops for four generations, but the father became a building workman, later employed by his own son as a manager. This son tells his story, not in terms of the building crafts which he learnt directly, but of an inherited instinct from a mythical ancestor:

Even at school . . . I didn't used to go out with mates, I was always doing something. I think it must be the Jewish blood in me: I was always thinking of ways to make money. Oh, we are going back ages, long way, me mum always laughs about that, cos that's what she reckons: she says, 'Oh, you're the lucky one, you have more Jewish blood in you.' . . .

I always did something better. . . . They're not lucky breaks, you only get what you work for. . . . Like on the way home from my junior school I used to pass a coupl'o joinery firms, and I always used to go in—'Could we have cuts of wood'—and I used to go home with the offcuts, and chop 'em all up into little bundles and put 'em in a little barrow and go round to the little old ladies and—I mean not a lot, only a few coppers—and, 'Want some firewood?'

There is Jewish blood in the family, going way back. Something like great, great, great, great- something like that.[20]

There were, it should be added, more genuine examples of not only Jewish but also other minority ethnic and religious cultural traditions. Some had proved incentives to social advance, others discouraging. One family of fallers had formerly been carpenters with their own small firms, but they had also been Christadelphians for over five generations, and it was this that counted. It was 'a sort of family religion community. . . . You live by the scriptures and God's word, you live that way. . . . I don't think the job was made to be a very important thing in life. . . . The main thing was they wanted you to join the meeting. That was more important than anything else.'[21] In their case family commitment to a religious minority resulted in an exclusive focus on religious at the expense of material advance.

The most widespread form of cultural transmission, however, is of specific occupational models. These can be passed between women as well as between men, and also between the female and the male lines. As a result, conventional social-mobility studies of fathers and sons have seriously underestimated their importance. Over two-thirds of our families reveal transmissions of at least one occupation over three generations or more. Even half of the risers and fallers show such a pattern.

Perhaps because these transmissions are so common, they are often taken for granted and scarcely discussed, let alone mystified. In a minority of families, however, the form of influence was more explicit. A family of ships' carpenters and shipping clerks, for example, lived in a 'house full of ships; it's all ships, water, and sea'. A Coventry miner treasured the first coal he had hacked from the pit-face when the colliery opened, and his son has it still: 'I've still got the first piece of coal that came up from that pit, what he brought up. The manager at the pit thinks he's got it, but he hasn't. It's in our family.' A skilled artisan could convey the powers of a 'master craftsman' at home by a constructive hobby such as making model aircraft, or by home improvements: 'he made that gate out there, it must be the most expensive gate in Bembridge'. Others were able to take their children to work. A future fisherman first went out to sea as a boy with his trawlerman father. A city tailor, 'all handstitching', worked in a big-windowed attic, and his son

used to go up there quite a lot. It was a marvellous place, I remember, because it was right in the centre of Manchester and it was right high up. . . . You could see all over Manchester. I used to like going up there. . . . He used to have a dirty raincoat hanging on the back of the door and all the work that wasn't for the boss was behind there. . . . He used to make all our clothes. He kept us in short trousers until we were about 13. We were always well dressed, always. He used to make my mother's suits as well.

A future bank chairman would go in as a boy with his father, a country branch manager, to the bank out of office hours. In a family of skilled engineers, father and son 'would discuss a problem like the car's engine's broke down so we need to get it bored, and things of that nature: you would talk to your father about that. And he would take a great pride, when I used to go down to his works, in showing me his latest jig. He absolutely adored his work and he loved people to come in and look at it. And I used to go down there from the age of 14.'[22]

An alternative work ethic to skill was that of service: ideally, of a mutual loyalty and assistance. A future footman was sent away from home at the age of 14 to serve as a page-boy in another family. 'My father said to me, "You'll be far better off with your feet under somebody else's table." . . . My father, as a young boy, worked for them, and they knew of him. . . . I cried my eyes out.' But he became equally trustworthy: so impeccably clean that, even to his last years, he insisted on changing his shirt three times daily. To an extent such attitudes could also be transferred to more public services. A naval physiotherapist, son of an ambulance driver married to a bus conductress, described himself as having

always been in the service of others. I think this is what they [his parents] were interested in. My father was in the St John's Ambulance Brigade and he spent a lot of his time looking after other people. Even when my mother died, he became a guide for a blind lady and he was honoured with the Order of the Serving Brother of St John. . . . And I think that is what they expected me to do as well.[23]

On the railways the two ethics, of skill and of service, were combined. John Read grew up in outer London.

My family were railway people. As we lived near the main line at Wimbledon, we used to go engine-spotting—getting the numbers: you used to see all these flash trains going through. . . . It was taken for granted that that was the way of life, that that was the way it was going to be.

He was close to his father from boyhood:

He was a great influence. He was the bloke who held the lamp and passed on the spanner. . . . How to do things . . . if I wasn't doing it right, he's take the hammer out me hand, 'I'll show you how to hit the nail.' . . . We had a common interest in the railway. . . . My father always said, 'Don't earn your living at the end of a shovel.' So when I said I wanted to be an engine-driver—'OK, I'll get you a job.'

So his father secured a letter from his own boss, 'saying this lad will be good for the railways because his father is a good servant', and John was asked down to interview at Portsmouth steam-engine shed, where he was greeted by a bowler-hatted official, who shook his hands, and 'nearly crippled me. "You gotta get your grip a bit better", he said, "because your life will rely on your hands." Which was quite true.' And indeed, he rose from boy cleaner to fireman, learning 'to maintain steam', to look to the lamps, the tools, to ensure 'everything is kept spotless'; and finally, to become an electric train-driver. Right through, he has kept his 'love of the railway'.[24]

Such explicit occupational inheritance seems to be almost always a form of transmission between fathers and sons. There are indeed instances of mothers who pushed their daughters to follow their own paths, like the office secretary and bookkeeper who sent her daughter for secretarial training, telling her, 'If you can type, you'll always be able to get a job.' But between women there were much less likely to be occupational traditions, because for the older generation work and marriage had been widely thought of as incompatible. Some families, indeed, continued to pass down attitudes which discouraged married women from paid work. In a Norfolk village family, for example, the mother felt that her own parents had been 'mainly more interested if I was going to make a good wife' then get a job:

run my own home . . . and I think that's why—I've been married nearly forty years—and I think that's perhaps why I turned out—perhaps with my home: I love my home, I love my cooking, I love anything to do with domesticated. And I think perhaps that was due to them . . . due to them.

Both her daughters have given up work on marriage too: and in the younger, especially, she sees much of herself. 'She's like me, you see. Now she love her home. She love her cooking. She's only 25 and . . . she's got the two young children. . . . She just loves being in the kitchen.'[25]

Nevertheless, if more often quietly, women do pass down strong family occupational traditions. We can take as a contrast an industrial Lancashire family, the Sims, in which not one of the multiple family occupations is in the direct male line, so that none could have been even perceived in a conventional mobility study. Yet on Pat Sim's mother's side, her grandfather and two uncles all worked in chemicals for ICI. The other connections are all made through the women in the family. Her husband was earlier a plumber; and so now is her daughter's boyfriend. Her husband then became an airport driver; and her sister's husband has followed him into the same job. Her son is a process operator for Shell—and her niece is marrying his mate. But the most sustained of all these work transmissions is among the women themselves, in service and catering. One of Pat's grandmothers was in service. Her mother worked for seven years in a local restaurant and cake shop. Both Pat and her sister worked later in the same shop. And now Pat's daughter wants to study Home Economics at a polytechnic.[26]

Pat has no brother so that, according to the terms normally used in studying social mobility, she does not belong to an observable family. Our approach at once reveals an unseen sociological phenomenon and helps to explain it.

Our second approach has been to examine each family as an intergenerational system of interlocking social and emotional relation-ships. We have been especially influenced in this by family systems theory, and have developed our ideas through a series of joint workshops at the Institute of Family Therapy in London. This way of looking at families has been developed for treating those in difficulties: thus the therapist assumes that the member of a family presenting for treatment may be manifesting the symptoms of a problem elsewhere in the system. The dominating ageing businessman father, for example, suffers acute but inexplicable pains because his son is a grown-up but still obedient boy who will not demand responsibility.[27] A series of deviant patterns has been identified, particularly in relationship to broken families: the child who becomes a parental figure, for example, not only taking adult roles at home but declining to go to school, or the child who fills the empty place as a substitute quasi-spousal confidant in bed or out.

Although the family-systems approach fits well with interactionist perspectives and also with the role theory commonly used in sociological work on marriage, as well as with more recent research on the distribution of power in families, it goes beyond it. Such studies do not take the individual family as a system in its own right. The only comparable sociological precedent of which we are aware is the earlier Chicago work of Bossard and Boll on large families, which was developed from role theory as a way of showing how each of a large group of siblings chose distinctive paths.[28]

We have certainly found among our hundred families instances of repeating difficulties. There are sixteen instances of transgenerational patterns of divorce: in many of them, each generation escaping from unhappy homes with early pregnancies and marriage, leading in turn to another unsatisfactory or broken marriage.[29] One of the most unhappily married women among our informants is Meg Jacks. Her story is part of a three-generational pattern. Her own daughter has left a drunken, violent first husband, by whom she had two children, and married for the second time to a draughtsman, Harry, and they now have a joint child too. Harry himself suffered emotionally as a child, not only from his father's death when he was a teenager, but also because even before that this parents, who ran a club together, were rarely at home and left him to be brought up by his sisters. He knows nothing at all about his own grandparents. But on his wife's side the roots certainly go back to Meg's childhood.

Meg's father, a miner, had died in his forties, when she was just 14. Very soon after her widowed mother

started going with this fellow. Not long after. Well I thought a lot about me dad and I suppose he spoiled me. . . . Well I—didn't like it. I didn't take to it at all. And she married him. And she moved in with him, into his home. And left this elder sister of mine in her home there. But I stopped with her. I wouldn't go over anyway.

Things got—this sister, you see I only realized when I got older—she couldn't keep me because I hadn't started work then. Her husband was in the war. So I finally drifted back to me mum and this fella.

But I never liked him. And I think that's how you get married sooner than you would do really. Because I weren't comfortable, you see, with him.

Meg married at 20. 'I was glad to get away. And then I wished I hadn't have.' Nor did the trouble in the family stop here. The wife of one of her two brothers had a child by another man during the war. 'They drifted back again. But I think she was always ashamed to—you never saw a lot of her, they sort of broke away through that. Like my parents didn't like the thought of her coming back into the family after doing that.' And one of Meg's two sisters has an illegitimate granddaughter, whom she unsuccessfully attempted to mother: the girl was 'knocking a lad' at 14 and stealing from within the home. A family tree, in short, burdened with bad starts.[30]

Such handicaps do not make downward mobility inevitable: this family is not in fact among our fallers. Normally falling is associated with a conjunction of factors. Typical transgenerational familial difficulties, in addition to divorce, include illness, physical or sexual abuse, alcoholism, large numbers of children, lack of parental support, low ambition, and poor communication between parents and children. With our cases such factors contributed to downward mobility in three situations. This first was when a middle-class family was forced to migrate from a deteriorating work context. The second is the reverse instance to the 'submerged middle-class' mother: the father who rises occupationally to a managerial level, while his wife and child remain culturally embedded in their original working-class neighbourhood, so that the children become occupationally downwardly mobile. The third situation is the working-class family, equally embedded, who are left high and dry by structural economic change and the ebbing of job opportunities in their own area.

We may take as an instance of the last type the family of Paddy O'Hara, grandson of skilled Irish stonemason and son of a South Wales labourer who himself, after working as an unskilled bakery worker, has been unemployed for the last twenty years. His wife and daughter, who have both worked as cleaners, and his son are all also unemployed. In each generation this family has suffered instances of serious illness or death by accident. One daughter who cohabits with a violent boyfriend also accuses her father of violence, attacking her as a teenager with a carving knife. There are broken marriages in both the older and younger generation. And right through runs a trans-generational thread of excessive drinking: Paddy's grandmother, father, himself, and his daughter's boyfriend are all picked out. All these handicaps combine with the positive pull of—in Paddy's words—'a close family' to rule out any thought of mobility, even to avoid the economic trap in which they now find themselves. 'We never did let it worry us. We carried on with our lives.' They are rooted in their neighbourhood by an extended family network which offers both a sense of belonging and support. When Paddy grew up, his father's sister lived next door, his mother's brother next door but one, and another of her sisters round the corner. When Paddy's brother married, he also lived round the corner, while his married sister settled into next door but one. Paddy's daughter was closer as a teenager to her stepgrandmother than to her mother and still goes on holiday with her: 'I was always up there.' And although family patterns in the 1980s have changed, the neighbourhood network remains as reassuring as ever. As she puts it: 'To be honest, most of my friends don't have fathers. Either their parents are divorced or their fathers are dead.'[31] Downward mobility here is part of a transgenerational fall in which the strengths of family culture have served to reinforce its handicaps.

At the opposite end of the spectrum there are families with positive transgenerational moral attitudes, such as love and encouragement in child-rearing, good communication, a commitment to work or to education, or a willingness to change or move in the pursuit of ambition. In an industrial managerial family, for example, the grandparents were 'always pushing ... anxious that I should get on and do well. Interested as to where I was and how I was coping.' They conveyed to their son an ambition which made him 'want the freedom of being my own boss and choosing what I did. And so I decided to get out and look after myself. ... I was able to take advantage of an opportunity to get out and I did.' The message that he passed on in turn to the grandchildren was of 'standing on their own two feet and making their own decisions ... pushing themselves as much as they possibly can without making their lives unhappy, and whatever they do, to try and do it well.' And indeed, the biggest hope of the granddaughter, now on a hotel management course, is 'to be successful ... It will really give me a thrill to get ahead. ... The thing I would really like to do is to have my own hotel group.'[32]

There are some respects in which these transmissions of attitudes can be remarkably precise: for example, in attitudes to money. John Read not only took his railway father as a work model, but of how to run the home as a married man. 'I thought, "Well, if I can model myself on them, on their financial affairs and how they set up home, I can do the same." ' He handed over his whole wage packet; they never got into debt. In another family of skilled workers the very phrases echo down the generations. The grandparents were brought up to believe 'the only thing was to be careful about money. Cos you had sixpence a week pocket money in those days, that was because you'd cleaned the knives and forks. But you always had to put it away, try to save it.' They passed on the same attitudes: 'if they wanted something, then they had to save it ... they had to make the effort. If they didn't make the effort, we wouldn't help 'em. That's the thing: if they wanted something, they gotta work for it.' Or, as their son put it, 'we had to earn it: like doing jobs. Because he wanted you to realize the value of things. "If you want something, you've gotta earn it." I suppose this is one thing he has given us.' And he is trying to impart the same message to the grandchildren: 'try to be careful with money. ... And now's the time, if they start saving now. It's a job to get 'em to do that.'[33]

One cluster of attitudes, emphasizing the social value of hard work and the importance of education, often linked to a political belief in socialism in at least the older generation, seemed a key factor in a small group of families upwardly mobile from the working class. The family of Cledwyn Roberts provides a very striking example.

Cledwyn's paternal grandfather had started life as a labourer on a hill farm and then migrated to become a South Wales coalminer in the boom years before the First World War. Of his four sons who survived childhood, three became miners, while his five daughters all went into domestic service and married working men, two of them also miners. There were, however, two breaches in this pattern. Firstly Cledwyn's father temporarily left the mines to work in London for a year, as a hotel servant, and there met his mother who was a hotel chambermaid. Although Cledwyn's mother's family was also working-class in occupation, it is noticeable that his maternal grandmother had been a schoolteacher before she married. Cledwyn thinks that his mother 'received informal education from my grandmother, who had done a little bit of teaching, and certainly she was able to assist me in doing my homework more ably than my father was'.

It was, however, Uncle Evan, Cledwyn's father's younger brother, who led the family's rise by winning a scholarship to the local grammar school, and then to university and a teaching job. He could not have followed this educational path without the help of his family, and indeed 'part of my aunt's contributions from service went to keeping and funding my uncle in his education, in university'. Later on Evan gave financial help to others in the family in turn: Cledwyn's father, for instance, in buying his house.

Evan married a teacher, but had no children of his own. But their example inspired three of his eight nieces to become teachers, as well as Cledwyn himself. 'There was a very strong drive towards education, in that particular generation in the mining valleys.' In the community as a whole there was provision of nursery schooling for all children and also an exceptionally high proportion of grammar-school places, reaching a quarter of all children by the 1950s. Cledwyn's own parents certainly 'had hopes for me', and for his sister: 'in their generation, becoming a teacher was one of the great aims for the children. . . . You find them all over Britain, brainwashing the English. Become a professional, have a professional qualification. I think this was an ambition they had.'

Cledwyn followed his uncle's educational path. But there was one point when, as a teenager, he hesitated. After all, the majority of sons did stay in the community and he wanted to stay with them. This time the crucial influence came from his father:

When I was about 15, I wanted to leave school. Some of my friends had left school: they were earning money—and I wanted to leave school. And he took me down the mine on a Sunday, and he took me in. It was an old mine. So we went down and we had to go three miles to where they actually dug the coal. And the last 300 yards you were crawling, and there was water. And he said, 'Now, this is what you've got to look forward to.' So I stayed in school.

Today Cledwyn lectures at a college in England. He has emphasized to his own children 'the value of education for providing better jobs and also just for the sake of education, to make a better person'. And his daughter, now a university student in turn, can also find encouragement in her grandfather. She describes him as a tiny man, a 'very strong socialist', now retired, who

likes sitting indoors and reading and listening to his music, and pottering about in the greenhouse. He's quite old-fashioned in his ideas. He is really nice. He takes a great interest in our education. He's always asking mum and dad what's going on. When we used to have reports he liked to read them and comment on them. And if they were good he'd give us a present.[34]

Upward mobility through education is a well-known phenomenon: but here it depends not only on formal education itself, but equally on transgenerational family culture.

We see the further exploration of these intergenerational patterns as a crucial future task. But as we have already noted in more than one case, transgenerational influence can take the form not only of continuities but equally of reversals. Thus the skilled working family who made their children save changed their attitude to the value of education. Whereas the grandmother had been made to leave school 'because I couldn't get a grant for the uniforms', the granddaughter felt her parents were sacrificing themselves to buy 'things like school uniforms . . . they've bought things that I've needed'. A dentist's wife, sent to boarding school as a child herself, ensured her own children had 'always been at home with us. At one time they wanted to go away to boarding school, and we didn't want them to: we talked them out of it. Yes, they've done a lot more with us than I did with my parents.' A miner's daughter who chose a timber foreman for her husband 'had vowed, I'd never marry a man that drank, because my father, when he wasn't—he'd got to work and come back and he was at the pub, and he was violent with it. He was always drunk.'[35] Each of these reversals is associated with a social rise. Undoubtedly, the assumption in family systems theory that influence can be handed down *either* through imitation *or* through rejection of a previous generation's pattern is particularly important, for it suggests how the averaging technique of statistical studies is likely to result in an underestimation of inter-generational influence.

It is equally important to recognize that most families offer not just a single tradition, but a choice of models. Betty Smith is an instance of a woman who achieved social mobility after leaving her lorry driver husband. All but one of her six siblings is in manual work and the only exception married a costermonger. Her father was a labourer, normally taciturn, but occasionally violent after drink; her mother an illiterate housewife. Neither her siblings nor her parents encouraged her. Betty from childhood has 'wanted to go into an office; but they wouldn't let me, because the money was more in a factory'. It was only much later, as a separated woman, that she rose to become a supervisor and bookkeeper, and she described this as a 'dream come true by sheer luck'. But it is striking how she picks out as the most influential member of her family her mother's sister, who also achieved fulfilment as an independent woman: 'it was all the scandal at the time, no one got divorced. She just used to enjoy life, really enjoy it. . . . She was always the gay one, always for a laugh. A right flirt, she was terrific. She was my favourite.'[36]

Sometimes the way in which such choices are made is also propelled by the family system of relationships. Brothers and sisters in some families can be close allies, in others irreconcilable rivals. In the exceptionally large family of a barber who went blind, the eleven children went in very diverse directions, some in pairs. Two of the daughters, for example, married two brothers who were fish whole-salers; two others found work in a sweet factory; two of the brothers disappeared as ne'er-do-wells to Saudi Arabia; and two other daughters, who 'used to always put airs and graces on', both became qualified nurses married to senior professional husbands.[37] Oliver Ridings, on the other hand, had only one brother: but the theme of his life story is how he surpassed him.

Born into a Lancashire mill-worker's family, to have fought his way up to a life of financial ease is a double triumph, for his older brother was always the family favourite. This brother was a model son, 'brilliant' at school, rising to the level of a mill under-manager before being cut off by wartime death. Oliver by contrast was 'a bit of a scarecrow', in frequent conflict with his Methodist father, who would warn him sternly, ' "You'll never be anything." . . . Me dad and me

wasn't the best of friends.' Nor did he get generous encouragement
when he chose to go in for a whole variety of dealing—houses, horses,
groceries—rather than a steady job at the mill. Sometimes he
borrowed from his father: 'he'd charge me full rate, oh aye! . . . He
said, "When he's spent it, he's back to clogs." ' But he stuck at it—'I
was a slave-driver in them days'—and made enough money to retire in
comfort in his forties, entertaining himself by playing at his shares. 'I
often think about my brother. He was so smart. He couldn't make
money and I could. And my father used to say, "You'll never be
anything." '[38]

This is a life story which again has a mythical dimension: a triumph
against apparent destiny laid down by family. This particular form of
transgenerational influence has been identified by the family therapist
John Byng-Hall as a 'family script'. Such powerful traditions can again
be either positive or negative in effect. In Byng-Hall's own family, the
family script goes back over two centuries, to the shooting of Admiral
Byng for cowardice in 1757 because of his failure to defend Minorca
against the French fleet: 'pour encourager les autres' as Voltaire put it.
Since that time, generations of male Byngs have sought to demonstrate
that they were certainly not cowards, whatever the verdict on their
legendary ancestor. John's own grandfather, as Governor in Nigeria,
quelled a revolt by confronting the rebels alone, standing unarmed in a
white smock on a hilltop. John's father farmed in Kenya gun in hand,
defying the surrounding Mau Mau. John's own life has been a triumph
against disablement from polio, which he suffered as a young man. At
the onset of the illness he was himself at sea, on a liner back to
England, and in his delirium he dreamt that he had been shot in the
back by a cannon-ball.[39]

A two-hundred-year family story is quite exceptional and none of
our families had any comparable script. But they do include examples
of disaster scripts against which the younger generation are struggling.
Most often these concern family breaches following desertion or
divorce. Significantly they often become compelling family legends
because of the mystery surrounding them. As a result of the bitterness
and anger engendered by separation, the grandparent or parent who
has gone is typically never spoken of, cut from the genealogical tree.
Again and again descendants know nothing at all about these
ancestors. This imposition of silence could be taken to extraordinary
lengths. A Kent village carpenter's daughter explained how her father
had broken with her grandfather when the grandparents split up.

My father fell out with his father about the time he got married, so we didn't ever know him as a grandfather, although we actually lived in the same road. So we knew of this chap but he was never mentioned as a grandfather. . . . We'd know everybody in the village and we'd know people who went past and we always used to say 'hello' to this old chap. . . . He used to cycle along on his bike. And it wasn't till ages afterwards that we said, 'Oh, there's only one person and he'll never say "hello".' And my mother said, 'Oh well, that's your grandfather!'[40]

She managed just one conversation with her grandfather before he died.

More often the secret was kept to death. Taking children to cemeteries is one form of telling the family story in many parts of Europe: the gravestones may incorporate working implements or portrait photographs, and the more architecturally ambitious tombs are almost family homes in themselves.[41] Such customs are rare in England and Wales—although Lancashire and parts of Scotland may have been different—and graveyards modest, reticent. But one grandmother, who had left southern England for Wales at the age of 17, would insist on returning from time to time to see the family graves, both revealing and keeping the family secret, for she would never say who her parents were:

she wouldn't talk about it. Just wouldn't. I spoke to me aunties and uncles and me father about it, and they all reckon that she had a very bad childhood. . . .

When she was alive and we used to take her over to Ampthill, she always used to go up to the graveyard for some reason. And she used to point out certain graves, and she used to say, 'Well, I knew her,' and 'I knew that person,' and 'I knew that.' But she wouldn't go into her past or anything like that. So it's a complete mystery about her.[42]

Mystery is a catalyst of myth; and when the mystery is repeated in more than one generation, it can become a particularly powerful family script. In Eileen Moriarty's family such transgenerational separations have, moreover, taken precisely the same form. Eileen's father's mother had 'left when he was very young as well, and it was an exact repetition of the situation that I had' in losing her own mother. After she had gone, her father never knowingly saw her again. Only after she died did they discover, through an uncle who read gas meters, that she had lived 200 yards away for years: 'and he's never known, all his life'. Yet when his own wife, Eileen's mother, deserted him in turn, the breach was as absolute, the absence even more total than after a death.

'She left, she just walked out one day, one night, and that was it. She was gone. She never returned.' Eileen's father pushed her out of their lives, just as his father had his own mother. 'It was never mentioned again, her family. . . . It was something that was never talked about, once she was gone. Everything was banished from the house one night; and that was it. Just like that. . . . It went straight to him. Just that day. And dad just—everything like, little photos, he cut her picture up and everything; it was just gone. Amazing. Strange.' Eileen is still haunted by the fear that her father will be the next to disappear. When she is away for any length of time she phones compulsively, not to talk, but to be sure he is still there. 'It's very strange, the same happened to him, as what happened to us. It's really awful to think that—I hope it will never happen again. Oh yeh, I often do [wonder], yeh; but to think that someone was so near . . .'.[43]

We return to where we started. Family stories are the grist of social description, the raw material for both history and social change; but we need to listen to them more attentively than that. They are also the symbolic coinage of exchange between the generations, of family transmission. They may haunt, or inspire, or be taken as commonplace. But the way in which they are told, the stories and images which are chosen and put together, and the matters on which silence is kept provides part of the mental map of family members. Each of these members has, at the same time, a place in their own particular family socio-emotional structure, their family system of relationships. Family myths, models, and denials, transmitted within a family system, provide for most people part of the context in which their crucial life choices must be made, propelling them into their own individual life paths: units for the social-mobility survey. And the 'I' in life-story interviews too: an 'I' who may also recount family stories. Such stories are not only remembered fragments of a real past, not only clues to collective consciousness and personal identity, but also a form of the past still active in the present: signposts.

Notes

1. Interview 5412AM, 3–4.
2. Ibid. 32, 87.
3. Elizabeth Tonkin, *Narrating our Pasts: The Social Construction of Oral History.* (Cambridge, 1992).
4. Raphael Samuel and Paul Thompson (eds.), *The Myths We Live By* (London, 1990).
5. Paul Thompson, 'Family as a Factor in Social Mobility', paper presented to Twelfth World Congress of Sociology, Madrid, July 1990.

6. For the classic recent studies, see John H. Goldthorpe, C. Llewelyn, and C. Payne, *Social Mobility and Class Structure in Modern Britain* (Oxford, 1980); and Robert Erikson and John Goldthorpe (eds.), *The Constant Flux: A Study of Class Mobility in Industrial Societies* (Oxford, 1992). On women and social mobility, see Goldthorpe, *Sociology*, 17 (1983), 465–88, and the ensuing debate; Pamela Abbot and Roger Sapsford, *Women and Social Class* (London, 1987), 47–87. An illuminating exception is Shirley Dex, *Women's Occupational Mobility: Lifetime Perspective* (London, 1987).

7. 'Families and Social Mobility: A Comparative Study', funded on the British side by the Economic and Social Research Council, and on the French side by CNRS. The Research Officers on the project were Catherine Itzin, Graham Smith, and John Cresswell. Interviews were also carried out by Michele Abendstern, Research Officer on our parallel project on 'Life Stories and Ageing', and by Sandra Lotti, Marion Haberhauer, Kay Sanderson, and Bob Little. The Research Officers also carried out some of the preliminary analysis, Catherine Itzin focusing on women's occupational mobility in relation to marriage, and Graham Smith on geographical mobility and espcially emigration. Of the 100 middle-generation informants on whom the figures cited here are based, 30 were classified as social risers, 16 as fallers, and 54 as stayers.

8. 'Growing up in Stepfamilies' project, funded by the Wates Foundation, and jointly conducted by Gill Gorell Barnes, Natasha Burchardt, Gwyn Daniel, and Paul Thompson. The informants are a sample from the National Child Development Study cohort who were all born in 1958.

9. 5701BF, 5; 5803BM, 13; 5609BM, 5–6, 19, 38. By the time of his father's decision, both grandfathers had lost a leg in a pit accident, and three of his four uncles were chronically sick.

10. Brian Jackson and Dennis Marsden, *Education and the Working Class* (London, 1962).

11. 5614AF, 5–6 (a son of the interviewee); 5900AM, 1.

12. Daniel Bertaux and Isabelle Bertaux-Wiame, 'Le patrimoine et sa lignée: Transmissions et mobilité sociale sur cinq générations', *Life Stories/Récits de vie*, 4 (1988), 2–26.

13. 5207AF, 5; 5403BM, 1.

14. 5607AF, 16–17; 5401AM, 43, BM, 4–50. There were no examples at all of the intergenerational transmission of education as a major value among either working-class stayers, or all fallers.

15. 6001BF, 39; 5404BM, 29.

16. This was less than a quarter of a skilled man's wage.

17. 5604BF, 14–15, 72, CM, 3, 6–7, 29.

18. Of the 83 English and Welsh families 14 include at least three generations of small entrepreneurs among their kin.

19. 5404BM, 5, 29, 36, 153.

20. 5302BM, 29, 31.

21. 5602BF, 33–4, 83.

22. 5809BF, 62; 5601BM, 8; 5207BM, 57, AF, 96; 5501BM, 11; 5607BM, 21.

23. 5204AM, 4–5; 5406 BM, 25.

24. 5102BM, 26, 31–2, 42, 64, 72, 74.

25. 5205CF, 30.

26. 5502BF, 18, 24, 35, 64, 66.

27. I discuss the relevance of this approach, with another more detailed case study of a north Italian family, in the 2nd edn. of *The Voice of the Past* (Oxford, 1988), 152–4; see also above, Introduction.

28. James H. S. Bossard and Eleanor S. Boll, *The Large Family System* (Philadelphia, 1956).

29. Since only informants living as couples with children were interviewed, excluding the single, separated, and childless, the general incidence must be much higher. In our stepfamily sample half of those whose parents had separated also had grandparents who had split up.
30. 5405BM; 5405AF, 3–5, 57, 74 (cited in *I Don't Feel Old*, 106).
31. 5805BM, 36, 44; 5805CF, 1, 48.
32. 5503BM, 28, 33, 62. For entrepreneurship and family culture, see also Paul Thompson, *Living the Fishing* (London, 1983).
33. 5102BM, 72; 5202AM, 24, AF, 61–2, BM, 31, 98.
34. 5301BM, 11, 12, 16, 28, 42, 76; 5301CF, 5.
35. 5202AF, 42; 5202CF, 16–17; 5410BF, 58.
36. 5005BF, 30, 58, 60–1.
37. 5408BF, 12–14.
38. 5413AM, 2–3, 6–7, 10–12, 17–23, 53, 87.
39. 'The Power of Family Myths', John Byng-Hall interviewed by Paul Thompson, in *The Myths We Live By*.
40. 5208BF, 3, 23.
41. The secular symbolism of cemetery monuments is most developed of all in Russia, where realistic portrait busts and figures are combined with huge sculptured artefacts, from violins to tanks, and the tombs of the most popular long-dead figures are regularly festooned with flowers left by anonymous visitors.
42. 5609BM, 1.
43. 'Growing up in Stepfamilies' project, interview 37, 1–3, 10, 15.

3

The Pull of Family Ties

Intergenerational Relationships and Life Paths

ISABELLE BERTAUX-WIAME

The speed and direction of each individual's life path is first set within the family of origin in childhood. As individuals grow into adulthood, their paths become autonomous, but rarely completely so. The long arm of family connection may reach out again at a later stage to exert a crucial influence on the path even of an adult child. My intention here is to demonstrate, with examples from two recent French research projects in which I have participated,[1] how the pull of family ties—'la force de rappel'—can continue to shape the lives of a younger generation into adulthood. I shall focus on families of relatively modest social standing: small entrepreneurs and workers in the provinces and the capital.

For the members of such families, the family itself was a crucial social resource, a form of capital which could give them a barely sufficient socio-economic margin for manœuvre within which they could develop viable life plans. Many of our interviews showed the decisive role played by family networks in the achievement of social status and the construction of a social identity. Conversely, the absence of family ties sometimes characterized life paths leading to social marginality or even exclusion—as, for example, in cases of homelessness or unemployment.

Family resources played a crucial role equally in conceiving and in achieving individual life projects. Some were directly instigated by family; for others, family was the source of inspiration. In achieving, maintaining, or improving a way of life, the possibility of drawing on family financial aid, exchanges of services or goods, and moral support could be crucial. Hence even the imagining of 'possible futures' took place within the context of the family network.

This runs counter to the assumption so common in novels that those

who rise socially need to achieve a distance from their parents'
generation, because family ties are inherently conservative, heavily
weighted towards the repetition of the life projects of earlier
generations. The truth is more complex. Some paths for social
advance, such as success in a scholarly or professional career, create
both discontinuities between generations and also approval in the
family circle. Anne Gotman has underlined how the existence of the
institution of inheritance side by side with the free labour market in
itself acts 'as a constraining system, contradicting the axiom of
independence between generations'.[2] By the same token, the persist-
ence of family solidarity undercuts the belief that social change is
brought about through the struggle of each new generation for its
autonomy. The maintenance of a balance between individual autonomy
and membership of a family network of solidarity remains a
fundamental characteristic of Western cultures.[3]

The various opportunities that can be found within each family
space thus carry a double meaning. They are resources for individual
life paths, but they can also constrain. The pull of family ties can be
especially powerful when exerted early in adult independence, when it
can have a particularly strong breaking effect. Yet even then members
of the younger generation will not always submit passively; facing
the challenge, they may still make something new of it for themselves.

The essential role of family solidarity among less educated social
groups is as a safeguard against social and economic marginalization.
Lacking formal credentials and skills, the family offers them an
essential protection against the consequences of illness, accident,
unemployment, and other risks to which they are continually exposed.
To draw on family support it is necessary to live relatively close to kin.
Hence the 'stubbornness' of women in refusing to move far from their
family of origin. The exchanges of help in housework and child-care
between grandmothers, mothers, and daughters are one means
through which young mothers can remain in the labour market and
sustain the economic independence of the younger generation through
the child-rearing phase. In this sense mutual aid between women can
be seen as a dynamic factor in social change and the raising of living
standards. The timing of such aid, however, does not only depend on
the needs of the younger generations: it also depends on how the older
generation has fared in its own paths. Thus in some families the older
generation have only become full home-owners late in life, and the

younger generation have to wait in turn; while in other families the emphasis and efforts are put on early access to property.

The forms of family support vary greatly between families. It is not even always between generations. When the timing of life phases makes intergenerational support difficult, the most important aid may come from siblings. In one family all the brothers and sisters were able to become home-owners at the same time, as the result of information supplied by the eldest, who works for a prefabricated housing factory firm. Another form, which may be particularly crucial after an unexpected personal catastrophe, is moral support. After the birth of a handicapped child, for example, the parents need not only practical help, but also the continuation of concern and approval through the family which helps to protect them from becoming socially isolated.

These positive aspects of different forms of family support have often been noted. Much less attention has been paid to their reverse aspect in holding back individual careers. In a working family the sudden and unexpected availability of small productive capital, for example through inheritance, may have a strong impact on its future. It may seem paradoxical to introduce this possibility as a form of braking rather than positive assistance. But our case studies show clearly how the availability through family of a house, a shop, a farm, or a workshop could suddenly transform a family's life by providing a new opportunity.[4] On the other hand, at this particular social level it was more often a poor opportunity: a small, half-abandoned farm, a café which had lost its customers, an artisan's workshop full of obsolete machines. If such a chance had not come through the family, it would have been more easily seen as a false opening and turned down. But coming from the family, it had symbolic value as well; and more crucially, there was also moral pressure to take it up. To refuse it because one had started a viable working career elsewhere might seem personal egoism, a rejection of family solidarity. To accept could imply the abandoning of a new way of life, the relinquishing of a dream of becoming different; but there would always be risks of such independence ending in failure. For both reasons, it might seem safer to accept.

The ties of family, in short, offer an encouragement that always remains ambivalent, capable always of calling back birds which have flown free from the nest. With this in mind, let us turn to some examples.

*　　*　　*

CLAUDE

When we met him, Claude had been a self-employed mason for five years. He had reached this situation not through a carefully nurtured plan, but through a chain of circumstances set off by an offer of land from his in-laws.

Claude had been employed as a mason by a construction company for a number of years. He lived with his wife, who worked as a cashier in a supermarket, and their child in a tiny apartment until his father-in-law suggested that they move into and renovate an old, unoccupied house belonging to the family in the village where his wife was born. The couple were happy to accept the offer. However, commuting to the city where Claude worked was a long, tiring, and fairly difficult journey. On the other hand, Claude's wife was unable to keep her job as a cashier, since it was too far away from their new home. In their new rural environment, there was a little hope that she would be able to find a new job very quickly.

When moving into the new house, the couple realized that their life would change. Undoubtedly, they would be able to adapt, but they found the daily commuting increasingly difficult to stand. In addition, they had to borrow to make the first essential renovations to the house. Thus, they decided to reorganize their life in the only way available to them.

Claude had never especially wanted to become a self-employed mason. During the course of his career, he had seen a number of co-workers quit their salaried jobs to set up their own businesses, and he himself had once been in a position to do so, following the bankruptcy of one of his employers. However, he had preferred to take another salaried job. His decision to become a self-employed mason at such a relatively late point in his life was the result of their move, and of the active support of his wife.

So Claude transformed the barn attached to their house into a workshop and obtained a licence as an independent worker. He knew that the reputation of his father-in-law, a well-known farmer in the area, would help him get clients. And indeed his wife now accompanies him to the work-sites, helping him to get projects started or to finish them. She also takes care of the paperwork. Professionally and domestically, their move seems to be a success. However, economic success is not yet assured.

The help of the in-laws, which was given to help resolve a housing problem, also had a significant effect on their working lives. At the same time, this brought them back to a familial place, and improved their family life. The couple were able to reorganize their projects in line with their opportunities, and to improve their social position. Without this support, such a move might have had a negative effect on their life paths.

ALBERT

Albert, the oldest son of a family of small farmers, had always made clear his intention to quit agriculture. Since the income from the farm was no longer sufficient to support a family, he intended to take advantage of the training that would be available at the end of his military service to become an aeronautical technician. But, for him, family ties had a much harsher effect. The death of his father, while Albert was off fighting in Algeria, put an end to his plans.

He could not leave his mother and sister, who was still quite young, to take care of the farm by themselves. Family solidarity imposed itself. He took care of the farm for ten years, and did not sell it until the future of his sister was taken care of. He now works as a chauffeur. His work schedule leaves him time to pursue other activities.

In his case, the pull of family ties seems only to have slowed his leaving the agricultural sector. Insufficient land and capital made it impossible to expand the amount of land under cultivation, and Albert knew that in the long run he could not keep the farm. Nevertheless, the suddenness of his recall prevented Albert from leaving the farm by getting appropriate training. It was as a farmer that Albert began his own family, and it was without any particular professional qualification that he left farming ten years later. But in the meantime Albert took advantage of his being under 'house arrest' to settle down in the community.

Albert is not the only one to settle down in the community. He married a farmer's daughter who also wanted to leave farming: 'crazy work, nobody feels like doing that any more'. Nevertheless, she married a farmer. Together, making use of their networks, they planned their move out of the agricultural sector, a move which neither of them had ever really given up on. Thus, even before selling the farm, Albert looked for employment while his wife took care of the farm with her mother-in-law for several years. At the same time, she took care of their first two children. She agreed to do this to put them in a better position to get out and, when the moment came, to look for employment herself: today, she is a nursing assistant at the hospital.

Leaving the farm meant also leaving their house; so they bought some land and built a house on it. Once the farm was sold, they reared ducks. The profits from this business allowed them to improve their standard of living and to 'take a trip now and then', which otherwise would have been impossible. Since both of them earn modest wages, and since neither had received much of an education, they have pinned their hopes on education to give their children better opportunities. In addition, their son, who will soon be doing his military service, might then be able to learn how to fly helicopters. Albert remembers the dreams he had when he was young, and if it hadn't been for the war in Algeria and for the early death of his father. . . . Thus Albert hopes his son may realize the same plans that he was unable to realize during his own youth.

By keeping him on the farm for ten years, family ties permanently influenced the lives of Albert and his family. Albert was able to use these constraints to anchor himself strongly in the local community. In accepting that he could not avoid taking over the farm, while knowing that he would not remain a farmer, Albert counted on the resources of his community to improve his social status. Their working lives today are much less important to Albert and his wife than their involvement in local organizations and responsibilities for the community on which they have built their renewed social identity as a family.

GEORGETTE

Georgette has a café-bar near Paris on the banks of a navigable river, whose boatmen provide the core of her customers. Her husband, a retired manual worker, helps her. They have a son who has just finished high school. The business was handed down to Georgette by her parents, now retired, who lived next door.

Georgette had enjoyed school, but her parents discouraged her from continuing with her education. Instead, they made her take a dressmaking apprenticeship. After completing this she was employed for several years as a much valued worker in a fashion house in Paris. The *esprit de corps* there made a strong impression on her, and she made many close friends. Eventually she was offered promotion by the fashion house.

Very soon afterwards, however, her mother became seriously ill and called her back to take up her job in the café. The business was the only source of income for her parents and they still had her younger brother to take care of. 'I, who'd spent so much time breaking into the fashion business, at any cost to have something at any price, I had to stop suddenly and found myself behind the bar in a café. It was horrible—horrible!'

She remained there helping her parents for two years. Once her mother had recovered her health, Georgette returned to Paris. She did not feel able to try to make up for two lost years in the fashion business, so she learned to type and got a job in an office. In the meantime, she married a skilled worker who made a good living, and they had a son.

After several years, her mother, tired out, decided to retire and 'only eight days before closing the café, asked me if I would be interested in taking it over, I swear!' It was a real ultimatum. Georgette had three days to decide. Her work situation was not good. She often had to stay home from work to take care of her son, who was frequently ill. As a result, she had been relegated to an unqualified and boring position at the office. In addition, the atmosphere there was worsening. Georgette was finding it increasingly difficult to reconcile work with her personal life.

Thus when her mother confronted her with a decision requiring a quick answer, Georgette could only opt for a future whose conditions she well knew. She accepted the offer for family reasons, although these reasons conflicted with her personal life goals. Georgette had tried to construct a life independent of her family. Accepting her mother's offer meant returning to the family sphere of influence which she had tried to escape. All the same, her attitude was ambiguous, because the possibility of one day taking over the family business had always been at the back of her mind. This was why she always chose jobs in the business sector. And the choice between the possibility of improving the social standing of her family, and continuing her independent professional life, now that its future had become uncertain, was made easier by its timing. Once again, Georgette decided to let herself be recalled by the family business, while at the same time concluding, 'I've never done what I wanted to do.'

Nevertheless, she made the most of her new life. Her husband, following an accident, was unable to get on well at work. After working for a while in a position beneath his qualifications, he asked for early retirement to help his wife run the café. The couple installed a fast-food service for lunch-hours and opened a terrace so that people could sit outside when the weather was good. There is plenty to do, but even if the business is back on its feet and better adapted to its clientele, Georgette feels that her 'choice' will be vindicated only by the success of her son, who is the focus of all her hopes.

BERNADETTE

Not all family ties are actually exercised. It was almost by accident that during her interview Bernadette mentioned something that nearly happened to her. If it had, she would have had a completely different story to tell about her life. In her case, the pull of family came, not from her parents or grandparents, but from an uncle and aunt.

Bernadette works as secretary to the mayor of a flourishing village. This position, of which she is very proud, is the result of a quiet, solitary fight to ensure an independent professional position, even though her family and husband are very kind.

Born and brought up on a small farm, Bernadette had always known that her younger brother would take it over and she would do 'something else'. She absorbed this assumption into her personal goals: 'I didn't like the farm, not at all. My brother, he loved it . . . he didn't want to do anything else.' Fortunately, Bernadette enjoyed school and got good marks. Nevertheless, she had to leave before receiving any professional training.

Her uncle and aunt had a well-known restaurant in the area. Since they had no children of their own, and were thinking of retiring, they asked her if she would like to come to work with them, and eventually take over the restaurant. Bernadette hesitated. She wanted to continue her education and felt too young to take on such a responsibility. Since she had not yet had time to decide what she wanted to do with her life, the only arguments she could come up with were that she was unsure and inexperienced. On the other hand, she knew restaurant work well, because she generally worked as waitress in the restaurant during vacations. Thus, it was nothing new for her or her parents, who saw in this offer a promising future for their daughter. Bernadette accepted the offer on condition that she be allowed to follow a correspondence accounting course.

She had been working in the restaurant for three months when her uncle died suddenly. Since Bernadette was still too young to be of much help to her aunt, her aunt had to sell the restaurant. For Bernadette, the death of her uncle cancelled out the previous pull of family on her life.

Nevertheless, it had an effect on her future. She resumed her studies but, adjusting her education plans to fit the changed situation, she decided to attend a course that provided secretarial training as well as accounting courses. Through staying with her family and thus in her original neighbourhood, Bernadette had the time to meet her future husband, an electrician in an adjoining neighbourhood. Pinned down by marriage, Bernadette refused an offer at the end of the course, from the law firm where she did an internship, and instead took a part-time job in a rural town hall closer to where she was to live. This job would make it possible for her to combine her professional and family responsibilities.

The offer from her uncle and aunt, which came at a time when she had not yet decided what she wanted to do with her life, fell through due to an event over which she had no control. However, this interlude had an effect on the course of her life, for it kept her within the family circle. Nevertheless, it left Bernadette with the desire to protect her professional independence from the demands of her husband as a self-employed worker and her family responsibilities. Eventually after a number of years, she was able to get a full-time job at the town hall of her community.

A family offer becomes a transmission between generations only when it is received as well as offered. And the form of what is passed down can be transformed in the transmission.[5] A network of clients can be used for many types of business, a workshop for many types of product. Nevertheless, the strength of such an offer can be the more compelling just because it comes from within the family, often as a result of a death, and because the recipients may not fully understand how its implications will reshape their life. It constitutes a form of family tie which cannot be ignored.

Yet, as these instances show, even those who accept such a call often contrive to make a life of their own from it. Bernadette almost became the owner of a restaurant; Albert continues to use the fact that he belongs to the farming community to improve his family's standard of living; and Georgette was probably expecting to be sacked from her job when she found a solution which reconciled her personal and

professional lives. Each in their own fashion has appropriated their
family inheritance for themselves.

MARCEL

For some, like Marcel, the call from family can come too late to make
an impact on their working career. Marcel's professional upward
mobility gave him some independence from his family and the ability
to resist a call of that kind. Even so, his inheritance, not of a working
property but of a house, has profoundly modified his personal life. And
again, its symbolic and emotional drawing power seems to have been
heightened through coming as the result of a death in the family, and
the feelings of emotional loss and the need to recover lost roots which
this evoked.

Marcel's parents were low-grade white-collar workers who lived
modestly. Their only advantages were job security and the fact that
they had decided not to have more than one child. To enable their son
to continue studying for so long, Marcel's parents relied on his
grandparents, who were better off financially. However, it was not so
much through financial means that Marcel's grandparents helped him,
but rather by always making him welcome in their home, and by
unconditional support. He would arrive every weekend and every
vacation at their house at the edge of a forest. There he could work and
rest. His parents were equally welcome to take advantage of such
favourable conditions, but they worked and often could not accompany
their son, who they knew to be in good hands. Thus, Marcel was
brought up mainly by his grandparents. In addition, since Marcel's
grandfather had become an engineer through in-house promotions, he
could help Marcel with his homework. Marcel successfully studied for
all his exams in their house, which thus represented for him and for his
parents an enviable sign of social success.

After graduating from a good engineering school, Marcel took a job
with a multinational corporation at a period when the corporation was
expanding rapidly, ensuring that Marcel was able to win rapid
promotion.

Marcel married a young woman who had a good education, but no
specific professional qualifications. His in-laws helped them to find
housing and to integrate socially through friendships with other
couples of the same professional milieu. Several years later, they
divorced. Marcel had been posted abroad at the time and asked for his

tour of duty abroad to be extended. When he returned to France, he
rented a spacious apartment close to his work and took up a very urban
lifestyle.

Within a very short time, however, both of his much loved
grandparents had died. They left him their house, the home he had
known since childhood. Although it was situated in a remote suburb he
was unable even to consider refusing this inheritance. He terminated
the lease on his apartment, and despite its distance from his work, he
moved into the old house.

As a result he has not been able to maintain his previous lifestyle. In
addition to the burden of paying for death duties on his inheritance
and the costs of renovating and maintaining the house, he now lives far
from the city centre. He goes out less and less.

Instead he has withdrawn into the old family home with all its
associations of the past. The house had symbolized the social identity
of the family to three generations. When it came to him, to refuse it
would have seemed infidelity to his ancestry. Instead of Marcel using
his inheritance to promote his own plans for the future, it is the family
home which has claimed Marcel for itself.

In any family network the ties of solidarity create both potential
opportunities and potential constraints for its members. The power of
family ties only becomes positively enabling when the younger
generation can find, in the openings provided through family
resources, a sense of personal discovery, so that it can turn these
chances into its own. Conversely every man and woman needs in order
to achieve and maintain a social position, not only to construct a sense
of self but to have this identity recognized by others. The family
provides the vital social space within which this process of construction
begins. For families with relatively restricted social resources, however,
the solidarity between generations is as likely to reinforce the limits on
the social movement for which family members can hope as it is to
encourage them to seize their individual life chances. In such families
especially, the power to launch their offspring is coupled with the
possibility that, right through their lives, they may be called back to the
paths of older generations.

Notes

1. The interviews discussed here are from two projects: 'La production des trajectoires
sociales: Articulation des événements de la vie familiale et de la vie professionnelle',

CNRS–MIRE, carried out with Françoise Battagliola, Michèle Ferrand, and Françoise Imbert; and 'Familles et mobilité sociale', CNRS, carried out with Daniel Bertaux.
2. A. Gotman, *Hériter* (Paris, 1988), 6.
3. See A. Pitrou, esp. 'Dépérissement des solidarités familiales?,' *L'Année Sociologique,* 37 (1987), 207–24.
4. There are in fact always two families, since each couple is composed of two people, each linked to a different family line. Consequently adult descendants who break with one line may find themselves at the same time continuing the traditions of the other. A further complication is that there are many different dimensions to continuity, e.g. place of residence as well as profession. See esp. F. Bloch, M. Buisson, and J. C. Mermet, *Dette et filiation: Analyse des interrelations entre activité féminine et vie familiale,* GRS/Université de Lyon 2, 1989.
5. D. Bertaux and I. Bertaux-Wiame, 'Le patrimoine et sa lignée: Transmissions et mobilité sociale sur cinq générations,' *Life Stories/Récits de vie,* 4 (1988), 8–25.

4

Religion, Family, and Industry in the Transmission of Values

The Case of Women Textile Workers in Antioquia (Colombia)

Luz Gabriela Arango

The region of Antioquia and its textile industry played a fundamental role in the formation of an industrial working class in Colombia. The modest industrial base consisting of small manufacturing companies that had been established at the end of the nineteenth century began to expand after the end of the Second World War. Colombia's industrialization process centred on the Antioquian region during the first half of the twentieth century and most consumer-goods industries were concentrated within its territory. Among the different social and cultural transformations that the industrialization process generated in this region, we have been particularly interested in examining the consolidation and evolution of values referring to women's work in industry, analysing the encounter of a tradition of Catholicism and a type of labour organization that determined the transmission of values in lower-class families and the production of new values arising from the world of the factory.

We will review the stages of renovation in the values referring to women's work in factories through a study of the Fabricato textile firm. This firm has been one of the most modern and productive in Colombia since the 1920s and has occupied second place among the nation's textile producers for many years. We will examine closely the relationship between the values transmitted by the family and those generated in the factory, arbitrated by Catholic values that attempted to ensure the unity and universality of the images of women's work and those of the working woman. This contradictory relationship initially, in the 1930s and 1940s, produced an apparently coherent symbolic

Translator: Carol O'Flynn

system that gave the working woman a unique place in the family and in production, sanctioned by Catholic values. Similar values were transmitted in the family circle and the factory, largely via the agency of the Church.

During a second period (the 1950s and 1960s), modifications in the organization of production and in industrial ideologies brought about important transformations in the values associated with women's work. Women workers became divided and were forced to choose between irreconcilable identities: that of the mother dedicated to her home or that of the celibate woman working in the factory. Paradoxically, new family and maternal ideals were exalted from within the factories, thus obliging countless families to modify their images of sex roles.

A new element that eventually displaced those values arose during a third period (the 1970s and 1980s). The interaction between family and factory took place in a larger arena in which the social, economic, political, and cultural transformations of the environment were to weigh increasingly heavily upon local dynamics, resulting in a further weakening of traditional relationships. Modernization has affected women's relationships with their families by making possible the emergence of an individual awareness that not even the conditions of proletarization predominating in the region until that time had been able to generate.

At the beginning of the twentieth century, a lower-class family model predominated in Antioquia. The families of small farmers, muleteers, and artisans were typically nuclear in kind, with widespread predomin- ance of Catholic marriage over common-law marriages and unwed motherhood. The stability of such marriages was built on the joint effort demanded by production and it established a clear and complementary division of sex roles: the father-producer wielded recognized authority in the home and the mother assumed an active role in managing the children and in co-ordinating household tasks.

The Catholic values that are socially recognized in Antioquia differ notably from those that predominate in other regions of the country. Antioquian Catholicism is pragmatic in nature. It values productive effort and economic success to the point that some scholars have claimed that it has assimilated the 'Puritan work ethic' described by Weber. Although the concept generally associated with this term does not reflect the Antioquian situation in an exact way, Catholic values and practices in the region have differed from the eclectic cults found in larger Indian populations with their heavy ritual content and deep-rooted institutions of servitude. The religious values of Antioquia combined ethical flexibility in economic behaviour with moral rigidity and rigorous social control of sexual behaviour, especially that of women.

The first generation of women workers,[1] who entered Fabricato between 1923 and 1944, were largely the daughters of small farmers, farm workers and muleteers of the region, though some were of urban origin: the daughters of artisans, small merchants, government employees, and factory workers. These young women initially entered the world of the factory as part of a family strategy that sought to complement the father's earnings. Their work must be understood within a context of scarce employment for women, other than temporary or poorly paid jobs. Lower-class families count on their working offspring to contribute to the subsistence of the household. The fact is that daughters working in paid jobs did not necessarily represent something new, since other alternatives such as temporary work in coffee-picking or in remunerated domestic work already existed. Nevertheless, the ways in which women entered industrial jobs generated in Fabricato represented a transformation in the patterns of female work. Having originally entered the factory on a temporary basis in order to complement family income, they later became the basic providers of household support.

Paternalism characterized the first decades of what would become the great Antioquian textile industry. Jorge Echavarría, a Fabricato administrator during the 1930s, was a prototype of the paternalistic employer who maintains a direct relationship with his workers: he knew them individually, was aware of their family histories, and intervened in their personal home lives without being asked to do so. This type of employer is very demanding regarding work, is frequently present on the factory floor, and has a thorough knowledge of the functioning of each machine.

The initial pragmatism of the factory owners in Antioquia was modified by the impact of Catholic Social Action on the region, particularly in organizing mutual aid societies among artisans, and in divulging the doctrines contained in the papal encyclicals. Catholic Action was a Church-sponsored institution that experienced a period of rapid development in the 1930s, when it co-ordinated a group of organizations involved in the workers' environment: Catholic Youth Organization, Workers' Centres, Convent Boarding School for

Women Workers, and the Catholic Press. In the 1940s it also began to influence the Catholic labour unions that were created in factories like Fabricato. Industrialists in Antioquia, who formed the ANDI (Asociación Nacional de Industriales) during the same period, maintained a close relationship with Catholic Action and adopted the social doctrine that this organization propagated as the framework in which to deal with labour relations. The institutional and symbolic support of the Catholic Church permitted the rising industrial class to solve two problems: the search for social legitimacy and the need to train a disciplined industrial working class.

At the beginning of the century female work in the incipient urban centres of Antioquia was the object of concern among journalists, politicians, and moralists. The questions they raised bring to mind the arguments of Jules Simon with respect to women workers in France in the nineteenth century. The visible misery of city life was clearly seen in these women and children in search of employment, the victims of a process of social transformation which still fails to call forth unanimous enthusiasm.

It is worth while calling attention to the fact that 9 per cent of the workers are girls of less than 15. Is it not painful to see that little girls as young as 5 are working in the factories in a Christian society, and that they are obliged to do so out of necessity or by their parents? Is it not high time to legislate on the matter in order to protect the children?[2]

In the face of similar doubts, the industrialists of the 1920s and 1930s carried out open campaigns calling for the 'moralization' of factories and of industrial employment for women. This was presented as an honourable alternative by means of which to rescue the lower classes from misery and to save the women from the risk of prostitution: 'the women, pulled out of misery and prostitution and dedicated to the easy work of watching over the weaving automats: the children, exercising their muscles and intelligence and acquiring a love for work, order, and precision in this school.'[3]

A famous administrator and owner of one of the first textile-manufacturing plants in the region, Don Emilio Restrepo, invited parents to place their daughters in the factories, as a means of ensuring that the family would be able to acquire its own home. The degree of exploitation of infant female labour was such that Don Emilio recognized that a family would have to have at least four daughters working in the factory in order to be able to purchase its own home.

Firms like Fabricato, aligned with the Catholic Church, later conducted campaigns to convince lower-class families and Antioquian society of the virtues of industrial work. In Fabricato, this was eventually translated into a 'sanctification' of the workplace thanks to permanent religious intervention. In the 1930s the creation of a chapel with its chaplain and a convent boarding school under the charge of Presentation nuns led to the 'sanctification' of two generations of chaste and celibate women workers dedicated to working for the benefit of their families and the factory.

Many of the female workers who went to work for Fabricato during that decade remained single, working in the factory until they reached retirement age. A good many others worked for a time and then resigned in order to marry. Company policies continued to favour growing stability among personnel and many families continued to elaborate survival strategies based on the wage work of their daughters.

A new and unique image of female work arose, encouraged from within the family circle and the factory floor, which assimilated it to a religious vocation, in which sacrifice and effort constituted the means of obtaining salvation. While it is true that there were antecedents of a Catholic tradition in the region, the origins of which have not been totally clarified, it seems even more certain that a Catholic work ethic, highly repressive of female sexuality, was propagated by Catholic Social Action in Antioquia from the 1930s on and reinforced by the policies of social legitimization of the local bourgeoisie, with a national dimension.

In its convent boarding-school, Fabricato applied the same methods employed by Catholic institutions such as convents, boarding-schools, and orphanages in the eighteenth and nineteenth centuries, where achieving the virtues of the faith for the soul required the taming of the body. In this context, religious discipline functioned together with industrial training in a symbiotic relationship.

The nuns' 'sermons', the humiliating punishments, and the discipline imposed on a daily basis constituted the principal mechanisms for transmitting values. Morality was taught with the rod. The bell would ring in the boarding-school announcing that it was time to go to six o'clock Mass, but it would also ring to announce the beginning of the work shift, lunch-time, the hour to take a bath or to do one's laundry or to attend edifying talks about the virgin Mary.

A lot of discipline, too much—There were six or seven nuns, one was always on watch to see that no one was smoking in the corridors or in the dormitories, and that no one was lying in bed in the dormitories. . . . After work we had sewing machines. They gave us sewing classes that were very cheap. We rested and then we did the laundry because the schedule allowed no time for anything else. And the bell rang a lot. If it was in the morning, we were obliged to go to Mass, even if we had got in at four o'clock in the morning; afterwards, we would get turns for taking a bath. . . . There was every type of Christian organization: the Children of Mary, the Eucharistic Crusade, a 'holy hour' every month, retreats that lasted all day. They gave us food and we could not talk. All in all, one is not entirely ungrateful. For all the unpleasant discipline, considering the instruction they gave us, the security of the place, the moral aspect, and the low cost, it was not so bad after all.

Although the search for salvation or the imitation of the Virgin were not the principal motivations of these women, religious vocations were recognized in the social environment and they provided gratifying models of femininity that compensated for the impossibility of achieving one of the patterns most highly valued by the culture of the region, the ideal of motherhood. For some female workers, factory work represented a substitute in the face of failure to achieve a full-fledged religious vocation:

The factory people themselves helped me. Don Rudesindo was delighted whenever the women workers became nuns. There were always some in the Presentation convent, in the Good Shepherd, in the Little Sisters of the Poor. I went off to enter the Barefoot Carmelites in Frontino. I was there about eighteen months, but since I was so poorly prepared I felt ashamed and humiliated. . . . eventually realized that I was not going to be accepted and although I lasted a year in the novitiate, I was rejected along with some other girls just three months before finishing the trial period as a novice. I went back to Fabricato.

While these religious values that 'moralized' factory work and cultivated physical self-discipline were widely propagated by the factories, other mechanisms operated within the family circle. Here, the employment of daughters in industry was in most cases the result of a need in the broadest sense. The family unit defined one's deepest sense of identity and purpose in life. Authority, affection, and economic necessity were not easily dissociated. Premature orphanhood, poverty, or a mother or father's request would result in the early incorporation of daughters into the workplace in order to face an inescapable imperative: the obligation to contribute to the support of the household.

But if the work of sons and daughters was an unquestionable part of their duties to their parents, the process that led to placing the entire 'obligation' on one or two daughters over a long period of time, demanding the indefinite postponement of such legitimate aspirations as marriage or motherhood, required other motivations and led to obvious contradictions.

Important decision-making moments in women workers' lives, especially the choice of continuing to work or of getting married, made it possible to express the conflict of values and the weight of the commitment that united them to their family of origin:

I didn't marry because I had many responsibilities at home from the beginning. I was the one that earned the most because they gave me a contract to work with the looms. My brothers went off one by one to organize their own lives until I was left alone with my mother after my father died.

I had a boyfriend in Fabricato when I first went to work there, but I was determined to work to help my family. I had to be 'the man of the house'; I had to work to help my mother and my brothers and sisters.

The sense of belonging to the home of origin that was inculcated in the daughters, combined with a domestic regime that emphasized submission and respect for paternal authority, were accepted as natural rules. It was not simply a matter of undeniable economic pressure, but of a moral duty that had been internalized with special intensity by women. The women's degree of commitment to the family of origin was much greater than that of their brothers, a factor which reflects the different expectations of parents.

We lived in Santa Rosa de Osos with the whole family and I entered the School of the Sacred Heart there but then the two oldest, my sister and I, had to begin to seek our fortune so we couldn't continue in school. There were seven of us, including three brothers, but one couldn't count on them.

The family unit established rules that determined the degree of commitment children owed to their home of origin. Daughters were considered to belong to the household to a greater degree than sons for whom a 'vocation' in the outside world was not only accepted but encouraged. Furthermore, older children had special duties with respect to the younger ones. They were required to contribute to the education of the younger ones once they themselves had completed a few years of primary school.

These values were transmitted within the coherent framework of Catholic representations and practices. The ideal that nourished the lives of women was the Marian cult. In school, the girls became

members of the congregation of the Children of Mary and proudly
exhibited their membership ribbons at Mass every Sunday.

This set of duties, and the factory work which went with it,
provisionally represented an acceptable option for many daughters. In
many cases, however, it was to become their 'destiny' just as
'obligation' would become the main point of existence. At some point
along the way, what seemed to be a temporary solution to surmountable
problems became a blind alley, once they lost hope of the possibility of
marriage or motherhood. Working daughters became the economic
pillars of their homes, assuming a role that did not correspond to
women within the culture and becoming, as they themselves have
expressed it, 'the men of the house'.

Assuming the role of essential providers in their homes of origin
permitted many women to accede to a position of status within the
family circle. They took on a mission of extended motherhood by
assuming responsibility for the welfare of the family, for the education
of nieces and nephews, and for solidarity with relatives in need,
especially widowed sisters or those who were abandoned by their
husbands. But this generally occurred only after many years of work,
when the parents were finally ready to surrender part of their authority.
Others, on the contrary, suffered frustration for years and the feeling
of having wasted their lives led some to a late marriage, often on the
threshold of retirement.

Nevertheless, even if the potentially negative ideals of duty and
'sacrifice' in favour of the family were associated with this form of
women's work, other values were also to be found that enhanced the
alternative of work and celibacy with positive connotations:

Over twenty years ago I had an opportunity to get married, but I couldn't
decide to go ahead with it. My responsibility for my mother held me back. I
didn't want to leave my job and I wasn't sure that I wanted to undertake the
adventure. I didn't want to marry just to get married and I had many personal
demands. Besides, the experiences of my sisters didn't encourage me very
much and I didn't want to give up my independence for a husband who would
shout at me.

Should these be considered mechanisms for achieving conformity, for
smoothing over the dissatisfactions of a journey that no longer permits
any change of course, or as a means of accommodation that offered
real advantages? Autonomy, independence, and eventual authority
within the household were consoling, though at best they provided
only a limited kind of empowerment.

During the 1950s, the implementation of an industrial engineering system in Fabricato began to bring about important transformations in the organization of production. This was accompanied by the spread of new values that would affect the image of women's work in notable ways.

The new type of worker that industry required corresponded in broad terms to the Ford ideal: productive workers, highly motivated by economic incentives, integrated into the company, and highly stable. Concern for the conditions in which these workers would reproduce the labour force arose with special emphasis during this period and the working-class family became the target of active policies for the first time in an attempt to adapt it to the Ford model.

The factory was no longer concerned about the disciplined single woman worker who was dedicated to her work and to the support of her family of origin, but rather about the workers' wives, the mothers of the future labour force. During this period female desertion and restricted recruitment of women decreased their participation within the workforce to 13 per cent in 1965. Like numerous other firms at that time, Fabricato undertook educational campaigns aimed at moulding a stable and 'rational' working-class family.

The company's chaplain and social workers were placed in charge of spreading these values by means of all types of courses, given in abundance throughout the period. The Social Secretariat, which was created in 1945, directed Centres for Improvement of the Home and primary schools for workers' children, and organized home visits to encourage the rationalization of family life. During the 1960s courses in sewing, embroidery, cooking, and home gardening were introduced. In addition, lectures were given on child education, alcoholism, and health, all of which were intended to increase women's qualifications as mothers. The Christian Family Movement, which 'works and exists for the purpose of strengthening the family as a healthy cell of civil society', has played an active role within the factory since 1960.

New agents and new mechanisms for the transmission of values arose: specialists, armed with academic knowledge—in this case, recently graduated social workers from the Universidad Pontificia Bolivariana (the Jesuit university in Medellín)—held conferences and short courses and supervised the effects of the learning process.

Working mothers continued to be ignored in the policies and the system of values promoted by industry. They were not even considered worthy of mention. Fabricato policies were concerned only with those women who served as support for the company's workers within the home. Social policy sanctioned this situation by introducing maternity bonuses for workers' wives and by excluding from the factory those single female workers who decided to marry or to have children. In discussing the issue of 'masculinizing' the production personnel, the engineer in charge of the industrial engineering implantation process argued that 'in giving a man a job, the problem of a woman was being solved'.

During the 1950s exaltation of the mother's role in the home and discrimination against women within the area of production became inseparable processes. Unmarried women workers who had been trained according to other standards in earlier decades suffered painfully in this process. Displaced from key jobs, such as weaving and spinning, and relegated to complementary tasks like cleaning machinery or folding towels, with the lowest salaries among all workers, they experienced a severe depreciation of their feminine image. They also found themselves deprived of their professional identity as the relative gratification of a job 'well done' disappeared as well. As some women workers have expressed it: 'one answered for one's work'; 'my contract work was among the best to be seen there, and all the bosses said so'.

The new nuclear family model centred upon itself and was the target of care, aid, and vigilance dispensed through the policies of private companies and the state. It was a model which ran counter to the interests of families of origin and with their value system in which the responsibility and duties of offspring sustained family solidarity.

The new working conditions created strong stimuli for males, reinforcing their vocation as providers who concentrated their efforts on the welfare of their family of procreation. Male workers who went to work for Fabricato quickly cut off ties with their families of origin and formed their own homes. Unmarried daughters employed in large factories had come to represent the hopes of their families of origin. Paradoxically, their commitment to their families of origin was reinforced just at the time when they were being expelled from industry. This brought about a stage of transition from the model of single women's work as a 'vocation', determined by daughters' 'privileged' relationship with the home of origin and protected by certain Catholic images, to a model of female work orientated to promoting the formation of families with access to the benefits of new social policies.

For a time, the working-class family, organized around the

industrial work of the father and the 'qualification' of the work of the mother in the home, coexisted with the old model now subject to contradictions and to increasing deterioration. Families of origin continued to stimulate the commitment of their wage-earning daughters in the hope that one of them would assume the long-term support of the household. Nevertheless, disciplinary mechanisms within the family circle and in the factory had been weakened and replaced by the company's new strategies, which sought to 'motivate', 'stimulate', and 'provide incentives' rather than to impose discipline and control. The sense of belonging to the home of origin and the internalization of a sense of 'obligation' on the part of daughters had little place in the new working-class model of exalted motherhood. In the face of these new conditions, female desertion increased, from the home of origin as well as from the factory.

At the same time, improved salaries and social benefits had repercussions for unmarried women workers' ability to aid their families:

Papa did not retire from Pantex. He worked for eleven years and then he quit. When he quit there was only my salary. I built the house, and sent them all to school and raised them as best I could. My sisters got married as they came of age. I had a chance to marry but I didn't because I was afraid to leave my mother and father alone since none of my sisters worked. Everything we have in the house: the TV, the radio, the refrigerator—I got us everything we have.

The close relationship that some daughters in recent generations maintain with their homes of origin is a result of freer choices. These daughters who assume responsibility for supporting their families of origin do so out of affection and also because they are stimulated by the possibility of assuming a much more gratifying role as providers than was the case in previous generations. It is no longer simply a question of ensuring the survival of the family, but of undertaking a more ambitious project: the improvement of living conditions, regardless of whether the decision to work was initially based on unfulfilled marriage expectations.

In these conditions, many women painfully perceive the lack of incentives available to them in the factory:

I have no right to anything for my nieces and nephews. Bachelors and single women, especially, have no right to anything. Everything is reserved for families. One is providing the same services as the married women, so I don't understand why we have no right to anything. One should have had something for one's family. We single women have no right but the right to die.

The Catholic Church invested its energies in promoting the mother's role in the home, her responsibility for her children's education and for her husband's performance on the job. Women workers were relatively neglected. Unmarried women workers no longer found images with which they could identify themselves socially. The convent-type image of female work no longer produced any enthusiasm; nor did it constitute a socially acceptable substitute for marriage. The gradual rise of secular values aimed at improving material conditions along with the legitimate search for access to 'consumer society' goods corroded Christian values that had associated female work with a morality based on the idea of sacrifice.

The Ford-style ideal of the worker whose salary was large enough to support a family was undermined by economic changes. Workers' purchasing power diminished, aggravated by the recession that affected industry in 1974 and 1975. Fabricato once again opened its doors to female workers between 1976 and 1978. Several factors motivated this reopening. The labour union and the chaplain's office exerted pressure for recruitment of workers' relatives. Their interest in employing workers' daughters was strictly as a means of complementing paternal income. During this same period, Fabricato lifted restrictions on employing married or pregnant women, a policy that had become both socially and legally unsustainable.

In this way, a new generation of women entered the factory: women of urban origin with several years of secondary-school education, most of them the daughters of Fabricato workers. The social context was thus marked by profound cultural transformations that the firm had failed to assimilate.

During the 1960s and 1970s when women's entry was restricted, Antioquian society had undergone a secularization process. It was characterized by a crisis of traditional Catholic values: a hitherto unknown inability of the Church to control private conduct, new tolerance of unorthodox family practices (unwed motherhood, common-law marriage, and widespread use of family planning). Finally, higher employment rates and educational aspirations were evident among growing sectors of the population and especially among women.

The new generation of women workers, educated according to the value system that Fabricato had spread among its Catholic Ford-style workers, was to achieve a true generational breakthrough. These women entered Fabricato as part of a familial strategy that required them to contribute a complementary salary to their families along with a personal commitment similar to that required of their predecessors:

I went to work because of the needs of my family. There were two of us to choose from, a brother of mine and me. My father had to choose and he preferred to have me go to work because girls bring home more of the money they earn than men do, so I went to work in Fabricato.

Working daughters initially became secondary providers with respect to their fathers but very quickly began to fulfil their own personal aspirations in preference to responding to the needs or pressures exerted by the home of origin. Although women still responded more readily to such pressures than men, often sacrificing years of study or postponing personal projects in favour of the family of origin, they only did so temporarily in this period. Distribution within the household of aid received from sons and daughters began to reveal greater equity and moreover there was growing respect for individual needs. This seems to have been facilitated by the improved economic conditions in homes in which the father contributed important earnings and managed to purchase housing for the family so that aid from older son and daughters was only required to cover the cost of educating the younger ones.

The seeds of a sense of individualism among the women workers were undoubtedly sown in secondary school. Nevertheless, none of them pointed out crisis or confrontations with their families during this period. These, when they did occur, seem to have originated more as a result of the opportunities to socialize which they encountered in the workplace and of salary earnings that opened up unsuspected options in the urban universe. Some of these women, in fact, went through a 'rebel stage' prior to going to work in the factory, but this was usually the result of a meaningful juvenile relationship, particularly with members of their peer group:

I have a daughter of 8. I met her father when he worked in a store in Medellín, when I was going through a rebel stage. I was 17 when I got pregnant. He was 18 and I met him in a little bar in the neighbourhood where he had parties. He was a rich boy (*hijo de papi*), well dressed and with money. I was about to marry him but my family didn't like him since he started to smoke marijuana. When I got pregnant my mother told me they would do whatever they could to help me and that I should be good, but that I shouldn't see the boy again because he had nothing to offer me. My mother talked to me a lot.

Access to a salary and to new social relationships at work constituted a real driving force that allowed these young women to liberate their personal aspirations. Most of them quickly established their own alternatives, in spite of their youth and their recent entry into the factory. Many got married, others became single mothers, and some opted for common-law marriage. Family attitudes towards unwed mothers reveal the difficulty these households experienced in developing greater tolerance towards the sexual behaviour of their daughters. The first reaction was generally one of rejection and may have included expulsion from the home. However, an agreement was usually reached based on an exchange of services: the unwed mother-daughter assumed greater economic commitment to her parents and they, in turn, assured her of domestic support in bringing up her child.

We had been living together for four months and we made the decision about the baby together, but when I got pregnant I left home because my mother took it very hard. His parents were my little girl's godparents. When I had to go back to work, my family had got over it and they called me back home. It was the best thing for me because I didn't know who to leave the baby with.

The cohesive system of values that had characterized the Ford-style family broke down without producing excessive trauma. Parents saw how their children adhered to values arising outside the family circle and, in many cases, they managed to introduce mechanisms of internal negotation that made it possible to conserve family solidarity and to tolerate diversity of behaviour and values among family members. Daughters abandoned many of their religious beliefs and practices. Most of them had been brought up according to strict Catholic norms in which religious rites and practices were closely associated with discipline in daily life. The tradition of the evening rosary had previously obliged the family to gather together before going to bed at early hours, and morning Mass on Sunday had been the only acceptable way to begin observance of the sabbath; but recent generations of women workers have broken away in varying degrees from these Catholic socialization ceremonies.

The rites and practices they still attend are generally limited to Sunday Mass. Novenas to saints and the evening rosary have practically disappeared. Some women workers have abandoned Catholic rituals altogether and only return to certain practices when they become mothers and seek to set 'a good example' for their children by baptizing them and taking them to make their First Communion.

Nevertheless, a clear differentiation between external practices and internal convictions has taken place. Without denying their Catholicism, these women workers have privatized their religious sentiments, asserting the right to live the faith in a personal way:

I was a Child of Mary in the nun's convent. My parents were very Catholic and went to Mass every Sunday. They brought us up very strictly, with First Fridays and the rosary every night, but I no longer go to Mass although I'm a believer and I communicate with God in a personal way.

Although working-class daughters' new attitudes signify fundamental changes with respect to the values and world view inculcated in them, their families of origin have adapted to these transformations. In vicariously entering the modern era through their children, they have interiorized change as a characteristic of the present day, have learned to tolerate differences, and have provided real support in raising the grandchildren and in offering temporary accommodation for young couples.

As old, rigid moral criteria were lifted, the heterogeneous sexual and family practices of the new generation made their way into the firm, causing great unease. Common-law marriages and children born out of wedlock became common among the young women workers, causing conflicts with older male and female workers who shared the moral criteria of the firm. The heads of production rooms reacted unfavourably, fiercely resisting the entry of women, whom they considered responsible for the upset that had occurred. Fabricato, accustomed for more than thirty years to exercising almost absolute control over the sexual behaviour of its female workers, proved incapable of designing new policies based on respect for the separation between the private lives of these young women and their work.

The textile crisis of the 1980s served as a pretext for interrupting women's moderate attempts to reclaim the space that they had once occupied in the factory. Despite the fact that these young women had demonstrated they could perform efficiently and productively in both specialized and semi-skilled tasks, numerous women workers who had recently joined the ranks of the factory workers were dismissed.

The few women workers who remained continued to transform, through practical action, the stereotypes predominating in the factory with respect to women's work. Not only did they refuse to tolerate any attempt on the part of the firm to control their private lives and their sexual behaviour, but they progressively asserted their status as women workers with equal rights to men. However, the crisis and the dismissals increased women's vulnerability in the factory and prevented consolidation of the process.

Women's relation to the workplace was indicative of the rise of a wage-earner's consciousness determined to a certain extent by the critical situation of belonging to Fabricato. Although they believe that they have a right to employment, identification with a particular job has tended to become weaker. They still believe in the personal satisfaction of a job well done, but this has not prevented them from seeking better economic and environmental conditions. Willing to change occupations and even firms if necessary, and clear in affirming that 'they were not born in Fabricato', given the precarious labour market they also value the advantages of working for the firm.

The changes that took place in society and in the aspirations of young women workers in the 1970s and 1980s raise the difficult question of the need for new images of women's work that will open up an equal place for them in the labour market. What is needed is a more positive image of a figure that has become increasingly common at Fabricato: the female worker who is also a mother.

The individualistic motivations of women with broad social experience (secondary school, access to mass communication) will permit progressive legitimation (still far from being generalized) of female autonomy and independence. Nevertheless, certain mediations are still necessary in order to 'justify' the industrial work of mothers socially. The main one stems from the need to legitimize the social-mobility project among young couples. In the present conditions of crisis of the Ford-style model, this objective requires the joint contribution of both spouses.

These women workers have assimilated a very rational attitude in defining their life projects with partners. Aspects such as the control of earnings and expenses, savings and investment planning, and decisions regarding the number of children and the timetable for conceiving them are all included in the new working-class family models. Increasing equity in managing income and in distributing domestic tasks suggests a profound transformation in sexual roles. Nevertheless, the problems involved in developing new values regarding maternity have yet to be solved. In many young households today, a mother's work is still considered a 'necessary evil' which many couples hope to be able to avoid.

In spite of growing collaboration on the part of men, those working mothers still have to face very difficult material conditions that have often made them long for the conditions of housewives:

My mother-in-law used to take care of the children. She's the one who has raised them for me, but she's sick now and is going to be hospitalized. I was used to leaving them with her and rushing home to do the housework. I'm exhausted when I go to bed now. I'm desperate. I have tried out four different maids but I haven't found a single one I liked. I'd like to stay at home now that we have paid off the house between the two of us. We built it and, although it's still unfinished, at least we don't owe anything on it. We are seriously considering the possibility of my staying at home to take care of the children.

Although women have achieved a positive image of themselves as workers and wage-earners, their role as mothers causes them profound uneasiness. Exacerbating this problem is a lack of positive social images of the working mother, along with a lack of support networks.

The evolution of values regarding women's work in industry, brought about under the influence of families and factory throughout four generations of female factory workers, reveals wide-reaching processes of social change. Local values were dominated by the Catholic Church within the context of a social organization marked by traditional relationships, which established no radical differentiation between family life and that of the factory. The efforts of the Church gave rise to *sui generis* images that legitimized the entry of women to industry during the first three decades of this century. Work became a semi-religious vocation that demanded abdication from motherhood and marriage in favour of economic productivity and commitment to the family of origin.

Later on, new values arose in the industrial world which eventually threw a shadow over images of female participation in industry. The male Ford-style worker was the ideal. His corollary, the mother of his children, was the educator and qualified administrator of a rationalized family. Eventually, individualistic values nourished by social transformations beyond the boundaries of factory, family, and region served as support for rebellion among a new generation of women workers in the 1970s and 1980s in their quest for control of their sexual, family, and workplace relationships.

68   *Luz Gabriela Arango*

The example of Fabricato illustrates a process that began with a value system moulded by religion and family, which regional industry exploited in order to ensure its legitimacy. Relationships between work, family, and religion were altered by the gradual integration of more individualistic values characteristic of modern societies. Social, economic, and cultural transformations during the past decades have transcended the factory, profoundly influencing the most recent generation of women workers. Women have become agents of change in family and industrial patterns, but will also have to face resistance and hardship along the way. Motherhood stands out as a key image associated with women's work. The first generation of Fabricato workers based their identities as women on notions of female celibacy. This was inculcated within the value system that imposed the ideal of women's work as a religious vocation. This ideal was partially eclipsed by the rationalization of the working-class family along the lines of the Ford-style model family. It is this model which recent generations of women have challenged in their search for new values.

Notes

1. We use the term 'generation' to indicate different groups of women workers classified according to the period in which they entered the factory. The series of periods we have established divide the history of the firm into four stages: 1923–44, Christian paternalism; 1945–59, Rationalization of work; 1960–73, Enterprise–Providence; 1974–82, Crisis and liberalization. Data were obtained from the résumés of 1,525 female workers classified as 'retired', 'pensioned', or 'actively employed' in the personnel files of Fabricato. From among the 836 female workers listed as pensioned or active workers in 1982, 20 cases were selected for the purpose of gathering information about their family and personal lives.
2. Jorge Rodriguez, in the *Anuario Estadístico del Distrito de Medellín*, 1915, 50, quoted by Fernando Botero in *La Industrialización en Antioquia, Genesis y Consolidación 1900–1930* (Medellín, Colombia, 1984), 139.
3. 'Una visita a la Fabrica de Tejidos Hernández', *El Sol*, Medellín, 20 Oct. 1916, quoted by Botero *La industrialización*, 150.

5

Social Change, Family Histories, and Attitudes to Money in a Rural Community in Epirus

KLIMIS NAVRIDIS

> Remembering is a commotion in the body.
>
> (Eleni Kosti, aged 46, potato farmer)

Sociological and ethnological research in rural Greece and in the Epirus region in particular has identified a number of changes in demography and family, economy and politics, society, and ways of thinking which have occurred in recent decades.[1] But all this research has one weakness: we almost never hear the voices of the villagers themselves. As a result, we do not know what part these people take as agents of change or of resistance, nor how they experience their participation.[2] Hence the method chosen for our research project in Chrysovitsa, a mountain community in Epirus, on the topic of social change and relations to money in a rural area.[3]

Another important starting-point for our research is the continuing close link in agriculture between family relationships and the relations of production. The ethnologists Claude Meillassoux and Pierre-Philippe Rey have respectively used the terms 'domestic mode of production' and 'lineage mode of production',[4] in analysing how, in a capitalist society, elements of the traditional agricultural society are locally articulated with features of the dominant mode of production.

The domestic unit preserves its productive role and is not transformed into a capitalist business. This restricts the monetarization of the relations of production and exchange. At the same time and on a different level, the development of agricultural co-operatives mediates in the village's relations with the town. In this way, a cheap agricultural

Translator: John Solman

workforce can be kept in place, and production prices held relatively low.[5]

This linking of different modes of production may end by strangling life at the local level. In the area around Chrysovitsa—that is, the north-east part of Epirus, astride the Pindus mountain chain—many villages which until early in this century enjoyed some prosperity thanks largely to stock-breeding have progressively declined and are now totally uninhabited. The Ministry of Culture protects these settlements as part of a campaign to preserve cultural heritage, but in the few houses which are still lived in one finds only old people.

Chrysovitsa is an exception to this rule. Not far from the village is a plateau with approximately 250 hectares of arable land which, owing to particularly favourable soil and climatic conditions, allowed the villagers gradually to move away from the breeding of sheep on to a single-crop system: the production of seed potatoes. As a result, this village, which is 43 kilometres from the city of Ioannina, started on a period of development after the Second World War and today is prosperous. It has a population of approximately 1,100, most of them farmers, with also a few stock-breeders and a woodcutter. The school complex includes two primary schools and a complete secondary school.

Chrysovitsa's production today far exceeds what can be consumed locally by the families or the community. In fact, the greater part of its production is sold, thanks to the support provided by two large agricultural co-operatives, a significant level of investment, and bank loans. This was why we chose Chrysovitsa: we wanted to study the relationship between the villagers and money against the changing relationships between family and production.

We used the biographical method from a largely psycho-sociological perspective.[6] We analysed twenty-two life-story narratives, allowing us both to reconstruct the histories of seven typical families and to provide a collective representation of the history of the community as a whole. We were also able to see how the villagers of Chrysovitsa talk about money, as a measure of the changes which have come about in recent years in their lives.

The psycho-sociological perspective entailed an examination of the relationship between the psychic and the social on the individual, group, and intergroup levels—the three fundamental levels present in an autobiography. Individuals present in their life stories an expression of specific individuality which also to some extent personifies the experience of their social relationships.[7] Thus the individual, the thinking and feeling person, evolves in relation both to larger social factors and to interaction between individuals on the level of the family or other groups. On the other hand, the individual becomes an active subject not only when in opposition to these shapings, but equally when submitting to them.[8]

A family history reveals both the processes of social reproduction such as the handing down of fortunes or occupations and signs of intergenerational identification and unconscious repetition, which lead us on to a more socio-psychoanalytic level of analysis. Sociological processes of transmission 'glide along', we might say, on these intergenerational identifications, and thanks to them. Equally, when an individual opposes a process of social transmission, this may be either consciously or in response to a different, unconscious intergenerational process which leads either to conformity or to an open rift.[9]

Equally significant are the framework in which the interview takes place and the interpersonal relationship between the research worker and the subject who is speaking. Among factors shaping the interview may be whether the interview takes place in the subject's house, or in a café, or in a location to which the research worker 'belongs'; the presence or absence of third parties; and the currents of transference which flow from the context.[10] It is important to note what may occur or be said outside the interview itself, for this too may be valuable for the subsequent analysis.

During our fieldwork we very soon encountered a problem familiar to social anthropologists: that is, cultural resistance within the interview itself. Our response was twofold: to note what happened before and after each interview; and also to accept the presence of third parties during the interview when this was suggested.

In examining the relationship between the individual and different social levels we have particularly looked for—to use a term from Max Pagès[11]—the socio-mental structures, which link emotion and ideas with social institutions such as the family household and, in our case here, the agricultural community or an agricultural co-operative. The family household, apart from its daily functions, is the place where plans are made for the future; and it also has symbolic dimensions. Like any group, it is both a social and a psychological unit: its members reside in it, and at the same time intertwine their individual unconscious through it.

Each life story is also an intersection of various times: not only the years through which the subject lived, but also his or her subjective view of time—which is of the greatest importance to villagers; the history of the community, and of the family; history as History; the time of the interview, and the time of analysis.[12] All these interact with official calendar time, objectified and objectifying. The relationship between the villagers of Chrysovitsa and this form of time is unusual: they have a very loose relationship with official and objective time. They do not remember dates, even in the very recent past, but they do remember events. They were almost never on time for their appointments with us, despite their moral and emotional consistency in personal relationships.

There is some similarity in the relationship with money. Just as family time binds up the life of the household with everyday work in the fields, so personal and family spending is confused with productive expenditure. No distinction is made between on the one hand the money which is spent on consumer goods, on building or maintaining the house, or on a daughter's dowry, and, on the other hand, the time used to buy seeds, fertilizers, or pesticides, to pay off instalments, or to purchase agricultural machinery. It was also striking that whenever they talked about money, the villagers always mentioned sums which were larger or smaller than the real figures. And certainly they measure their dependence on the bank in their own terms.

'Money's a greedy thing,' one of them said to us during an interview.[13] Their dependence is sustained by credit policy and the system through which the banks finance the cycle of production. But nearly all the villagers of Chrysovitsa whom we interviewed see themselves as lenders rather than borrowers. They may borrow from the bank, but the money which is 'due to them' is more than that which they themselves owe.

They grant some loans, but so what? They get the money back, don't they? I don't say they should give it away, but when they do give it they shouldn't charge interest on it. You should pay it back just like that. Couldn't the state say go on, take it? But they want a lot of interest back. They want us to live on lies—that's why they call life a liar.[14]

There are two types of loan: 'crop loans', which are intended to finance the cycle of production, and investment loans. It is interesting that in the case of crop loans the transaction between the farmers and the bank is neither direct nor monetary: it is mediated by the co-operatives or by the state agency for the central purchasing of agricultural produce (KYDEP).

The bank finances the co-operative to purchase from KYDEP what is called 'first-generation' seed potatoes imported from abroad. In March each year, the co-operative distributes this seed to the farmers. Planting takes place in the spring, and the potatoes are harvested in late summer. In the autumn, after sorting, the product—that is, 'second-generation' seed potatoes—is collected by the co-operatives. The co-operatives then deduct from the value of the product the sum which corresponds to each farmer's debt to the bank, pay the farmers the balance, and sell the product to potato farmers throughout Greece. It is thus the co-operative which repays the bank and not the farmers themselves.

As a result, the Agricultural Bank is seen as a 'good mother' which guarantees the farmers what might be called 'easy money', by contrast with the situation before 1960, when, as one interviewee told us, money was in short supply: 'The conditions in which people worked then were very tough. Not just tough—very tough. Money then was in short supply, it wasn't easy to earn it; it was very difficult to make.'[15]

Nevertheless, there is a 'break' in the 'genealogy' of the seed: the raw materials, the 'first-generation' seed potatoes, are imported. In a similar manner, we could talk about a break in the genealogy of the farmers themselves: producers under the age of 50 who are currently growing seed potatoes may have inherited the capacity of farmers, but they are certainly not farming as their forebears did. The cultivation of potato seed is an innovation which divides generations and attitudes at a specific point. Before that point was the old system; after it is the new system.

One example in changed attitudes concerns how money is managed within the family household. In earlier days, when money was in short supply, there was never any question that the money should be managed by 'the old man' or, if he was no longer alive or was absent, by 'the old woman' or the eldest son. Today, when 'money is greedy', things are more complex.

Let us consider the Lambrou family. Christos, aged 71, is a retired postman and cantor in church. His father, the son of a muleteer, married the daughter of a rich stock-breeder ('he was the first man in the village', said Christos[16]), but he himself became a postman. In the late 1950s, the family lived in conditions of some deprivation, as did the rest of the village then. What put Christos's family in a slightly better position than the others was the fact that Christos had a steady and guaranteed income. They also had one or two very small fields,

which were worked principally by his wife Evangelia and which
provided food solely for the family.

Christos tried to get his eldest son Mitsos a job in the post office, but
failed for political reasons. As a result, Mitsos went to Germany as a
migrant worker around 1965. The next son settled in a town in
Macedonia, married, and became an unskilled manual worker. The
third son stayed in the village and lived with the family of his father-in-
law.

About 1970 Mitsos returned from Germany with some money
saved. He got married and began to grow seed potatoes. He made the
best possible use of the Agricultural Bank loans, buying fields, building
a barn, purchasing a tractor, and taking on his three younger brothers.
All four together built up a sizeable farm. Today, the four brothers
have the highest production in the village. They cultivate 9–10
hectares of their own and rent an area of an equal size. They own two
tractors in addition to the original one and have a large truck.

In 1982, Mitsos was elected mayor of the village and in the same
year played a leading part in setting up the second co-operative of the
two which we have already mentioned, rallying around himself
approximately one hundred disaffected small producers. Since then he
has been president of the co-operative. This co-operative is known in
Chrysovitsa as the 'private co-operative' to contrast it with the other,
the 'state co-operative', because it is extremely dynamic, and
embarked on a series of business initiatives after 1986. One of these
initiatives was to circumvent KYDEP and make direct imports of seed
potatoes. KYDEP challenged their legality, and the case came before
the courts. They have plans to set up a unit to produce the potatoes on
the spot, so as to obviate the need for imports.

Mitsos made sure that one of his three brothers was taken on as a
warehouseman at the co-operative, while the other two work there on a
seasonal basis whenever seed is being delivered or distributed. The
relationship between the four brothers is thus quite complex. For the
others, Mitsos is at the same time a brother, a power in the land, a
boss, and a partner. They work together in the fields and share the
profits they make from production, making complicated calculations
which take into account the amount of land that falls to the lot of each
and also the fact that Mitsos owns the tractors and the truck.

The brothers describe their arrangements differently. Mitsos says:

My brothers and I grow the crops together, but we don't split the money down
the middle. Each gets money according to his needs. For example, the

youngest one's got married now, and he lives over with father. He gets his fair share—he doesn't get what I get. My other brother is a warehouseman at the Co-operative—well, I'm the president, aren't I?—and he has a salary from there. . . . We're rather an unusual case: most of the brothers here aren't on speaking terms. Let's hope and pray it goes on like that. Nowadays three of us work up there. One of us spreads the dung, another one ploughs, and I—well, as the eldest I've got to give the orders, haven't I? I get a bit angry sometimes.[17]

This may be compared with Babis the warehouseman's account:

My brothers and I have nothing to do with each other any more. We're members of the same co-operative. . . . We work together on the product. Then a ratio is worked out—each of us gets what he put in, whether he has tractors or not. If he does, he gets a bigger share of the profits. Here it's what we call 'brotherhood' that counts—the fact that Mitsos has the machinery, that he worked hard to get those machines. I've only just started here.

I don't have any claim on a larger share. . . . As for my relations with Mitsos in the co-operative, I could say that just because he's my brother he's less co-operative than he would be with someone outside the family. I don't like going to him and saying, 'Look, I've got to have this or that.' If he wasn't my brother, perhaps there would be things I wanted. I can't ask anything like that of my brother, because that would be letting myself in for criticism. And he wouldn't want it either. But that's not a problem. In any case—and it's strange given the situation—he's very nice to all the workers. . . . If he ever said to me, 'Look, you're doing that wrong'—not like a brother, about my work, for instance—I'd have my own way of accepting that.[18]

Mitsos, his father, and the youngest of the brothers all live around the same courtyard, but not in the same building. Christos and the youngest brother's family live in the old house. Mitsos has built a new house directly opposite. In effect, there are three households with three different sets of finances (the 'old man' and the 'old woman' have their pension), linked by the shared courtyard and the shared eating arrangements. One day one of the daughters-in-law cooks in her house, the next the other in her house, and on the third day Evangelia is responsible for the cooking; they all eat the same meals. The doors of the various parts of the house are always open to everyone.

The picture given by the Petrou family is rather different. The grandfather Leonidas is a stock-breeder with a small herd of sheep. He also has a little field, where Dimitris, the youngest of his children (three other sons and two daughters have already left home), first began experimentally to grow seed potatoes five or six years ago. Leonidas insists on confining his work exclusively to the sheep, and has little time for his son's innovations.

During the interview with Leonidas, Dimitris was also present, interrupting now and again, sometimes to comment and explain and sometimes to disagree with his father. It was as if the father and son were playing out in front of the researcher a family conflict which is also a conflict of generations and a cultural conflict.

LEONIDAS. Working the potatoes is more tiring than doing the sheep.
DIMITRIS. Yes, but there's more money in potatoes.
LEONIDAS. Yes, but the potatoes could ruin you. [Here Leonidas was alluding to the conflict between the co-operative and KYDEP, and the losses producers suffered when KYDEP refused to buy their potatoes.] And everything has to go on your own back. Is everyone able to shift 50 tons of potatoes? You have to be young. If you're an old man—and that's what I say to my son—if you carry on working like that all the time, you'll burst one day. Whereas with the sheep, you put on your cape and you take your stick and you go and milk them. It isn't—what's the word—it isn't a burden.
DIMITRIS. If you're modernized, if you've got a tractor with a grab on the front, you can load and unload the potatoes in no time at all. If you're going to grow a crop, you should do it properly.
LEONIDAS. Yes, but to have all that you've got to have a big unit. Machines cost money, don't they?[19]

In this household, Leonidas is clearly the challenged leader. None the less, he controls the money and manages it with great caution.

In the Zissis family, Periclis, his wife, his parents-in-law, his son, his son's wife, and their two children all live in the same house. Periclis was born into a very poor family. When he married he went to live with the family of his father-in-law, whom he describes as extremely authoritarian and avaricious. For twenty years, the father-in-law made Periclis suffer and humiliated him without ever giving him a penny.

When Periclis's son Georgos was 14, Periclis sent him to Athens to learn the trade of house-painting. A year later he and his wife also moved to Athens to seek their fortunes. Threatened with complete abandonment, the father-in-law made his property and house over to Periclis. This occurred in the early 1970s, when the cultivation of seed potatoes was just beginning in Chrysovitsa. Helped by his wife, his mother-in-law, and his son, Periclis soon made considerable progress. Today they, too, are among the largest producers in the village.

In complete contrast to his father-in-law, Periclis is flexible and permissive about money. He says:

Do you know what I need for myself? If I have a thousand drachmas in my pocket, it'll still be there a month later. I don't drink. . . . If I go to a *glendi* [secular feasting and dancing on the occasion of a religious feast], I'll have a good time, I like that sort of thing. I mean, I'll dance a lot, I like enjoying myself, I like standing people drinks, I like being able to stand drinks. I mean, I don't spend money on things which aren't necessary. But I like my grandchildren. I'm not used to having money. If I don't have any, I don't care a bit. Today it's my son who manages all that. I don't have to worry at all. Georgos goes to sell the potatoes now. He goes in, he comes back in the evening with meat, with fruit, with all sorts of things. I don't know how much he spends. He says, 'Take the money.' I reply, 'What am I supposed to do with the money? You're in charge of things now.' I can't tie a young man down. A young man will want to spend a bit extra, take his wife out to a nice place and have a drink or two.[20]

Glykeria, his daughter-in-law, says that 'the money's in a drawer and anyone who needs some goes and gets it'.[21] This applies to all those who live in the same house, except for Periclis's parents, who have their pension.

Dimosthenis, the grandfather in the Rigas family, is a carpenter. He inherited the carpenter's shop from his father. He had two sons: the elder was killed five years ago, leaving Lambrini a widow at the age of 25, and three children. The younger son, Christos, is married to Katerina and they have two children. They all live together in the same house, and the five adults work in the carpenter's shop.

There .is permanent but unspoken rivalry between the two daughters-in-law, and when her children are a little older Lambrini plans to move to a house of her own. As Katerina puts it:

It's wrong for one person to have more than another. Each of us should have what he needs, as long as my father-in-law knows. Later [meaning when Lambrini moves to a house of her own] we'll split things down the middle. It won't be possible for me to ask for more or for her to ask for more. Each will have what she's entitled to. Of course, the work's the same for both of us, but that'll be divided too. She'll get half and her children can do what they like with it. As things are, she doesn't enjoy life and neither do I. . . . We're all on top of each other, you can't get things in order in the house—or arrange things as you'd like them. You can't put something where you'd like to have it. One of us wants things this way round, the other a different way—impossible.[22]

In this household the money is kept in a suitcase and anyone who needs some takes it, says Christos. None the less, Dimosthenis is always complaining about how wasteful young people are today. He says:

Unfortunately, young people today are not just as they ought to be. They like enjoying themselves and having a good time. They don't know that you have to deprive yourself of some things today so as to be able to live well tomorrow. . . . Young people today are wasteful. If a family is wasteful or a community, or even the state, we'll end up going backwards, not forwards.[23]

If it can be said that in the previous case the drawer symbolizes a form of mobility between the two generations in the management of money, the suitcase in this example seems to symbolize the tug-of-war between the two daughters-in-law and the unresolved differences between Dimosthenis and his children.

It will thus be seen that money, a sign of exchange which has an objective and historical value as a general equivalent for transactions, can also provide a potent symbol for the tensions inherent in the transmission of attitudes between generations in a context of radical economic change.

Notes

1. S. Damianakos, 'Rural Community Studies in Greece', in J. L. Durand-Drouhin and L. M. Szwengrub (eds.), *Rural Community Studies in Europe*, iii (New York, 1985), 73–123.
2. P. Thompson, 'Des récits de vie à l'analyse du changement social', *Cahiers Internationaux de Sociologie*, 69 (1980), 249–68.
3. K. Navridis, J. Archondaki, and K. Doxiadis, 'Social Change and Relationship with Money in a Rural Milieu: The Case of a Community in Epirus', Educational Institute of Agricultural Bank of Greece, unpublished report (Athens, 1989).
4. C. Meillassoux, *Femmes, greniers et capitaux* (Paris, 1982); P. P. Rey, *Les alliances de classe* (Paris, 1978).
5. Cf. M. Pagès, M. Bonetti, V. de Gaulejac, and D. Descendre, *L'emprise de l'organisation* (Paris, 1979) (on a Breton fishermen's co-operative).
6. V. de Gaulejac, 'Approche socio-psychologique des histoires de vie', *Éducation Permanente*, 72–3 (1984), 33–45.
7. F. Ferrarotti, *Histoire et histoires de vie* (Paris, 1983), 66.
8. D. Bertaux and I. Bertaux-Wiame, 'Le patrimoine et sa lignée: Transmissions et mobilité sociale sur cinq générations', *Life Stories/Récits de vie*, 4 (1988), 8–25, esp. 22–3.
9. V. de Gaulejac, 'Irréductible social, irréducible psychique, éléments d'une problématique', *Bulletin de Psychologie*, 36 (1983); V. de Gaulejac, 'L'héritage', *Connexions*, 41 (1983).
10. F. Ben Slama, 'La question du contre-transfert dans la recherche', in C. Revault d'Allonnes *et al.*, *La démarche clinique en sciences humaines* (Paris, 1989), 139–53.
11. M. Pagès, 'Systèmes socio-mentaux', *Bulletin de Psychologie*, 34 (1980–1), 350.
12. V. de Gaulejac, *La nevrose de classe* (Paris, 1987), 45–8. See also Ferrarotti, *Histoire*, 87, 27–34; H. B. Brose, 'Zeit und Biographie', Habilitationsschrift, Marburg, 1989; M. Burgos, 'Life Stories, Narrativity, and the Search for the Self', *Life Stories/Récits de vie*, 5 (1989), 29–37; P. Ricœur, *Temps et récit*, 3 vols. (Paris, 1983), II 5.
13. Kostas Vlahos, aged 42, potato farmer.
14. Anastasia Lambrou aged 60, potato farmer.

15. Christos Lambrou, aged 71, retired postman.
16. Ibid.
17. Mitsos Lambrou, aged 47, co-operative president.
18. Babis Lambrou, aged 25, potato co-operative warehouseman.
19. Leonidas Petrou, aged 63, sheep stock-breeder, and Dimitris Petrou, aged 27, potato farmer.
20. Periclis Zissis, aged 56, potato farmer.
21. Glykeria Zissis, aged 30, painter's wife.
22. Katerina Riga, aged 19, carpenter's wife.
23. Dimosthenis Rigas, aged 64, carpenter.

6

Attitudes towards Marriage and Divorce among Women in Modern China

Weiyan Farmer

Old Li was born in 1912 and married a railway worker in 1925; she is a housewife and lives with her 56-year-old daughter.

In the old society [before 1949], people had to get married and bear children, especially male ones, according to Chinese tradition. For people in our generation, marriages were usually arranged. An arranged marriage could be made through a matchmaker or by the parents of both families, depending on their relative social status, economic ability, and the relations between the two families. We did not know what marriage meant because we were too young to understand this kind of thing. We just knew that no girl could avoid going that way, that the wedding day would come. I saw some girls who were older than me in my neighbourhood get married and suffer a great deal from their husbands' families. Like other girls, I knew that marriage meant tears. Girls often cried for several days before their wedding day and did not want to leave their parents' home.

I was married at the age of 13. Most girls married around this age. The marriage was arranged by both of our parents. At that time I knew nothing about marriage, and my periods had not come. I met my husband for the first time at the wedding. For the first week of my marriage, I cried continuously.

My husband was five years older than me. He beat me every day for fun, and my mother-in-law praised him for doing it. When, about ten years later, I asked him why he had beaten me, he said he thought that beating a wife showed he was a man, not a woman.

Actually, he treated me nicely later on when he realized that I was his wife, not a servant. After I got married, I was always the first person of the family to get up in the morning. I cooked the food and cleaned the house. After everyone in the family had got up, I served the food, but I could not eat until everyone else had finished. I was not allowed to eat at the table, so I just ate in a corner. Women had no freedom, I was just like a slave in the house.

Now the situation is different. All girls have the chance to go to school. Life is much better than in the past. They choose their partners freely, which is a good thing. They can date for a few years before they decide to get married.

Women now are very lucky. They have jobs and do not suffer in their husbands' families, not like our generation. Of course, everyone should get married and have children, otherwise life is terrible. In our generation women were never allowed to divorce, not like now. Any kind of marriage is better than being divorced. Divorce is no good for parents or their children.

In traditional China, romantic love was a kind of taboo; marriage was perceived not as a romantic union between husband and wife, but as a family function. Romantic love was no part of what a husband and wife expected in marriage. Love had to be suppressed and was considered abnormal. It was believed that only prostitutes could meet men freely.[1] Romantic love was not permitted for fear that it would disrupt social and family life. Until a few decades ago, the notion that love between a man and a woman could lead to marriage was an alien concept to the Chinese. So too was the belief that women had any control over whom they would marry. Moreover, it was not the relationship between husband and wife, but that between their two families, which decided the stability of a marriage. The precedence of the parents over the husband is reflected in the common Chinese saying that marriage is a family 'gaining a daughter-in-law' rather than a husband 'gaining a bride'.[2]

Confucius defined marriage as a bond of affection between two surnames, serving the ancestral temple on the one hand and continuing the family line on the other.[3] It was the family's survival, not the individual's, that was important. Since the successful marriage of a son was essential for the survival of a family line, marriage was considered much too important to be based on the feelings of either the husband or the wife, who often met for the first time on their wedding day. It is easy to understand, therefore, that it was the duty of parents to arrange their children's marriage. They could do this themselves, or they could employ the services of representatives such as family elders, relatives, and even professional matchmakers. The traditional family system penetrated Chinese society so deeply that arranged marriages were still practised well into this century. After marriage, a woman became a daughter-in-law and a servant for life in her husband's family, rather than a wife. Patience and self-denial were considered the two essential virtues for a married woman, in order to maintain harmony in the new household. Young married women had to accept their fate and learn to act properly. Such sayings as 'Obey heaven and follow fate' and 'When you marry a chicken, stick with a chicken. When you marry a dog, stick with a dog' were constantly used to remind a wife that her situation could not be changed. The proverb 'A woman married is like a pony bought—to be ridden or whipped at the master's pleasure' sums up women's low marital status.[4] Women had no real legal redress with which to protect themselves. While the husband's family could freely divorce her, a women could not initiate a divorce against her husband. This situation continued for more than two thousand years up to the mid-nineteenth century. In the short span of history since then, China has been fighting to free itself from this oppressive system.

The annexation of parts of China by various foreign powers in the mid-nineteenth century was important in precipitating change and marked the start of a turbulent period, spanning about a century, in which foreign intervention, internal rebellion, and civil war rocked society. These social crises of the nineteenth and early twentieth centuries resulted in an increased emphasis on the importance of the individual, and so brought about an erosion of Confucian patriarchal dominance and a radical change in the political and social position of women.

Considerable change has come under the Communist regime, which came to power in 1949. In particular, the 1950 marriage law was the first formally to give legal status to women and lead the way to their economic independence. However, the constant subsequent political turmoils also left their mark on the people and, in practice, limited the implementation of the marriage law. Thus, freedom of marriage was never truly achieved during this time: rather, love came to hold a political meaning. Since the death of Mao Zedong [Mao Tse-tung], however, the Chinese political situation has stabilized. In this new climate, the latest marriage law, promulgated in 1981, has had a far more extensive impact on the attitudes of the Chinese people. The ideals of love and freedom of marriage have become normal and are no longer linked to political meaning as in the past.

Owing to the short time-frame in which these changes have occurred, different generations within a family can have had very different experiences of marriage. My interviews, taken over the summer of 1990 with twelve women from six families living in Nanjing, highlight the changes that have occurred, as well as the different attitudes and practical responses of women from different age-groups—the old, the middle-aged, and the young—to the current trends in marriage and divorce. The experiences and views of these women can help us to understand both the past and the future of the Chinese family.

Let us begin with the oldest generation. We have already heard from Old Li. Old Liu, 68 years old, is a retired scientist. She and her husband had studied in Japan and returned after the Chinese Communist Party (CCP) came to power. They married in 1947 and have three daughters. Old Liu's family was sent to the countryside during the Cultural Revolution. After eight years' labour reform on a farm, they returned to Nanjing, where she worked as a director of a glass fibre institute until she retired. Young Liu, 42 years old, is Old Liu's eldest daughter. She is an engineer. Old Liu:

Parents and matchmakers arranged marriages with little if any consultation with the bride or groom-to-be. Love? Marriage in traditional families had nothing to do with romance and love in China. What was marriage? Marriage was about sons bringing daughters-in-law, not wives, into their family. That was it. It was your duty to get married. You had to do it to show filial piety to your parents.

We did not know or understand what love or marriage meant. Love stories were probably only found in novels, not in real life. Interestingly enough, love could be hostile to marriage. In Chinese literature, romantic love always ended in tragedy, such as in the *Dream of the Red Chamber* [written by Chao Xeiqin] or the folk-tale *Love Story of Butterflies* [a Chinese *Romeo and Juliet*], etc. Men and women married, not because they loved each other, but to unite families and continue the family line. Everyone had to choose this way.

You seldom find stories of happy brides. Brides in my memory were inevitably linked to separation, tears, and fear. Whether one married 'up' or 'down', a woman learned obedience and tolerance for an uncertain future. Women only wanted their husband to be healthy, because many women were afraid of marrying an opium addict or a leper. [This was a serious problem before 1949.] An opium addict could spend all of the money and ruin the family. Even worse, he might sell his wife and children to buy opium. There were other threats facing a wife. Some suffered the humiliation of their husband taking several concubines, while others had to suffer the nagging of a mother-in-law.

Since Liberation, with financial independence and education, women are becoming more dominant in the family. There are more and more henpecked husbands. Young women are more and more picky in choosing mates. Divorce is increasing. In the past, divorce for women meant committing suicide. Divorce is not necessarily good since it can also cause suffering, especially for the children of a marriage. Sometimes, however, it is the only answer.

The interviews provide vivid testimony of the very low position of women in traditional Chinese society. The central importance of the family's survival and the dominance of males is clear. The older generation emphasize the family bond; for them, the parent–child relationship is more important than the relationship between husband and wife. They disapprove of divorce, out of concern for the children of a marriage, and, like Old Li, most prefer to stick with unhappy marriages rather than disrupt the family by divorce. However, an important change in attitude towards marriage and divorce is evident among the older generation. All of them have a very positive attitude towards the new freedom of mate selection, a freedom they themselves never had. Implicit within this is an acceptance of the right to freedom of divorce. It is clear too that, in accepting this, the old now see marriage and divorce as a personal rather than a family issue. This change is evident in the interview with Old Wang, who puts aside her dislike for her daughter's husband, because she respects her daughter's individual freedom. Furthermore, while she is against her children getting divorced, she accepts that it is their own decision. Thus, a shift in power from the family to the individual is evident.

Old Wang, a 71-year-old housewife, married in the 1940s. Her husband was killed in Sichuan Province in a Red Guard fight during the Cultural Revolution. She has two daughters and married again five years ago. When I interviewed her she told me that her two daughters had stopped coming to see her for nearly two years because of her remarriage, but now she is very pleased that her two daughters together with their husbands and grandchildren often come to see her and her new husband. Young Wang, 44 years old, is Old Wang's eldest daughter. She is a worker in a textile factory. Old Wang:

You had to be very good at housework, otherwise you would be beaten by your husband and in-laws. Nobody sympathized with you in your sufferings. It was the fate of being a woman. It was common sense. Girlhood was preparation for nothing but marriage. My mother always told me that. A woman was taught from birth that she must prepare herself for lifelong servitude. The function of a woman during that time [1940s] was very clear and simple, to get married and bear children. In the old society we had no freedom and we had to suffer everything.

But now things are different. Women do not have as many restrictions as we had in the past. Most of them have their own jobs and feel free to do anything they want. Parents hardly control their children, especially over personal things, such as marriage and divorce. I think this is good for them. For example, at first I did not like my elder daughter's husband. But my daughter loves him, so I gave up all my bad thoughts about him. I don't want to interfere in their life if they are happy, that's okay.

Divorce? Divorce is a bad thing. One of my friends' sons divorced, and now she has to look after her grandson. If my daughter wants to divorce, I would not agree with her doing it. But whether or not she would listen to me, I do not know. That is her choice. I don't want to take the responsibility if she later regrets her decision.

After the establishment of the People's Republic of China, the CCP continued and extended the policy of family reform which they had begun in their controlled areas prior to Liberation. Their aim was the destruction of the traditional feudal society and its values, and the formation of a new society based on their socialist principles. The Communists saw freeing women from patriarchal dominance as essential to achieving this goal.[5]

Significantly, the implementation of the 1950 marriage law gave women political and legal equality with men. Marriage and divorce were to be based on the free choice of partners. Since the majority of marriages formed before 1950 were made forcibly, according to the will of parents, and law gave the CCP the means by which to abolish the traditional family system. And indeed, in the first few years after implementation of the law, at least three million divorces were granted, mostly to women.[6]

However, the change to socialism was not smooth, and a series of political turmoils, such as the Anti-Rightist Campaign (1957–8), the Great Leap Forward (1958–61), and the Cultural Revolution (1966–76) relentlessly attacked normal social and family life, which were brought into a political arena of fierce class rivalry. This caused great suffering, particularly among the middle-aged generation.

Let us listen first to two of the daughters of the three older women from whom we have heard. The changes affected Young Wang (b. 1946) through her mother's experience as well as her own:

To our surprise, my mother broke with tradition and remarried some years after my father died. My stepfather was my father's friend. His wife had died of cancer. When my mother told me she had decided to remarry, both my sister and I disagreed with her decision and thought she was mad. We felt that since we were already grown up and married there was no need for another man to look after the family, but my mother refused to listen to us and married him. We felt we had lost face because of my mother's action, and so we stopped visiting her.

However, an educated couple who lived next door to my mother persuaded us not to treat my mother like this, and gradually we realized that we were wrong. Society was changing, and so were people's ideas. We were being left behind and needed to change ourselves as well.

My husband and I were workers at a textile factory; we knew each other through a relative. Both of us were from workers' families, so there was no political problem between us. Political background in our time was considered very seriously in marriage. No need to explain why. We got married on National Day in 1967. [In China, many people choose to marry on state holidays.] In those days, a wedding ceremony was very simple. We bowed three times before a portrait of Chairman Mao and sang revolutionary songs. Wedding presents were the works of Mao. We had two children. We were lucky that our second child was born in 1978, just before the 'one-child family policy' was set out.

Divorce has now become a major social issue, especially amongst our age-group. There were many unhappy marriages as a result of political pressure. My feeling is that if couples cannot get on well, why should they maintain their marriages just in name? Divorce is the way to end dead marriages. In the 1960s–1970s, people felt embarrassed to divorce, even if their marriages were unhappy. People would easily succumb to social pressure, especially women, who usually had more difficulties to overcome than men. Now, things are easier, though no matter how society is, divorce is a terrible risk.

Young Li, born in 1934, has recently retired from lecturing at Nanjing University.

By the time of Liberation, the government had become very corrupt, and inflation was very high. The Nationalist government had lost the confidence of the people. When the CCP took power, people expected the new system would be better for China. People were full of idealism. The CCP was supported by the people, and it was true that the CCP did some good things. The first marriage law meant that people could choose their partner freely. Women had equal legal status with men, as well as an equal chance to go to school and to work.

Of course, there were still some problems. Soon after the CCP took power, one after another political movement followed. During the Hundred Flowers Campaign in 1956, intellectuals were called on to criticize the CCP. However, in the 1957 Anti-Rightist Campaign, the intellectuals who had spoken out earlier were persecuted. After graduation from university in 1956, I became a lecturer in a university. My boyfriend and I wanted to save some money for a few years before getting married. Unfortunately, I was attacked and labelled as a rightist in 1958 and, a few years later, I was sent to the countryside for re-education in a village town outside the city of Nanjing. Actually, the re-education was a kind of physical punishment. They made me clean pigsties and lavatories in the countryside. My boyfriend's parents were against him marrying me because the life in the countryside was a living hell. If he married me, it was obvious that his future would be ruined.

I stayed in the countryside about twelve years. After the Lin Biao incident

[Lin Biao, Mao's officially designated successor, was killed in a plane crash after a failed coup in 1971], government policy loosened a little bit, so I was able to return to the city of Nanjing in 1972. Still I was not allowed to teach. At first, my job was to clean lavatories in a university. Later, I looked after equipment in the chemistry department. My job was to clean and wash bottles. Eventually, I was allowed to teach.

After I came back to the city, I found out that my ex-boyfriend had married. I was told he did not want to divorce, though his marriage was unhappy. He had two daughters. We used to meet each other secretly in parks or restaurants. My husband, a university lecturer in chemistry, and I married in 1975. He is very kind to me. We have one son. My husband does not know about the relationship between me and my ex-boyfriend. I have stopped meeting my ex-boyfriend regularly. If I had continued to see him, I would have felt guilty. The past is just the past. I will forget everything in the past and look forward to the future. I believe that many people have had similar experiences to mine. Our lives were destroyed by political catastrophe. We were fortunate to survive.

From my own experience, it seems that during that time people were restricted in how they chose their partners. A person's political background was the most important criterion to be considered in marriage. Nowadays, young people never worry about political beliefs. Divorce has been increasing in recent years. Divorce is no longer considered a forbidden zone as it was before. My feeling is that if both husband and wife really don't have a happy marriage, divorce should be possible. Because if they don't divorce, the continuing conflicts are not good for their health or their children.

From the outset, the CCP had wanted to abolish the traditional family, seen as the cornerstone of the feudal system which they opposed. The 1950 marriage law formalized their attack on the feudal system, opposing arranged marriages and the interference of parents. However, propaganda aimed at drawing a clear distinction between the different political classes made correct political ideology a major criterion for both mate selection and divorce. It is clear from the interviews that political prohibition in choosing mates freely, such as bad family background and political class, put much political pressure on the people. Thus, Old Zhen was prevented from marrying her boyfriend by the cadres at her workplace. She is an engineer, born in 1932:

My father used to teach in a Guomindang (GMD) air force school in Nanjing [now the Nanjing Air Force Institute]. Near the end of the Liberation war [1949], many Guomindang officials fled with Jiang Jeishi [Chiang Kai-shek] to Taiwan. My father could have gone too. My father did not think Jiang's government could save China, because it was so corrupt. People's standard of living was very low. Seeing that the Communist Party was doing a lot of good things and had massive support from the people, he decided to stay behind. Just after Liberation, my father was accused as a GMD spy and reactionary. He was sent to a labour camp outside Nanjing.

After I graduated from the Nanjing Engineering and Technology Institute in 1964, I was assigned a job in a small factory. I could not get any academic job because of my father's political problem. At least I was lucky to get a job, good or not. Sometimes you could be jobless because of political problems. My boyfriend and I wanted to get married, but we could not get permission from our workplaces. The cadres from my workplace said that I was corrupting a son of a working-class family. We were told that there was only love with a class base. If I married him, it would be an insult to the working class. We had to be parted.

Later, he married the daughter of a cadre. My future ruined by my father's political problems, I became disillusioned with this human world. I decided to remain single for all my life, but God gave me the chance to know my husband who sympathized with me. He is from a landlord's family. It is common sense that life is always full of setbacks and misfortunes.

The Communist regime's efforts to realize their new social order were abrupt and brutal. Romantic love was considered as suitable only for capitalists or the bourgeoisie. There is no doubt that attitudes towards marriage and divorce were controlled by the political movements. The philosophy ordained by propaganda slogans, such as 'Love for revolution or Chairman Mao, not for love' and 'The sun is reddest and Chairman Mao is dearest', came to govern people's daily lives completely. Young Liu, born in 1948 and married in the 1970s, is now contemplating divorce from such a marriage:

During the 1960s and 1970s, the criterion for marriage was very different from today. Many young people wanted to marry Party members or army people. My parents were accused as spies because they had once studied abroad, and before I was able to finish my university studies, we were all sent to the countryside. After about eight years of struggling in the countryside, we finally came back to Nanjing in 1972, where I became a technician in a medical apparatus and instruments factory.

It was there that I met my husband. He was a demobilized solider and a Party member. Unlike now, intellectuals were regarded as 'snakes and monsters', and having an education was nothing to be proud of in those days. [To the Chinese, an intellectual is anyone with education beyond high school.] The political aspect was the first thing to be considered in marriage during that time. Encouraged by my friends and relatives, I married my husband, though my parents were not pleased with my decision. We had two children, one daughter and one son.

However, after a few years of married life, I felt we viewed things very differently. He is from a high official's family and is the eldest son. He is spoiled by his parents and is chauvinistic. He thinks that housework is a wife's duty, so he never helps me. We always quarrel about family matters. Our cultural level is not the same, I spend money on books while he spends it on drinking and smoking. Gradually, we have come to have little in common. I regret having married him.

In fact, it was not my fault. It was very naïve of me to choose the wrong person, but during that time propaganda slogans such as 'Love is found in a common political faith and revolutionary purpose' were so powerful. There are many people like me who are suffering, because they based their marriage on political considerations. Now young people do not have this kind of political problem. They consider other aspects, such as economic situation and cultural level, but never political status. Now, you will have difficulty in finding a partner if you are a Party member. Society has been totally changed. We were born at the wrong time.

I am filing for divorce now. Divorce is also a difficult thing, but I have wanted this for a long time; I have made up my mind. My husband does not want a divorce and accuses me of looking down upon him because he is only a primary-school graduate. The mediation in the lawcourt will usually take a long time if one partner does not agree to the divorce. It can be quicker if you have connections with lawyers or judges. Although women have jobs now, and feel less afraid of divorce than before, I know that a divorced woman faces a terrible future because of social bias. Of course, the ideology is changing fast. But actually, I am very brave in deciding to divorce. When I told my friends they said I was a heroine. I know a lot of people whose marital situation is similar to mine, who admire my decision, but do not want to choose this way, because they think their lives would not get any better after divorce. They would rather remain in their loveless marriages than risk divorce. Probably they are right, but I don't care that much. You should write something to support victims like me.

In contrast, Old Wu, born in 1932 and now a retired nurse, was pressurized into divorcing a husband whom she did love:

My ex-husband was from a capitalist family in Shanghai. Just before the CCP took power his parents and younger sisters and brothers left China for America. He stayed behind because he had to finish his studies at medical college in Shanghai. Honestly, he was quite a progressive person. Like other liberal intellectuals, he thought the Nationalist Party was useless and was full of faith in the CCP's promise to build a socialist China. So he wanted to use his knowledge to contribute to the construction effort of the country. After graduation, he became a doctor at a hospital.

During the Hundred Flowers Campaign in 1956, the Communist Party asked intellectuals to give their criticisms of the Party. My ex-husband had a quiet personality and did not like to talk much in public because of being the son of a capitalist. At a certain meeting, everyone was supposed to have a turn to air their own views. Many gave their honest opinions of the Party's wrongdoers, and so did my ex-husband. He only said one sentence: 'Non-professionals cannot be leaders of experts.' He said this because after Liberation, many uneducated army officials had been promoted to high positions above more qualified professionals.

Soon, the criticism of the Party was so blunt that the Anti-Rightist Campaign started. My ex-husband was accused of vilifying the Party and was labelled a rightist. In China the Communist Party exercises leadership in everything. My ex-husband was jailed for being a counter-revolutionary and a suspected spy for speaking out and having overseas relatives.

For the future of the family, and especially for the children, he thought it would be better that I divorced him. The Party secretary from my workplace had discussed my case at a mass meeting and suggested that I get a divorce. He told me that love was not just for love's sake; love must have a political base. My husband was an enemy of the people and did not deserve my love; if I didn't divorce him, then I supported the enemy. The Party secretary told me not to be afraid, as the masses would support and help me to divorce my husband. It seems inconceivable and ridiculous to young people nowadays, but this kind of propaganda beguiled our generation for several decades. I thought my children would suffer for ever if I did not divorce him. Furthermore, because my husband was in prison, he could not get any salary. I was a nurse and did not earn much. In the end, I decided to get a divorce and I married another man who was a worker.

My son was only a teenager and was strongly against my divorce. After five years of prison life, my ex-husband died of some illness in prison. When my son heard the news of his death, he could not control himself and went mad. It was a great tragedy for my family. I am very fond of my son, and his mental illness has led me to suffer spiritually ever since.

My ex-husband was not pardoned until 1981. I am not fully satisfied with my second marriage. I don't think I have enough courage to divorce again. Divorce belongs to the young. I am too old to divorce, I do not want to catch the vogue. I love my children more than myself. That is the great love of Chinese women.

Thus, love was distorted. Love for the Party and Chairman Mao were placed above individual love; marriage was based not on love, but on class division. Very quickly the 1950 marriage law's proclamations of free choice in marriage and divorce became hollow and meaningless. This has created millions of loveless marriages. For others, like Old Fang, a retired middle-school teacher born in 1930, finding a husband at all was made very difficult:

Our family was wealthy before 1949. My mother was a housewife and my father was a government official in Nanjing. After the CCP took power, my father was accused as a counter-revolutionary and was put into prison. Ten years passed before my sister found out that my father had died in prison long before. We still do not know how or exactly when he had died. That was my 'black' family background.

We have never told anyone anything about my father because it is shameful to tell people this kind of thing, even now. Although policy has changed a lot now, my family history is certainly not glorious. People would look down upon us if they knew it. I was lucky to go to a teacher's university in Nanjing in 1953. In China, the political sins of the old generation are inevitably carried by the younger one.

Owing to my family background I was destined to suffer. I was not allowed to teach, for fear I might corrupt the children; so I was sent into a factory to reform through labour. It was there that I met my husband, who was a son of a capitalist and also a university graduate. Both of us thought that we suited each other because of our same 'black' background. I was quite pretty when I was young, so men were always interested to know me. However, as soon as they knew my 'black' background, they left me immediately.

In traditional China, marriage and divorce were an issue for the family, not the individual. Under Mao's regime, marriage and divorce became a public and political issue. Thus, while the CCP got rid of family interference in marriage, in its place came political interference. In doing this, the CCP changed the centre of loyalty from the family to the Party.

With the death of Mao and the arrest of the 'Gang of Four', the years of turmoil were brought to an end. A second marriage law was promulgated in 1981. Unlike the previous law, the 1981 law makes the absence of love a sufficient criterion for divorce. By affirming love as a requirement for marriage in this way, the present law has removed political interference in marriage. True love has returned to people's lives as a realizable ideal, and they have begun to examine the quality of their marriages by this criterion. Nevertheless, in general, the middle-aged generation choose to maintain their loveless marriages rather than end them by divorce, even though they now believe that marriage must be based on love and admire those who do divorce: Young Liu was considered a heroine for divorcing her husband. Most rationalize their fear of divorce, using excuses such as age and the love of children, or social prejudice. Many of them indeed regard the family and children as more important than the individual, and they depend on their family or husbands for support. But the younger generation challenge such hesitant attitudes. The daughters of Old Wu, Old Zhen, and Old Fang have all asserted their belief in a marriage based on love and equality—to the point of divorce.

Young Wu, 31 years old, is a worker in a food products factory:

Can you believe I want to divorce even though I've been married less than one year? I cannot bear him any more. I don't care whether it is good or not. I have not had a child yet, so I think it's okay. My parents were very worried about my marriage because I had not had any boyfriends though I was already 30 years old. In China, if you [women] are over 25, not to say over 30, and still unmarried, you are nicknamed 'old girl', and are considered as a social problem by the government, and as an eccentric by the people around you. People in the neighbourhood and at your workplace start gossiping, and all your actions are under supervision. People think you must have something wrong with you, that you were rejected by an ex-boyfriend and were deeply wounded by love, or that your high expectations were unrealistic, and so on. The Chinese are so sensitive about people's private matters.

I knew my husband through my father's friend. He is an only son from a peasant family and is a university graduate. In China, the only way for young peasants to get to the city is to go to college. He works in a scientific research institute. I want my husband to have higher education, because I failed to go to university. We got married having known each other about three months. One reason why I married quickly was because my younger sister wanted to get married but couldn't get an apartment. My husband could get an apartment from his workplace as soon as we got married. So if I married, my sister could have my room to get married.

However, since our marriage, I feel that we seldom have a common language. Although he is a graduate, he does not like studying. He is a chauvinist and expects me to do the housework. I like studying and am taking teach-yourself university exams. I go to evening school four times a week after work, but he just wants me to stay at home. He also suspects that I am having an affair.

I would rather remain single than remain in a loveless marriage. Now the law has made divorce much easier than before, so I can get a divorce. He does not want a divorce. You have to be patient about divorce. I must say that divorcees will face some pressures, but our generation seems to suffer less than in the past. We are rebellious and we think differently.

I don't want to be like my mother and be a woman of traditional virtues, maintaining a loveless marriage rather than getting a divorce. I have had several discussions with her to try to change her traditional ideas. My mother didn't agree with the idea of divorce at first but, seeing that I was insistent, she gave up her opposition. I am still young and full of hope for life. You will hear my good news very soon.

She divorced at the end of May 1991.

Young Zhen, aged 27, is a legal consultant in a wireless company:

I graduated in law at university. I found it difficult to find boyfriends, though everyone knows I have a kind heart. I was not only fat but also very tall, 1.71 metres. In China, no boy wants his wife to be taller than himself. I didn't have any boyfriends. I tried to diet and even fainted several times from dieting, but it didn't work for me because I was born fat. I told myself I would never marry.

I was introduced by a friend to my ex-husband, who is a policeman. After we had known each other for about one year, we married and had a lovely son who is now 4 years old. After marriage we couldn't get on well. I regretted getting married so soon, before I totally understood him. I really lacked life experience, though I am a legal consultant. Our life views were not the same. He doesn't like a woman with a strong personality. I wanted to divorce. He agreed. My parents did not mind my wanting a divorce. So we got divorced in 1988.

He has my son. I have to pay him 60 yuan a month to help raise my son, though my salary is only about 100 yuan per month, including bonus. My ex-in laws don't allow me to see my son, which makes me very miserable.

I am taking English classes almost every evening, because I want to go abroad to make a living there. I am free now and can do what I want to do. I know going abroad is a risk, but I don't want to stay in Nanjing any more, because my ex-husband and son are here. Everything here reminds me of them. Our minds [the young] are very open and our spiritual life has changed greatly. For example, I divorced, and no one around me feels there is anything strange. I think the important thing is it's up to you. If you don't care about others' gossip, that's okay.

Young Fang, 36 years old, is an English interpreter:

Once I read an article which said that about 85 per cent of marriages in China are of the 'firewood, rice, oil, and salt'—basic daily necessities—type. That was because most marriages were made during the national turmoil and political terror. Different people have different life and marriage views. Of course, life is not life without 'firewood, rice, oil, and salt', but life is not only these things: there is a spiritual demand.

My husband and I were educated urban youth and were sent to the countryside. We started to date when we came back to Nanjing after graduation. He is an English teacher in a middle school, and I am an English interpreter. We got married after half a year's dating and have a daughter.

In the 1980s, China has changed so much, so have people's life views. Increasing material living standards lead to a rise in people's spiritual life. Our peaceful life began to stir when I was sent to work in Iraq. I felt it was a good chance for my career, but my husband was strongly against it. I suddenly felt I didn't belong to myself, but to him and the family. I didn't want to be controlled. I insisted on going. I stayed in Iraq three years and learned a lot. After I came back home, I felt the three years of separation had left us with nothing to say to each other. Thus, I often go out to see friends, but he doesn't like me to do that. I feel my home is like a prison and I don't want to go back after work.

My friend persuaded me to make it up, but our conflict came up again during the student demonstration in 1989. We intellectuals supported the students, but I couldn't believe that my husband was so ultra-left and strongly against the demonstration. I was not political. Since then, our life view has been completely different. How can I live with him? Marriage is not a make-do business. I want to divorce. He is concerned about his reputation, so doesn't agree. He cooked up a story that I am having an affair. He told our daughter that I was bad and irresponsible. Although my mother doesn't mind divorce in general, when it came to her daughter wanting a divorce, she was at first against it. However, after discussing it several times, she has gradually come to agree with my choice. If people think that divorce is immoral, I want to ask them whether a loveless marriage is moral.

In China since 1980, in short, the concept of marital love is no longer based on class division or political background, but on individual feeling. Romantic love is considered essential for marriage by the younger generation. Financial independence gives modern women more chance to choose the kind of a partner they want. They are no longer content with 'basic daily necessities' marriages: they also hope for spiritual co-operation. This is particularly true among the educated. It is clear that enactment of the 1981 marriage law has made divorce easier, though there is still some negative social pressure. Nevertheless, the young are now quick to petition for divorce when they feel their marriage to be inadequate.

At the same time, the relationship of parent and child is no longer closer than that of husband and wife. In traditional China, the purpose of marriage was mainly to bear children, especially male ones, to carry on the family line. But for the younger generation, especially since 1980, the relationship between spouses has begun to take precedence over the production of children. Women now have the chance of education, of paid work, and even of involvement in politics, increasing their financial and cultural independence. Since 1980, the one-child family policy has been particularly important in helping to remove the emphasis on child-bearing from the marriage relationship. It cannot be denied that in some of the more traditional countryside areas this policy has created difficulties for some women. Nevertheless, the strong feeling that came across in these interviews is that, for many city women, the one-child family policy has freed them from the heavy burden of child-care, giving them more opportunities to enjoy social life outside the home.

In the past the family, represented by its eldest generation, was the centre of loyalty. Children had an absolute duty to obey their parents, as Old Liu points out in clear terms: 'It was your duty to get married . . . to show filial piety to your parents.' The Communists have broken this cycle, and now attitudes of the young towards marriage and divorce are formed mainly from influences external to the family. As Young Fang's case reveals, the younger generation are unwilling to follow the traditional way of marriage and now demand a new style of life. This new independence of the younger generation from the old is also evident in other interviews. Young Wu describes how her mother opposed her divorce, but later gave in. Old Wang feels that marriage and divorce are a personal choice and, while she disagrees with divorce, she will not interfere in her children's decision. 'If my daughter wants to divorce, I would not agree with her doing it. But whether or not she would listen to me, I do not know. That is her choice. I don't want to take the responsibility if she later regrets her decision.' Young Li rejects her mother's advice that 'any kind of marriage is better than divorce' and insists that divorce is acceptable, although there is some social pressure.

The link between the generations is not completely gone, and the younger generation will accept advice from the older generation, particularly when the advice agrees with modern social attitudes. Thus, we see that Young Wang comes to accept her mother's modern ideas regarding remarriage, and Young Liu is encouraged by her mother to divorce from her failed marriage.

What is also evident is that the transmission of attitudes in China has taken an entirely new direction. That is, the old are now being influenced by the young. Thus, Young Wu describes how, after several discussions, she persuaded her mother to accept her divorce, and although Old Fang is actually in favour of divorce, her daughter points out that it took her a while to come to accept her daughter's decision. Old Fang sums up this gradual acceptance of the attitudes of the young by the old:

Our generation probably think differently from the younger generation. It is customary for us to think about the family first, but now people think of themselves first. The situation is completely different. In the long term, I think they are probably right. So I generally agree with their choice.

The older generation may resist the new ideas on marriage and divorce; but through communication with their children they are gradually coming to realize that such modern views are acceptable.

Thus the most significant change that the interviews revealed in the attitudes of Nanjing women towards marriage and divorce is their new acceptance of the idea of marriage based on love, and thus also of the freedom to divorce. This means that an important shift in power from the family to the individual has occurred. It has not come unproblematically. The middle-aged generation especially suffered political pressure in choosing a partner. Social disapproval of divorce remains, though it is much less than in the past. The young seem able to ignore this pressure but both the older generations tend to continue in unhappy marriages, emphasizing family happiness at the expense of that of the individual. Yet while not choosing divorce themselves, they are able to accept the new freedoms of the young. The transmission of attitudes between mothers and daughters, in short, continues: but the former imposition of tradition by older generations on the younger has given way to an exchange of both new and old views which is not only more open, but also mutual.

Notes

I would like to thank all those I interviewed for their openness, trust, and honesty in telling me about their experiences. I also wish to thank Paul Thompson for giving me much encouragement and advice with my work, and my husband, Andrew Farmer, for his suggestions and kind help with my English. This work was supported in part by a grant from the Fuller Fund, and by donations from the Sidney Perry Foundation and the Sino-British Fellowship Trust. While conducting this research, I held an ORS Scholarship at Essex University.

1. Olga Lang, *Chinese Family and Society* (New Haven, Conn., 1946), 32; Marion J. Levy, jun., *The Family Revolution in Modern China* (Cambridge, 1949), 177.
2. Lin Yutang, *My Country and my People* (London, 1939), 148.
3. Richard W. Guisso and Stanley Johannesen, *Women in China: Current Directions in Historical Scholarship* (Youngstown, NY, 1981), 68.
4. Elisabeth J. Croll, *Feminism and Socialism in China* (London and Boston, 1978), 28, 32.
5. Mao Tse-tung, *Selected works of Mao Tse-tung* (Beijing, 1965), i. 44.
6. M. J. Meijer, *Marriage Law and Policy in the Chinese People's Republic* (Hong Kong, 1971), 114; Teng Ying-chao, 'On the Marriage Law of the People's Republic of China', in *The Marriage Law of the People's Republic of China together with Other Relevant Articles* (Beijing, 1950), 31.

7

A Hitler Youth from a Respectable Family

The Narrative Composition and Deconstruction of a Life Story

REINHARD SIEDER

At the beginning of his autobiographical narrative,[1] Peter Treumann, born in Vienna in 1921, leads us to the house in Wachaustrasse 28[2] where he spent his childhood. Built in 1924 under a socialist communal housing project, this social housing complex was situated in a neighbourhood near the Prater whose working population was for the most part employed at the local power station and the nearby freight-harbour of the Austrian steamship-line navigating on the Danube. In the early twenties the Wachaustrasse 28 complex, Peter Treumann recalls, was inhabited by a 'real variety of people':

a harbour boat skipper, dockers, and unskilled workers; a managing clerk, Brandstätters, lived on the third floor, ordinary people; above them a Hungarian Jew, a functionary of the socialists, and so on. . . . Across the street a brushmaker had his shop in the basement, Serva was his name, a Polish Jew, who immigrated, I believe, in 1919, with shoe-laces in his pedlar's bag, short, inconspicuous, but he was one of those I liked best there. (2/13–14)

If we consider the family's historical perception of themselves, the Treumanns did not fit into this neighbourhood at all. Peter's father, Alexander Treumann, was at that time a retired officer of the former Habsburg army. Lieutenant-Colonel Treumann (retd.) belonged to those who would deplore the disbandment of the army and the disintegration of the monarchy their whole lives. The family's tradition of high-ranking military service dates back to the great-grandfather, who had already been an officer under Field-Marshal Radetzky. The second family tradition emphasized by the narrator is acting. According to Peter Treumann, several members of the family had had a career on the stage, above all a great-aunt who, says Treumann, is still considered one of the greatest actresses of the German theatre today.

Translator: Maria Gutknecht.

Alexander Treumann combined both traditions. He was a retired officer and—at least according to him—an actor, a director of silent films and a writer. To him the family heritage was both an obligation and a burden. He suffered from being forever cast into the shade by the fame of his celebrated great-aunt. Yet he prided himself on belonging to one of the 'oldest dynasties of actors in the German-speaking countries'. From his early years, as Peter relates his father's stories, Alexander Treumann had grown into the life of an officer. When he was forced to discard his uniform in October 1918, his world collapsed. He missed the stage and the corset previously afforded him by the military attire. Moreover he was unable to develop a bourgeois discipline of any sort. Above all he lacked a rational approach to money: 'Whenever he had money, he squandered it lavishly; when he had none, everybody had to see about how to manage. . . . He was one of those stranded people who had been robbed of the Emperor's uniform' (2/12).

In the late 1920s, at the time of the Great Depression, as Peter recalls the family's financial situation deteriorated dramatically. His mother spread stale bread with old oil and heated it in the oven. During the winter months fuel was scarce. Like the children of the working class, the two sons of the retired lieutenant-colonel, Peter and Paul, had to stay home from elementary school in cold and icy weather for lack of winter shoes.

The year 1928/29, the hard winter, the Danube froze, the ice packed solid, people rode across the Danube with horses. Officer Treumann's family had nothing to heat the furnace with. We stayed in bed for eight days. . . . Until the age of 16, I had no long trousers that covered my knees, neither in summer nor in winter. I wore short trousers, knee-length socks, the soles of my shoes were tied together with wire. This was the son of a decorated officer of the Emperor's army. And the incongruity: we had absolutely nothing, but we had to sit at the table bolt-upright, a phoney make-believe.

In retrospect, Peter Treumann believes that his personal development was greatly influenced by the effort to attain the 'bourgeois discipline' his father lacked.

I think I am very much like my father. Except that I learned from childhood what duty is. For this, I must say, I am still grateful to the Hitler-Jugend [HJ, Hitler Youth]. And this runs through like a red thread. In my civilian life, from 1945 until today, I have always taken duties regarding my family seriously, quite unlike my father. (2/11)

In the memories of his son, Alexander Treumann was a stern and detached father. There was no tender physical contact between father and son. From his early years the boy was trained to be hard towards himself. Slaps in the face—'that was normal' (2/3)—and cuts with the riding-whip—'that was unpleasant' (2/3)—were frequently used to enforce discipline.

I was brought up by my father in an absolutely militaristic style. From childhood I had a firm notion what officer and army meant. Father said: 'You are the son of an officer, you have to become an officer yourself.' Completely schizophrenic idea at the time. We had nothing to eat, nothing to wear, and my father said, 'Well, the first thing you have to learn is to ride a horse, to shoot, and to fence!' (1/24)

Quite often Peter accompanied his father to the officers' mess. There the former 'k.u.k.' (*kaiserliche und königliche*, imperial and royal) officers would meet in an attempt to continue their old life. There the old titles were still in use, there the officers' code of honour was still in force—a monarchic-military island within the small republic the officers disliked from the bottom of their hearts.

And little Peter was perfect at it: he stood bolt-upright—full marks, he sat upright—full marks, clicked his heels; I knew the ranks from Lance-Corporal to Fieldmarshal-Lieutenant by heart. I have always been some kind of tin soldier. . . . He said to his wartime comrades, 'Look, what a splendid soldier he'll make!' (1/34)

The mother worked as a secretary in an attorney's office, a rather prosaic occupation compared to her husband's. With her meagre salary she tried to make ends meet. 'Through endless patience and diligence and hard work' (1/26) she attempted to compensate for the dire straits caused by her husband's 'extravagant' demeanour. She was, however, not capable of creating an atmosphere of security in the family: 'My mother tried, but she was too weak' (1/35).

When he looks back upon his childhood days Peter complains first and foremost that the family lacked a sense of solidarity. The resulting isolation of its members was extremely painful for him. Above all, he seems to have missed a feeling of security and safety. To illustrate his own resolution not to follow in his father's footsteps, Peter Treumann tells several stories about his relationship to his younger brother Paul. He used to feel extremely responsible for his brother, whom he would defend against their parents and against any other adults for that matter. In 1927 Paul died of diphtheria. Peter's younger sister fell sick with tuberculosis of the bone during the first year of her life and was taken to the tuberculosis ward, where she spent three years in a plaster cast before she died. Her death left Peter as the only child until the birth of another in 1931: 'So then I was all alone' (1/30).

From the age of 6 Peter spent most of his free afternoons—'every free minute'—in the streets. The Wachaustrasse, where traffic was not heavy, was the usual meeting-place for the children from the complex. At play they split into gendered groups. While the girls were busy with their dolls, their skipping-ropes, and the like, and generally stayed in the courtyard of the complex or at least near the house, the boys formed a gang—as was common in many streets in Vienna[3]—and time and again sought 'military' conflicts with gangs from nearby streets.

Our enemy was the Hillerstrasse on the other side of the complex. And they were quite rough and also resorted to rather rough methods. But in these confrontations I saw what a difference a leader makes, one who is not afraid. ... Girls were never present, never, never. That was impossible, that was impossible with us, girls were out of the question! (2/24)

According to Peter Treumann, '90 per cent' of the other children's parents were 'socialists', 'reds', some of them even communists. He used to stop by some of his playmates' homes to get something to eat. The boys either helped themselves, or mothers, grandmothers, and sisters gave them slices of bread spread with lard and the like: 'one was really grateful for that' (1/19). Looking back Peter Treumann today regards this solidarity among the neighbours, which was based on mutual help, as an experience that marked the beginning of his social and political consciousness. He contrasts the lack of attachment within his own bourgeois family with the solidarity of the boys 'in the street' and the predominantly 'red' neighbourhood: 'Here I had learned that one person alone doesn't amount to much.' At that time he 'pressed towards community', as he calls it. In particular the sharing of food, which was constantly becoming more scarce, among his playmates made a great impression on him: to this day he still considers it to be a primary experience of solidarity. A few years later this experience was renewed through the feeling of togetherness in the HJ. There his notion of 'community' became ideologically explicit and the 'social aspect merged with the political' (1/20), the haphazard community that was formed out of a state of emergency became a political community. At this point, the structural opposition of family and street is implicitly used by Peter Treumann as an argument for the necessity of organizations for children and adolescents. He maintains that these organizations represent a microcosm of solidarity and therefore could also provide a model for more justice in society as a whole. Peter Treumann himself found this microcosm, against which the *Volksgemeinschaft* was to be measured, in the HJ.[4]

Even though Peter Treumann asserts that he 'pressed towards community' at that stage of his life, he obviously felt that he did not quite belong with the members of his street-gang. Presumably, his playmates also sensed that he came from a 'better', that is, bourgeois family. Peter's awareness of his élitist family background and the expectations thrust upon him by his father prevented his natural integration into the group.

They built a cathedral in front of me which, for all that, did not match my experiences in the street. And this heritage was not easy to digest in the confrontation with the street. So I always went out into the street. I mean, I talked like the street, I reacted like the street, and everything that goes with it. But inside of me the awareness, 'you are the son of an officer', lay dormant. Still, this never meant arrogance on my part or a rebuke for the others; it rather meant an obligation. (1/26)

According to Peter Treumann, this explains why he felt called upon to be the leader of 'his' gang. He was predestined for this role not because of his physical strength but rather because of his mental superiority and exceptional courage, both of which he attributed to his origin and his upbringing: 'I never gave way, not one step. There were boys who were much stronger, I was mentally more agile and I was terribly quick. I was not a member of the gang, I was the boss' (2/24).

My first hypothesis is that the structural opposition of a bourgeois family marked by social deprivation, on the one hand, and the solidarity in the street and the neighbourhood, on the other, caused Peter to develop a proto-political stance which was determined by the following ideology. Human beings are not equal since they possess different hereditary faculties. This is why human beings also bear different responsibilities. This Darwinistic understanding of societal structures was transmitted to Peter Treumann first and foremost by his father and the narrative tradition of the family history. After the disintegration of the monarchy in 1918 and the material decline of the family in the 1920s, the above concept was grossly at variance with the experience that only the solidarity of the street-gang or of the grown-ups in the neighbourhood respectively could ease the material plight.

Until now, the discussion of Peter's family has focused primarily on his father, while his mother has hardly been mentioned. This also reflects the remarkable absence of Peter's mother in his stories. In retrospect, the relationship with his mother strikes him as physically restrained. He could never stand his mother's kisses: 'This was rather disagreeable. I have always respected my mother, but the truth is that I probably never loved my mother. . . . To this day I have always been closer to my father than to my mother' (1/26–7). The only detailed story Peter tells about his mother is a story of painful separation. When his mother was about to give birth to her fourth child in 1931, the 10-year-old Peter accompanied her to the general hospital. Peter stands in for his father who—as so often when family matters are concerned—was not on the spot:

We rode on the tram together. She was right before delivery. And I took her hand and went to the admission with her, where pregnant women go, you know. And there we said goodbye and then my mother went in and I was standing in front of the hospital all alone. And this aloneness was awfully depressing. It was on a scale I could not cope with. It weighed upon me terribly for a long time even though I never talked about it. (1/35).

Following this story the narrator gives a short but concise evaluation: 'All these many, many, many small scars you got, they did matter later on. You became tough in a way, although perhaps you weren't tough at all. It became apparent afterwards, during the war' (1/36).

At about this time the then 10-year-old was recruited into the HJ by his classmates in school. When his father, who was strictly opposed to Peter's joining the Nazis, refused to sign the application form, the father–son conflict—and this is my second hypothesis—gradually turned political. Peter forged his father's signature and started to take part in the meetings of the HJ without his father's knowledge. The personal became increasingly political: the conflict between father and son intensified and was carried out more and more with explicitly ideological arguments. Moreover, Alexander Treumann drew his closest friend, Emil Fey, into the conflict by insisting that Peter choose him as his godfather at confirmation. Fey was the head of the Viennese squad of the Heimwehr[5] in the 1920s and early 1930s, and from January 1934 Minister of Defence and Public Security in the Dollfuss Cabinet. During the First World War he had also served as an officer and had fought side by side with Alexander Treumann in the battles at the Isonzo.

And these two officers were inseparable. . . . And when Fey became minister and head of the Heimwehr, my father also joined the Heimwehr. . . . I liked him [Fey] personally. Because of all the stories I heard in those days, I knew that he was an excellent officer. But I didn't like his politics because I didn't like those members of the Heimwehr. So again there was the HJ and all this conflict. (1/35)

Peter rejected Fey as his godfather; the political explanation of this rejection points to an early development of a political consciousness. Or has the 70-year-old narrator, who has become thoroughly political, politicized the private in retrospect? I would venture to suggest that Peter Treumann developed his early political opposition to the Heimwehr under the influence of both the HJ and the 'red' neighbourhood he lived in: HJ functionaries and National Socialist (NS)[6] propaganda made a strong impression on Peter, as did the social problems and political discussions of the Social Democrats on the block.

Even though Peter's father, owing to his belief in the monarchy and its restoration, opposed his son's participation in the HJ, his method of child-rearing nevertheless prepared his son for the paramilitary activities of the HJ only too well. In fact, the training of 'the little soldier' provided Peter with a head start over the other children and—after his success as leader of the street-gang—again predestined him for a career as a leader. 'I liked it, it was military and I knew all about this from my father. And what made a tremendous impression on me was that there were no class distinctions. No matter whether one's father was an engineer or an unskilled worker in the harbour, everybody was equal' (1/32). It is not, however, a question here of the concept of equality used in bourgeois-democratic or leftist discourses. Instead, the equality praised by the narrator is the equality of the dutiful and therefore an ideology of Social Darwinism; the admission ticket to this club of equals was race and performance. As to performance, the central criterion among the boys of Peter's age was physical performance and will-power.

We went into the woods with our rucksacks, played scouting games, and had to prove our courage, ate a kilogram of bread and 30 grams of cheese, and the cheese wasn't fresh any more, and we had to run the last 5 kilometres of the 20 kilometres, and so forth, according, as it were, to the old principle, to praise what makes us tough. And that meant a lot to us. (2/24)

In this Social Darwinistic system of values, equality meant solely liberation from the constraints of an unjust society and a stepping-stone for the rise of the natural leaders. Peter Treumann was absolutely positive that he was not to remain an ordinary Hitler Youth, but that he was in for a career. 'It was clear to me that I wanted to bear responsibility sometime, that was what I wanted originally, and that because of this, let's say, that I also had to be above average' (3/2).

Peter's time with the *Pimpfen*[7] came to an end in the summer of 1933 when the NSDAP was banned after a wave of National Socialist terror which had claimed numerous victims. After the official dissolution of the HJ and the confiscation of its homes, only the hard core still met at certain places, in the Viennese Woods, at public pools, and the like. Most of the former Hitler Youth preferred not to take part any more. Peter Treumann, however, set about a subversive and conspiratorial political activism which he was to continue for several years.

The small size of his group notwithstanding, Peter Treumann describes it as particularly activist, radical, and assertive. As in other districts of Vienna, the members of the illegal groups were for the most part grammar-school students and unemployed youths. The fact that they were able to frighten 'the other' youths was proof of their energy and effectiveness: 'It silenced them when we marched!' The 'others' were the members of the *Vaterländische Jugend*, the official youth organization of the *Ständestaat*[8], which was organized after the model of fascist youth organizations like the Balilla in Mussolini's Italy or the Hitler Youth in Nazi Germany; even formal and aesthetic details were copied. The first principle of the Austrofascists was in fact to take the edge off the attractiveness of German National Socialism by imitation. Thus an odd competition emerged: the Austrian *Ständestaat* (corporate state) equipped its *Staatsjugend* (state youth movement) with uniforms, symbols, and hierarchies copied from the *Staatsjugend* in the Third Reich in order to attract as many young people as possible. The illegal Hitler Youth, however, had to content themselves with plain clothes for they were not allowed to hold paramilitary marches nor to identify themselves through uniforms, flags, and the like. Yet their desire to wear uniform was so great that they devised a quasi-uniform: leather shorts, white shirts, grey socks, and close-cropped hair.

The events of February 1934 are described by Peter Treumann as a
further stage in his ideological-political conflict with his father, a
veritable crisis. The Viennese Heimwehr, the police department, and
the army opened fire on the housing complexes of 'Red Vienna', where
members of the *Republikanischer Schutzbund*, who for the most part had
already lost their leaders through treachery and arrests before the
beginning of the fighting, had entrenched themselves.[9] In this conflict
Fey played a crucial role. He had been appointed Minister of Defence
and Public Safety under the pressure of Mussolini in January of the
same year and therefore was in control not only of the Heimwehr but
also of the police and the federal troops.[9] Alexander Treumann was
engaged in the fighting in the working-class district of Favoriten as
battalion commander of the Heimwehr.

After the violent confrontations came to an end, Peter accompanied
a man called Habitzl, a retired employee of the power-station company
and *Armenrat* (voluntary welfare worker) of the housing complex, on an
inspection tour to the places where the fighting had occurred. Even
though fifty years have now passed since that incident, Peter
Treumann still regards the fact that his father sided with the seemingly
unjust government powers as particularly tragic.

I was boiling, I was boiling with rage! Now they are shooting at the workers!
The tragedy was, Habitzl took me along and said: 'Peter, I know you are a
Nazi. But come along, I will show you how workers fight!' Then he led me to
the Schlingerhof, to the Goethehof, and that was dreadful for me! And the
tragedy was—otherwise it would have just been an inspection tour—that my
father was serving as battalion commander of the Heimwehr in the tenth
district near the water tower and was shooting at the workers as well. It was
that whole Fey-offensive [*sic*]! And inside of me so much, so much was
crushed. (2/17)

Immediately after this story Peter Treumann tells about the
National Socialists' attempted *putsch* in July 1934.[10] The dramatic
thread of his narrative is much more than a mere chronology of events.
In fact, in his account the incidents of civil war in February 1934 are
linked to the NS *putsch* later that year in a specific and very personal
manner. His evaluative commentaries show that he regards the *putsch*
of the National Socialists as an act of retaliation on the Austrofascistic
system which had directed its guns against the people and their
symbolic home base, the housing complexes, a few months earlier. As
a result of the juxtaposition of these two stories, the members of the
illegal Viennese 'SS Unit 89' who prepared and carried out the

storming of the office of the Chancellor appear to be the more determined adversaries of the regime. After all, they were ready to fight for a just political system with weapons in their hands. Peter Treumann considered them to be 'rebels for a just cause' back in the 1930s and still holds this opinion today. The *putsch* was a failure. Wounded by the insurgents, Engelbert Dollfuss, the Chancellor, bled to death in his office. On 30 July Otto Planetta and Franz Holzweber, two young SS members, were charged with insurrection and with the murder of Dollfuss; they were sentenced to death and hanged the next day. Numerous executions followed. Peter Treumann identifies himself in the first place with the young SS men. On the night of their execution

in the little room I had there was a table and that's where I put a candle, and there was a picture I had cut out from a newspaper showing Planetta and Holzweber. When they were hanged, I, well, I held a sort of wake or a minute's silence for them; and my father wrote the book *The Hero-Chancellor*. That's where we parted company. So there was this confict again, which was brought into the family by politics, this perseverance of my father in something that didn't exist anymore, for only the future existed for me, not these old stories. (2/18)

At grammar school Peter Treumann had a teacher who sympathized with the National Socialists even though this meant putting one's life into jeopardy during the *Ständestaat*: 'He understood me as neither my father nor anybody else had ever understood me' (1/31). He was the first teacher Peter Treumann got along with well—as a rule he had always been rebellious against his teachers—'because he shuffled responsibility on me' (1/31). Once in a while the malaria-stricken professor had to stay home for a few days during his fits of fever, and he made Peter Treumann his representative: 'I made it known in class, if anything happens during those two weeks, then ... In short, I thrived on responsibility! He developed my sense of responsibility a lot' (1/32). When Peter Treumann carved a swastika into a school bench and the assembly of teachers decreed his expulsion from school, Professor Jurenka delivered an ultimatum to his colleagues: ' "If Treumann has to leave this school, I'll be off, too." I thought that was great. For the first time I saw one person standing up for another, now, a grown-up, a respectable person' (1/32). In the dramaturgical setting of the narrative Professor Jurenka is the first male adult who—unlike Peter's father and Fey—is not opposed to the political ambitions of his student but encourages the disposition Peter has already developed in his relationship to his younger brother, in the street-gang, and in the HJ: the attitude of 'responsibility' in peer groups.

While the Jewish brushmaker Serva is depicted as a clearly positive figure and as his first mentor in social consciousness, Peter Treumann's image of 'the Jews' apparently changes with the widening of his experiences and the gradual consolidation of his political beliefs. In the ideological training courses of the HJ, Peter encountered the anti-Semitic discourse, whose phantasmagorias he gradually internalized. My hypothesis is that an effective and lasting indoctrination can take place only when the ideological phantasmagorias have situational equivalents in the perception and interpretation of the adolescent.

In the years of illegal political activity as a Hitler Youth, Peter was searched by the police several times and taken to the police station in the Prater for questioning.

And there was a police superintendent who was half-Jewish, he belonged to . . . the political police, and this man—now, I hated this man like hell. Not the police-officer who beat me, but *him*. . . . And the worst thing was when we once heard BDM-girls[11] being beaten in the next room, who were screaming like mad. Well, I could have killed him on the spot, now, not the one who deals the blows, but—how should I say—the desk-perpetrator, so to speak. I hated him, I can't say how much. (2/4–5)

For the first time Peter Treumann mentions 'BDM-girls' in a compassionate manner. The 'half-Jew' is pictured as an assailant of the 'German' girl. Is it not the well-known anti-Semitic stereotype of the Jew who abuses an 'Aryan' girl which surfaces here—as text within the text, so to speak? Can we consider the incident at the police station as one of those experiences which caused Peter Treumann to turn the abstract concept of the demonic Jew into a subjective truth?

During the fourth interview, that is, only after nine hours of narrating his life, Peter Treumann relates a violent incident involving Jewish youths. Treumann and his group of illegal Hitler Youth were assigned to distribute leaflets and small iron swastikas in the streets and to paint the walls with anti-Jewish slogans. Their precinct was the second district, the district with the highest percentage of Jews. Here, the activities of the HJ were levelled not only at the regime but also at the Jewish population.

They had better know something was going on and they had better be careful. Things also escalated. One Sunday, for instance, we went to the cinema . . .

and there were Jews, young Jews our age. Well, and I think there were two
BDM-girls there, Anni Mayreder, for instance, and the Jews started calling us
names. . . . If I analyse it today, what did they actually say? To us they said: the
'goys' are coming. Now, the goy is the Christian. We shouldn't have felt as
insulted as we did for we weren't that great Christians anyway. But . . . this
again coincided with this early form of anti-Semitism, [conveyed to us]
through religious instruction at school. . . . What triggered the whole thing was
when they said to these two girls, who were wearing dirndls and braids: 'Nazi
Schicksen!' (4/2)

In the beginning the narrator touches upon the dissemination of
anti-Semitic stereotypes by Catholic teachers and catechists in the
schools of the christian *Ständestaat*. Yet only the social labelling of the
BDM-girls in their company as Nazi Schicksen has a 'triggering'
effect. The Yiddish word *Schicksen* also has a derogatory connotation
meaning *Flittchen* (floozie) and obviously was interpreted by Peter in
this sense. Apparently, the young Jews had struck a painful chord with
Peter and his friends. Though not being able to elaborate on this
problem at length in this article, I still want to point out an essential
connection. The problem of the male youth in developing a sexual
identity was linked to the fantasy of the male Jew who violates the
blonde Aryan girl. Thus the enemy remained outside the *Volksgemeinschaft*. Out there evil, lust, and syphilis were to be found. Between
'Aryan' girls and boys, on the other hand, only comradeship and
brotherly/sisterly affection existed.[12] The sexual problem of the male
youth was thus transferred on to the Jewish race; in other words, the
sexual problem was concealed by an anti-Semitism which specifically
had its roots in the particular problems of male adolescents.[13]

In the following part of the interview Treumann uses the rhetorical
device of homologization. From the generalized passive behaviour of
the Jewish youths in the street he deduces the behaviour of the Jews in
the concentration camps of the Third Reich. He contrasts their
'defencelessness' with the militancy of his peers. In the competition of
the street, which is determined by physical strength and a cult of
physical aggressiveness, the orthodox Jewish youths strike him as
inferior opponents:

most of all they disliked the confrontation on the street because that was not in
keeping with their way of life at all. This means they never defended
themselves. It is well known that later on they marched to the slaughter patient
as lambs and cried and wailed all right but nobody did anything. That was

something we never understood. Now, if I were being led to the slaughter and I knew that out there in front was the end, well, I would try to take at least two with me who will open the door for me in hell. . . . Now, I have not known of any Jew who was in for a fight or anything. As I said, that was not much of a confrontation! (4/3)

Whereas the Catholic *Staatsjugend* of the *Ständestaat* and the Orthodox Jewish youths were not taken seriously in the competition in the street, an entirely different type of youth did attract the attention of the HJ: those youths who did not join the *vaterländische* or the National Socialist youth organizations, and equally shunned the illegal organizations of the socialists or the communists. Their contemporaries coined the derogatory expression *Schlurfs* for these youths,[14] who—completely against the then current trend—were not interested in politics at all. These young people—predominantly apprentices and unskilled workers, but also students—took a fancy to contemporary, mainly American, light music, to swing and the dance that went with it, to fashionable hair-styles and elegant casual clothes. The lifestyle of the *Schlurfs* was in many respects a continuation of a childhood in the street into adolescence. Most of them came from working-class neighbour-hoods and—just like Peter Treumann—had spent their childhood in the street. After entering into the social stage of youth, they held on to the forms of group life they had learned and practised from childhood: the principle of territoriality, the ritualized fights between the groups, the hierarchical structure, and the collective forms of reproducing themselves and their identities. Yet, after a phase of complete banishment of girls during childhood, relations between the sexes began to play a paramount role. In almost every group of *Schlurfs*, girls could be found.

Since Peter Treumann had spent a great part of his youth in the Prater, he had known the favourite spots of the *Schlurfs* from childhood. While he had shared their experiences in the street prior to puberty, they parted ways at about the age of 10. Some grew into the youth culture of the *Schlurfs*, whereas others associated themselves with confessional or political organizations like the HJ. Many who like Peter Treumann had come to know the permissiveness and the specific requirements of street-life in childhood soon felt disappointed and turned their backs on the HJ. They perceived the paramilitary discipline enforced by the organization as mere chicanery. The required self-restraint was completely alien to them and, moreover, completely inconsistent with their strategy of living from day to day. Peter Treumann was a different case. He belonged to those who thrived on the comradeship of ascetic and soldierly young people. The dispositions he had acquired in his family, in school, and in the street met the requirements of the HJ. He rejected those parts of his personality which were diametrically opposed to the ideal of the HJ and his own dispositions: everything that had to do with physical desire, sexuality, and tenderness. In his imagination Peter Treumann projected what he had warded off for himself on to the *Schlurfs*; apart from their consumerism and their refusal to perform in school or at work, it was above all their relations to girls and their liberal approach to sexuality which indicated their social inferiority. They embodied, so to speak, the negation of the HJ ideal and therefore appeared to be the natural enemies. Unlike the Jewish youths, they were children of the street. They knew the rules of gang-fights and they readily faced confrontations. With the escalation of the conflict after the *Anschluss*, the *Schlurfs* for their part took the initiative and attacked the HJ time and again.[15]

Peter Treumann's relations with girls were remarkably rare and—until after the war—marked by abstinence from any kind of sexual contact. A BDM-girl was adored by him in a bashful and chaste manner.

She was a BDM leader. . . . And she was a typical BDM-girl. She was blonde and had braids and was really attractive. She was so attractive that she appeared in several German magazines as BDM-girl. And we adored her, sure enough, secretly that is. . . . But to go up to her and ask her for a date—I believe, if one looks back today and analyses carefully: we were, I think, much too immature for that, we were inhibited, we simply didn't dare to, we were ill at ease and disguised it, no doubt about it, with coarse 'masculine' behaviour and so on. . . . I mean, in theory we knew everything, we were perfect at that. But this was a sphere where we were completely at a loss, where we felt totally insecure. And above all with a BDM-girl, from our area at that—well, for God's sake, if you make a fool of yourself in a case like *this*—for life! Until death that is, you see! (5/14–16)

In contrast to the military and physically aggressive interrelations between the boys, their contact with girls was thus marked by a dread of failure. The extension of adolescence through the status of the National Socialist youth functionary in itself afforded few chances to try out sexual relations. If—as in the case of Treumann—a particularly military upbringing, which entailed extreme discipline and hatred of the body, had preceded adolescence, youth was nothing more than a period of waiting filled with sexual anxiety. In this light, the willingness of the young men to take upon themselves any kind of hardships for 'the Reich' appears to be not only a corollary of the adjustment to the requirements and career-opportunities of the regime but also a flight from sexuality. Among HJ functionaries BDM-girls were considered to be the ones who were most suited for marriage, for they belonged not only to the same race but also to the community of values and the élite of the dutiful. Yet this only aggravated the fear of sexual failure in male youths, since their own status within the élite was at stake.

In the months prior to the *Anschluss* Peter Treumann served as a courier in the illegal SA (*Sturmabteilung*). After the annexation of Austria by Germany in March 1938, he went back to the HJ. The first weeks and months after the *Anschluss* he lived in a state of exaltation: 'An endless high from which only work brought you down quite fast. But in this high, a tremendous amount of work got done' (2/36). In this phase, many old Viennese HJ functionaries believed they would be rewarded for the risks they had taken and the steadfastness they had displayed during the times of illegality. Peter Treumann also hoped for a promotion in the hierarchy of the HJ leaders. Yet a further career was thwarted by the policies of Berlin. They sent HJ functionaries to Vienna in order to organize a *Staatsjugend* as fast as possible. It was to be modelled after the *Staatsjugend* in the *Altreich* which had already been established in 1933: the HJ was to become a mandatory organization for all 14- to 18-year-olds (with the exception of those who had been banned according to racist criteria, of course). Instead of a Viennese functionary, the Saxon *Gebietsführer* Busch was appointed to the leading position in the *Befehlsstelle Südost*. With the transformation of the HJ into a *Staatsjugend*, it lost its élitist nature. Furthermore, new qualifications were required: bureaucratic abilities instead of conspiracy and cunning.

These changes naturally posed a threat to the identity of Peter Treumann and his Viennese comrades of many years. They began to fight against their gradual relegation to insignificance. To this end they organized an informal network of former illegal Austrian HJ function-aries. They spread subversive leaflets saying: 'Gauleiter Bürckel deliver us from Busch!'[16] Yet the informal organization of Austrian illegals apparently did not have much of an influence. Many of the illegals turned away from the HJ eventually and joined the *Wehrmacht* or the units of the SS. Among them was Peter Treumann. He gave up his hopes for a future HJ career and enlisted in the Wehrmacht.

*   *   *

The story of Peter Treumann's childhood and early youth as I have arranged it is an account of accounts. As a matter of course, telling stories always implies adherence to certain structures.[17] This is the basis for the affinity between the story of everyday life and the historiographical narrative on the one hand and the impact of form, which a priori moulds our perception and comprehension. Reflections upon our own lives and the lives of others are in themselves always stories, since a chronology of events (the before and the after) is already implied. As a rule, a life story is perceived as a continuous development and—at least in the middle and upper classes to which Peter Treumann unquestionably belonged—as a teleology of education, advancement, and development of one's personality—in short as a career. Behind the stories we can thus detect a culturally determined meta-narrative of the life story. For that very reason our epistemological vigilance must be directed at the persuasive impact of the story. Regarding the interpretation of the narrative we are dealing with in this article, nothing is more enticing than to transfer the efforts of the narrator to construct a career into a historical case theory. If we consider Peter Treumann's background, the tradition of his family, the general political development, and so forth, was it not inevitable that he became a National Socialist? Yet this would mean the construction of a subject which is deprived of every possibility to act and interpret of its own accord, a puppet of history, so to speak. Therefore let us ask for the purpose of deconstruction: by what means is the evolution of a personal identity constructed in this autobiographical narrative?

First and foremost, three processes attract our attention: allegorization, typification, and homologization. Allegorization signifies the comprehension and interpretation of an abstract context by means of personification. The persons used for this purpose usually belong to the world of primary experiences (father, mother, godfather, Nazi teacher, the socialist *Armenrat*). Typification denotes the application of auto- and hetero-stereotypes to social groups: the solidarity of the street-gang, the antisocial attitude of the *Schlurfs*, the passivity of the Jews, the cowardice of the socialist fighters of February 1934, and so forth. Persons and groups such as these are already known from everyday experiences and can easily be used for the interpretation of the larger political-economic and cultural context. In other words, they nurture the political orientation in general and Utopian ideas in particular by providing empirical evidence. Consequently, they remain inconsistent and confined to particular aspects. Homologization means that within the family, the street-gang, the HJ group and so forth, the historical subject discovers equivalents of the general social conditions. The patterns of interpretation, the ideological elements and phantasmagorias used in this process, are taken from the discourses the subject partakes in through hearsay, written texts and images. The social roles, positions, and characteristics of both family members, neighbours, and friends on the one hand and of the respective adversaries on the other hand are projected on to society or parts of society by the adolescent. One's own family does not function any better than the system of the *Ständestaat*; the *Volksgemeinschaft* operates in the same way as the HJ, only on a larger scale; in the competition in the street the young Jews show the same kind of behaviour as the Jews on the ramp at Auschwitz.

Through all three processes the political sphere merely appears as the private increased in intensity. For the active subject, the world is by no means empirically divided into the political on the one hand and a completely different private sphere on the other. At first sight the narrative might seem to be a distorted presentation of the private as political. If examined more closely, however, it is rather a reconstruction of the private turning political through the above procedures. These processes are neither individual nor voluntary, but they occur in a social context and in communicative co-operation.

A further process is the social labelling of persons and groups, which can also be observed throughout the stages of personal development. At the beginning the family's tradition is referred to at some length. By affiliating himself to the family name, the narrator constructs his tradition and his heritage. Because of the continuity of the family name for about two centuries, the narrator lays claim to a nobility of 'German race' and 'culture' which, in his opinion, ensures the superiority of himself and people like him over the Slavic and Jewish 'races'. In connection with the contemporary discourse, which mistakes differences of class for genetic differences, the timely perspective of a successful life governed by will-power and performance emerges. The labelling becomes particularly important whenever the social or political identity of the narrator and his group are at stake. This is the case in the conflicts between the street-gangs, and in the attacks on the *Schlurfs* and on the Jewish youths for instance. Name-calling by the respective adversaries ('Nazis!', 'goys!', 'Nazi Schicksen!', 'Schlurfs!') functions as a signal for attack.[18]

At the centre of autobiographical perception we can find not only the intellect of the narrator but also his bodily sensations. The stories about his childhood and adolescence clearly show the impact of physical experiences. The masculine identity develops—to put it into the metaphors of the narrator—from the 'little soldier', who is not allowed to show pain, to the clever boss of a street-gang with the slashed cheek, from the tough marathon-runner in the HJ to the soldier and officer, who—as the boss of the street-gang—'never gives way'. Moreover, the dimension of the body and its sensations are of paramount importance whenever the enemies are attacked physically. Physical aggressiveness and assertiveness almost represent *the* system of orientation for the perception of the world: it defines adversaries as dangerous or ridiculous. By the same token, it separates Peter Treumann's own male world from the female, which is entirely alien to him. In dealing with this female world, the criterion of military fitness is of no use whatsoever. The willingness to disregard the physical and psychological costs of standing up for one's values, the latent tendency to self-destruction, and the identification with dead (murdered) heroes seem to have become habitual from childhood. These traits are constantly promoted by the various agencies of socialization (street-gang, *Pimpfengruppe*, illegal Hitler Youth, Staatsjugend, *Führerschule*, Wehrmacht) and are lauded as 'duty', 'loyalty', 'courage', and so forth. The subject took in the rewards for auto-aggression in order to pass them on again—for instance as leader of the HJ.

The HJ became the site of Peter Treumann's social life in adolescence. This social space organized and structured the dispositions of the adolescent. It continued to mould what had had its beginning in other social spaces (in the family, in the street-gang). On the other hand, Peter Treumann also took part in the forming of his social space through his actions and interpretations. According to psychoanalytic theory, a personal identity can only be developed through this reciprocity of the social space and the adolescent person. 'Ego-Identity', as Erik Erikson defines it, signifies the mutual relations between an inner feeling of continuity of the self and a constant participation in the symbols and values of certain social groups.[19] We can add to this: Ego-Identity also entails the warding off of and, if need be, the militant fight against other groups which represent precisely that which has to be denied. The group that an illegal Hitler Youth in Vienna was above all opposed to were those youths who lived according to an alternative, hedonistic concept of life, the *Schlurfs*.

To sum up, the material of an autobiographical narrative allows for a consideration of both the structuring effects of the social place on the subject and the actions of the subject, which in turn structure the social place.[20] The biographical efforts of the narrator certainly aim at providing the illusion of a coherent, meaningful continuity of life. Still, the narrator is by no means as blind to the social construction of his identity as Bourdieu alleges in his short text on the 'biographical illusion'. The stories—as was demonstrated by the quotations—contain a good deal of information on the structures of those social places and narrator frequented as one among other actors and on the actions and the interpretations of the actors there. Which other technique, after all, could provide us with more valid information on past(!) social places and practices than the narrative autobiographical interview? Admittedly though, only through the efforts of analysis, that is, by breaking with the construct of the narrator, can we see through the narrator's artefact of a successful life and discern the social-historical constituents of the processes of life behind it.[21]

Notes

1. I conducted fifteen narrative autobiographical interviews (3 hours each) with Peter Treumann between Oct. 1990 and autumn 1991. The sound recordings of these interviews are in my possession. To protect the rights of the interviewee and his relatives, I have altered his last name. Verbatim quotations from the interviews are followed in parentheses by the number of the interview and page number of the transcript.

2. A short street connecting the Vorgartenstrasse and the Engertstrasse in the second district of Vienna.

3. Cf. Reinhard Sieder, 'Gassenkinder', *Aufrisse: Zeitschrift für politische Bildung* 5 (1984) 4, 8 ff.

4. *Volksgemeinschaft* was a central term of Nazi ideology meaning the whole non-Jewish population as a community, no longer divided into opposing social or economic classes.

5. The *Heimwehren*, which were organized by states and were supported primarily by Mussolini, who supplied them with money and arms, were a paramilitary auxiliary squad of the *Ständestaat* under Dollfuss and Schuschnigg.

6. The Austrian National Socialist (NS) movement was formally separate from the German NSDAP (National Socialist German Workers Party) until the Anschluss in March 1938. But after a split in 1926 the majority of the Austrian Nazis acknowledged Hitler's and Goering's leadership. The Austrian NS movement adopted the ideology and the political concepts as well as the means and topics of propaganda from the German NSDAP.

7. *Pimpfen* was a Nazi slang term for boys starting their career within the HJ; after demonstrating knowledge of ideology and Nazi history, and athletic ability, they could graduate to full membership.

8. *Ständestaat* was the name given by the Austrofascist leaders Dollfuss and Schuschnigg to the corporate state established after the civil war in February 1934; it lasted until the *Anschluss* of March 1938.

9. The *Republikanischer Schutzbund* (Republican Defence Corps), a paramilitary socialist organization founded in 1923, was dissolved in March 1933, but continued to work underground. See Hans Safrian and Reinhard Sieder, 'Gassenkinder— Strassenkämpfer: Zur politischen Sozialisation einer Arbeitergeneration in Wien 1900 bis 1938', in Lutz Niethammer and Alexander von Plato (eds.), *'Wir kriegen jetzt andere Zeiten': Auf der Suche nach der Erfahrung des Volkes in nachfaschistischen Ländern* (Berlin and Bonn, 1985), 117–51. On Fey's role: Anson Rabinbach, *Vom Roten Wien zum Bürgerkrieg* (Vienna, 1989), 174 ff.

10. Gerhard Jagschitz, *Der Putsch: Die Nationalsozialisten 1934 in Österreich* (Graz, 1976).

11. Bund Deutscher Mädchen (BDM) was the organization for girls within the HJ.

12. The asexual 'comradeship' between boys and girls is no invention of the National Socialists, but already surfaces in the German youth movement at about the time of the First World War. It can also be found in socialistic youth élites in the 1920s. Wherever it was employed, comradeship was nothing more than a synonym of chastity. See Ulrich Linse, ' "Geschlechtsnot der Jugend": Über Jugendbewegung und Sexualität', in Thomas Koebner et al. (eds.), *Mit uns zieht die neue Zeit: Der Mythos Jugend* (Frankfurt am Main, 1985), 245 ff.; see also Safrian and Sieder, Gassenkinder—Strassenkämpfer', esp. the detailed explanation of 'homeless eroticism'.

13. In her study of the Viennese National Socialist youth of Austria Johanna Gehmacher has shown that the very first address to Austrian adolescents in a leaflet of the NS already linked the adolescent sex-problem to anti-Semitism. Tellingly enough, one of the first actions of the NS Youth was directed at the lectures of the Jewish sexologist Magnus Hirschfeld. 'The sexual difference comes to the fore as the "Jew's" sexual assault on the "German girl". . . . The "German girls" are perceived as the Achilles' heel of the "German people", the site from which the "Jewish corruption", the "deterioration of the race" can be launched.' Johanna Gehmacher, 'Nationalsozialistische Jugendorganisationen in Österreich: Eine Untersuchung zum Geschlecht in der Politik' (Ph.D., Vienna, 1992), 75 ff.

14. Christian Gerbel, Alexander Mejstrik, and Reinhard Sieder, 'Die *Schlurfs*: Verweigerung und Opposition von Wiener Arbeiterjugendlichen im "Dritten Reich" ', in Emmerich Talos et al. (eds.), *NS-Herrschaft in Österreich 1938–1945* (Vienna, 1988), 243–68. The term *Schlurf* had been widely used as a derogatory name for adolescent 'loafers' and 'tramps' in Vienna since the early 1930s. Subsequently, the term was applied more specifically to youths who dressed and behaved in a certain way. After the Nazi takeover in Austria in March 1938, the term was adopted by the state authorities (school administration, police, public youth welfare, judicial authorities).

15. Gerbel, Mejstrik, and Sieder, 'Die *Schlurfs*, 261.

16. Archiv der Republik, Gestapo Wien an Bürckel, 14. 12. 1938, RKfWö 165.

17. For an analysis of the structural composition of stories, see Wolfram Fischer, 'Struktur und Fiktion erzählter Lebensgeschichten', in Martin Kohli, (ed.), *Soziologie des Lebenslaufs* (Darmstadt and Neuwied, 1978), 311 ff.

18. Pierre Bourdieu, 'Die biographische Illusion', in *BIOS: Zeitschrift für Biographieforschung und Oral History* (1990/1), 75 ff. at 77. Bourdieu, however, merely discusses the proper name bestowed upon someone at baptism. Our current discussion also comprises the names for social groups and how the act of naming turns into an explicit and explosive social action: into an action embedded in a social conflict. Whereas, as a rule, the proper name is not contested, the name of a social group is frequently at stake.

19. Erik H. Erikson, *Identität und Lebenszyklus* (Frankfurt am Main, 1966), 124.

20. R. Sieder, 'Auf dem Weg zu einer neuen Kulturgeschichte?', in Eva Brücker and Heike Dieckwisch (eds.), *Alltagsgeschichte* (forthcoming).

21. The expression 'narrative artefact of a "successful life" ' stands for a story which—in the opinion of the narrator—provides a seemingly coherent composition of stories and descriptions. The outcome of this story, however, need not always be positive. See Christian Gerbel and Reinhard Sieder, 'Erzählungen sind nicht nur "wahr": Abstraktionen, Typisierungen und Geltungsansprüche in Interviewtexten', in Gerhard Botz *et al.* (eds.), *'Quantität und Qualität' Zur Praxis der Methoden der Historischen Sozialwissenschaft* (Frankfurt am Main und New York, 1988), 189 ff. at 208.

8

Transgenerational Transmission in the Families of Holocaust Survivors in England

NATASHA BURCHARDT

The lives of every one of us are shaped and developed from a tangled mesh: genetic endowment, family and cultural influence, the chance fate of time and place. Each one of us leaves his or her own trace in the world, itself dependent on the legacy of the preceding generation or generations. For children born to survivors of the Holocaust, the specific and uniquely powerful legacy was nevertheless individually shaped, not only by the previous and subsequent circumstances of their parents' lives, but by the course of their own life itself.

My concept of transgenerational transmission in families is derived from my work as a clinician and family therapist. In family therapy, the symptoms of the referred patient are seen as arising from family interactions, or interactions of the patient and family with the outside world. Usually, family members are seen together, rather than individually. One of the techniques frequently used in the therapy session, when exploring issues relating to transmitted beliefs, family values or behaviour, is the construction of family trees or genograms. This gives an opportunity for family members themselves to reflect on what influences from their own or previous generations may have been important to them.[1]

There is, of course, an extensive literature on the Holocaust, including survivors' own accounts, and a psychoanalytic literature which has reported on the treatment of survivors. Interest in the children of survivors, who have come to be known as 'the second generation', and are now themselves mostly approaching middle age, has increased over the last few years. But published work has still principally been concerned with the second generation in Israel and in the United States, and has consisted of accounts by journalist children of survivors themselves, and the reports of therapists who have been involved in their treatment.[2] As long ago as 1971, Klein, who studied Holocaust survivors and their families in the kibbutz, called for more cross-cultural research, drawing attention to the differential adjustment and adaptation of survivors living in Israel.[3] There has been some work on children of survivors in Scandinavia, The Netherlands, and Hungary; but to date there has been no published work specifically on the second generation in Britain.[4]

The life-story interviews on which this work is based are with children of Holocaust survivors living in England, born between 1943 and 1967.[5] The scope of the material is insufficient to allow general conclusions to be drawn, for example about the influence of birth order or gender on the experience of the second generation. Sometimes within a life story such effects are clearly significant. To take one example, the oldest of three daughters of two survivor parents describes how throughout her childhood there was a lot of pressure to succeed: 'it was an abstract pressure. "You must be best and you must be best at everything" . . . and nothing was ever good enough, at least to your face.'[6] The expectations of her as the eldest were even greater than of her two younger sisters. But when it came to her choosing a subject for university study, her parents had no apparent interest in the direction of her career: 'I was a girl—okay, I'd go to university . . . they were proud, they were very, very proud of that. Quite what I did didn't matter as much, because they expected I'd get married soon. I think that's the way it was in their head.'[7]

How much did the children of survivor parents know of their parents' experiences and how did they learn about them? Among these children of survivors, most seem to have become aware of their parents' survivor status at an early age, often because they had noticed a tattoo, or because one or other of their parents would frequently talk about their past experiences. One woman tells how she remembers overhearing her mother's family talking together about their time in a labour camp in Siberia, where they were permitted to live as a family group. But although she knew that her father was also a survivor, he would often say 'I want to put it behind me and get on with my own life.'[8] As a young child, she knew that her father's parents had been murdered. But it was only about five years before she was interviewed that she had learned the details: his parents had been shot in Buchenwald before his eyes when he was only 9 years old. He had escaped during the last weeks of the war with a group of teenagers by burrowing under the perimeter fence. She tells how her father took her when she was only 12, together with her two younger sisters, to a reunion of Buchenwald survivors. But 'we didn't go to the reunion. We stayed in the hotel in Munich while he went to meet people. And he didn't want us to go to Buchenwald with him. I didn't really know why we were there. It was a long time later that I found out.'[9]

There are many instances of survivor parents who were unable to talk about their experiences. One woman describes her mother as being 'reticent',[10] and tells how when she eventually talked it was to her son-in-law rather than to her own children. But she had been conscious of her mother as a survivor from an early age, because she had asked about the scars on her legs, and her tattoo; and when she was 8 or 9, she knew that 'she had a problem that she kept having nightmares at that time'.[11] She had her own nightmares about German soldiers and Hitler. But her mother would not discuss her experiences with her: 'you'd ask a question and you got half an answer.'[12] She would put her off by saying, 'Why don't you go and read a book or something?'[13]

It was not only the difficulty that many survivors had in talking about their experiences, nor the common mutually protective collusion of silence between parents and children that prevented many of the children from gaining an understanding which made sense to them. Survivors often felt unable to communicate about the brutalities and degradations of the times they had lived through, except with other survivors. As one woman put it: 'maybe I've picked up the atmosphere of it more than the details. Filling in the details just bring back the atmosphere.'[14] The lived experience of overwhelming fear, disorientation, exposure to constant humiliations, sickness, starvation, and an ever-present threat of death might prove possible to convey in a general way. But what was not possible was to pass on an ordered story, which would have violated a fundamental aspect of the personal experience—the all-pervasive chaos which gathered momentum from the moment of the abrupt rupture of the old life following the occupation. Many survivor accounts tell of the sense of personal confusion, loss of identity, and increasing focus on the minutiae of life in the camps, a state of alertness to the particular which alone might contribute to survival.[15] The victims of transports were usually unaware of where they were being sent, an ignorance deliberately fostered by the calculated deceptions of their German captors. The chance of survival in the camps was marginally greater for those who were German-speaking than for those who were not, partly because they had more chance of understanding where they were and what was happening around them.[16] Out of this nightmarish chaos, it is hardly surprising that many of the memories that were handed down were incoherent or incomplete, even when memory was supplemented, as it inevitably was, by subsequent knowledge.

A few survivor parents deliberately taught their children as much as possible, not only about their own experience but about the Holocaust as a whole. Some children themselves became preoccupied with the subject at an early age, finding out about it from their own parents and from other survivors, and by avidly reading. Faced with the difficulties of absorbing the unimaginable, often at an age when they were developmentally unequipped for the task, fantasy was a natural by-product for the second generation. Fantasy worked in various ways at different levels: horrifying fantasies might supplement the information gleaned from parents and be woven into a child's nightmares. The woman mentioned above remembers 'when I was 5 or 6 he [Hitler] was behind the bathroom door at night'.[17] More positively, fantasy might help to construct a continuity with the past which was painfully absent in the family, and which might surface on occasions of family celebration, in particular, such as weddings or barmitzvahs.[18] Conversely, fantasy might be used to ward off the contaminating and all-enveloping consciousness of the reality of genocide; or more specifically to distance a child from the persecutory images which a survivor parent might unconsciously project into them. Fantasy allowed the development of an alternative, life-affirming world of the mind, which might be expressed through specific activities: a passionate interest in art or music or in growing beautiful flowers.[19]

Some children learned details of their survivor parents' lives for the first time when they accompanied them to the country of their birth. Here they often visited sites of personal significance: the former homes of their parents, murdered relatives, and friends, and lost communities; sites where loved ones had been shot or other atrocities had been committed and where the endurance of the survivor had been tested to the limit.[20] Such visits sometimes unleashed emotions whose impact on the children varied according to temperament, and according to how closely a particular child identified with a survivor parent. One woman who had immersed herself in the Holocaust from early childhood had been given *Exodus* to read when she was only 7 by her survivor parent. She tells how she imagined all that she read as having happened to her father. As an adult she made films about the ghetto and about her father's birthplace, now transformed out of recognition. She identified so closely with her father that she was able to describe herself as always having had 'this sense of really not having survived'.[21] When she visited a Jewish cemetery in Cracow, she found herself overcome by fear. Her identification is such that she says: 'I died in Auschwitz . . . I really do think I've got a memory of what I've no right to remember.'[22]

By contrast, an adopted daughter of a survivor of the Lodz ghetto, Auschwitz, the death marches and Bergen–Belsen, whose mother was infertile as a result of her experiences, describes her mother's stories as 'like a novel, very remote'.[23] Nevertheless, as the only girl in the family (there were also two adopted sons) she saw herself as having a special responsibility to support her mother. She went with her mother to Prague, and encouraged her to continue her Holocaust paintings, which she thought were 'liberating' for her. She had a sympathetic understanding of the underlying cause of her mother's overprotectiveness and her constant irrational fears. Her mother's excessive fearfulness of others, of sickness, death, and contamination had weighed heavily through her childhood. Later, her mother opposed her becoming a laboratory technician because the job involved dissecting animals—for her mother a reminder of the torture inflicted on humans. This interviewee had always known that she was adopted and that her own parents were not Jewish. In spite of her closeness to her adoptive mother and her interest in her story, she in no way identified with her. She continued to live with her parents until she was well into her twenties and was keen to be interviewed as a second-generation person. But she was aware of a deep sense of insecurity within herself and a lack of understanding of her own identity, which lay somewhere else. As the adopted daughter of a non-believing Jewish mother, married to a non-Jewish husband, herself born to a 16-year-old non-Jew, it is perhaps hardly surprising that she does not identify herself as Jewish. But the meaning of the experience which her adoptive mother has conveyed to her so powerfully has shaped many of her attitudes, for example her fierce and active opposition to racism.

The life story of this adopted daughter and her survivor mother graphically illustrates the complexities of transgenerational transmission. Survivor parents sometimes offered models of strength and courage to their children through their active attempts to find ways of living with intrusive, burdensome memories. In the case of this mother, only when external events (for example, the Six Day War) brought her past painfully to the fore, would she turn to painting her memories of Theresienstadt, to help her achieve some peace of mind.

Although the intense emotional involvement of many survivor parents with their children could result in a stiflingly claustrophobic atmosphere within the family, which made it difficult for children to achieve adult autonomy, they also tended to be the recipients of unstinting love, which in itself sometimes helped them in the long run to overcome those very difficulties to which their upbringing had led.

Parents' desire for their children's future security frequently led them to place great emphasis on their educational progress. In some cases, however, this can be seen to be an intrinsic feature of the family culture: for example, the daughter of an Auschwitz survivor, whose academic mother had married her father, a non-Jewish Cambridge professor, after the war, tells how the family would sometimes play a game of counting the number of degrees they had between them—'it added up to quite a few one way or another'.[24] Idealizing their children, investing them with all their own frustrated hopes, and sometimes also with the hopes they had had for previous dead children, parents often placed high, and even unrealistic, expectations on them. But many children did strive successfully to fulfil their parents' high expectations.

Some children undoubtedly suffered from their parents' inability to escape from their own sufferings. The physical and mental scars of the survivors' experiences continued to reverberate in their post-war lives, adding to the difficulties of establishing themselves as immigrants in an unfamiliar English culture. The scale of their suffering was just not appreciated at the time. Survivors were treated with tremendous insensitivity by the non-Jewish and Jewish community alike.[25] They were greeted with indifference, and even sometimes outright hostility.

At the extreme, one traumatized survivor of the camps who met her British Army husband during the liberation, was harshly rejected by his working-class English family as 'the foreigner'. Her mother-in-law

was jealous of me and accusing me of—of—alienating her son from her. And there was always these accusations . . . I felt 'I am being hated'. . . . Once . . . when my pregnancy began, I didn't know what is happening to my body. . . . And I remember one lunchtime I felt nausea very badly and I couldn't eat at all. And my brother-in-law turned round and said, 'while you ate the potato peels in the concentration camp, we try to give you good food and you turn your nose up'. . . . I left the room, I went upstairs and I was just sobbing my heart out. My husband didn't say a word.[26]

Many of the interviews with survivors reveal that they suffered from symptoms of the 'concentration camp syndrome', which was described many years ago,[27] in relation not only to the Holocaust but also to the Japanese prisoner-of-war camps, where brutality, starvation, and severe physical illness took their toll on the inmates, and continued to do so in the ensuing years. Indeed, before the emphasis shifted from the physical trauma undergone, and the consequent long-term effects on health, to the psychological trauma and its consequences, evidence accumulated of the possibility of the development of organic brain disease, which in itself could lead to a reduced life expectancy for victims. More recently, the rapidly expanding literature on post-traumatic stress disorder has focused on the immediate and long-term psychological reactions to overwhelming stress.[28] Among the features which appear frequently in the interviews are the mention of recurrent persecutory images, both waking and sleeping; crippling fearfulness, hypervigilance, and paranoia; over-reaction to trivial incidents in daily life; and a blocking of the normal range of emotion, interfering with responsiveness to pleasurable experience. Such reactions necessarily affected the survivor's parenting capacities.

Even those survivors whose own post-war lives have been productive and energetic, and whose family lives have been exceptionally fulfilling are commonly affected by enduring physical and mental ill-effects. The youngest child of a French Auschwitz survivor, born in 1950,[29] describes her mother with great admiration, emphasizing her close involvement with her children and grandchildren, her loyalty to her survivor friends, her vigorous intellect, and her tireless zest for life. But she also mentions her mother's tendency to worry excessively and irrationally about trivialities, at the same time as being able to meet calmly the challenge of a real crisis: a serious accident, illness, or death of a friend. And her mother speaks in her own interview of her continued nightmares.[30]

This young woman had grown up with some knowledge of her mother's experience from an early age: 'not something that a mother could get away with very easily when they've got something tattooed on their arm.'[31] But she blamed herself for not having taken in enough of what her mother had told her as a child, explaining her reluctance to question her mother as a wish not to risk offending her by making it apparent that she had not listened attentively enough to her in the first place. Similar attitudes were expressed by a number of those interviewed: self-blame for lack of knowledge, together with a reluctance to enquire because of the risk of upsetting a parent. Sometimes it was a child who deliberately avoided the risk of exposure to the burden of the overwhelming horror of a parent's experiences. As one young woman put it, she did not want to hear about 'the unspeakably horrible'.[32]

The mutual protectiveness of parents and children is expressed in one account of a father who had remained silent until he took his whole family, his wife, two daughters, and son-in-law to visit the camp where he had been held: 'My father spent the whole time talking about it and telling stories, which he'd never done before.'[33] He was able to say the mourning prayers (Kaddish) at his father's grave, at which point he broke down. Afterwards, in England again, his previous silence returned. But for the first time his recurrent nightmares ceased, perhaps because he had at last had the opportunity to begin to mourn his father effectively.

Some survivor parents remained compulsively preoccupied by their need to tell their children about their sufferings. One young woman, an only child, born in 1948, describes her mother as having 'rammed all the information down my throat', though she considered herself 'much too young to absorb it'.[34] As a child she found herself powerless to fend her mother off. It was only when her mother started to behave the same way with her grandchildren that her daughter felt able to intervene. (The perception of her mother as discussed in her own interview was, on the contrary, that she 'did not really talk about it'.[35])

In some cases, the survivor parents' inability to speak of their experience appears to have pervaded all family communications to the extent that one man interviewed, the elder of two boys who describes himself as 'making allowances' for his mother's neurotic reactions, says naïvely: 'the unfortunate thing is . . . I don't think we've ever really had the time, somehow, to sit down and specifically direct the line of thoughts . . . to this particular issue.'[36] His own perception of himself seems distorted—for example he describes himself as always having excelled in everything he attempted, though he goes on to say that he failed his school leaving exams and subsequently failed to qualify as a dentist, which had been his life-long ambition. He attributes his own asthma as a child to physiological causes, whereas he describes his younger brother's similar symptoms dismissively as hypochondriacal. It is apparent from his interview that he knows little of the details of his mother's camp experiences, and very little indeed about how his father (who served in the Polish Army) had succeeded in escaping the camps. It is clear that his own and his brother's lives were deeply influenced by their mother's problems, from the time of her breakdown when he was 8 years old, and throughout his childhood. His mother's own interview graphically conveys the effects of the burden of her suffering as her life unfolded. She describes how as a young child in a Czech ghetto, 'I was just a father, a husband, and a daughter to my mother. She just was going to pieces.'[37] The subsequent murder of all her close relatives and the brutality and degradations she herself suffered in the camps were superimposed on the massive shock of the abrupt end to her previous family life, and the loss of her own childhood. She tells her story vividly but with a partial incoherence that only adds to its poignancy. Her story also conveys some of the problems that her own difficulties must inevitably have posed for her two sons in their attempts to make sense of the world.

Survivors who married very soon after their release from the camps, or almost immediately after their escape to Britain, sometimes found fellow survivors as partners and clung to them regardless of underlying social, cultural, and temperamental differences. Such marriages sometimes resulted in a stifling family life, in which simmering marital conflict was the backdrop against which parental overprotectiveness, and projection of fears on to the children, were played out. These were the families whose children recurrently use the image of a survivor parent always 'having their mental suitcase packed'.[38] One man was repeatedly warned by his mother throughout his childhood that 'they'll come for you in the night'. 'Be careful'; 'don't do anything disruptive'; 'they'll come for you'.[39] As a young girl, his mother had returned home from work one day to find that both her parents had been arrested: 'she came home and they'd been taken, her parents had been taken. Now, I don't know if that's actually correct, but that was what she expressed to me. And I think—I mean I just get the sense of the suddenness of it, you know.'[40] She continued not only to be excessively fearful but also irrationally angry. 'I couldn't cope with her anger, I suppose, and her bitterness, not directed to me, I couldn't make sense of it.' His mother would talk about her suffering every day, at the same time as refusing to discuss it, saying 'I don't want to hear about this, this is in the past.' She frequently repeated, 'I wish I was with my little mother', 'I wish I'd died instead of her.' Neither of his parents had friends, nor did he himself. 'My mother wouldn't let go, you know. My mother would have actually bathed us all until we were 21.'[41] His middle brother was slow to develop, which seems to have resulted in an even greater degree of overprotectiveness of him than of her other two sons. The result was that the middle brother failed to learn basic skills of self-care, and it was not until after his mother's death, when he was already in his thirties, that he began to be able to express his own needs.

In this family, the father is described as temperamentally an evasive man, and his reluctance to talk about either his own experiences in Dachau or his wife's experiences is attributed to lack of interest. He would say, 'these things end up in arguments. I don't want to discuss it.'[42] The eldest son became his mother's confidant, and thus received the full impact of her distorted view of the world. Nevertheless, he also absorbed the benefits of the close engagement with her searching mind, and in spite of his ambivalence about the 'evasiveness' of his father, he is able to convey a memory of his father's tenderness towards himself and his brothers as young children. More problematic was the lack of help that his fearful refugee parents were able to give him in guiding him through the English educational system. This, combined with the family's self-imposed, almost total, social isolation, resulted in his finding himself woefully ignorant of ordinary educational and social conventions, which was especially difficult for him when he eventually arrived, through a series of fortunate chances, at university. While he continued to achieve successes in the academic world, he found difficulty in sustaining intimate relationships, though it was through his relationships with significant women in his life that he was eventually led to an interest in exploring for himself his sense of Jewish identity. Only he among the three brothers retained the German form of his name, and only he was allowed inklings of his Jewishness by his parents. But he grew up without a clear understanding of Jewishness other than as a source of pain.

By contrast, the majority of these second-generation interviewees had been brought up with a strong consciousness of their Jewish traditions. Many had attended Jewish schools and had mixed throughout their childhoods mainly in Jewish circles. Even those who reacted against their upbringing as teenagers or young adults tended to return to it at a later stage. One woman tells how it was the experience of meeting anti-Semitism as a teacher of primary-school children that encouraged her to identify her own Jewishness once again.

Children of survivors seem frequently to have found that they were drawn to other children of survivors;[43] seeking each other out, for instance, within a Jewish school, though their shared consciousness of their parents' suffering usually remained unspoken. It is not clear how this attraction of children of survivors to each other can be explained, though their differences from the children of Anglo-Jewish families was often obvious—their parents had foreign accents and foreign customs, tended to suffer from more ill health than the parents of their schoolmates, and sometimes behaved strangely. As one young woman puts it: 'our parents were different. The other children were children of English parents who spoke English and did English things, whereas our parents all had these odd accents, and sometimes crazy approaches to life, which we shared.'[44] Among those who are members of active second-generation groups, some find a closeness which leads them to think of themselves as cousins, perhaps compensating for their own lack of relatives by these means. Within such groups, and in the friendships of fellow-children of survivors, there is often a shared consciousness 'tacitly understood'. 'Maybe what we share is knowing what terrible pain our parents have gone through. I cry for him. I feel unbearably sad.' 'There's a look in the eye of other children of survivors. A look of sadness. And it's not our sadness. We identify with our survivor parents and feel their pain.'[45]

A continued intergenerational issue for many survivor parents and their children is that of coping with separation. For some survivors, even minor experiences of separation risked evoking the spectre of traumatic separations in the past. Crises sometimes arose within a family when children moved away from home for the first time. One father became severely depressed when his second daughter went to university; another found it intolerable when his daughter chose a university many miles from home, in a deliberate attempt to get away from her suffocating home life. Sometimes survivors found even brief separations from a particular child difficult to bear, and often daily contact was maintained even after marriage. One women recalls how her mother was in the habit of quizzing her at length about her movements when she went out as a teenager. Another tells how her mother could not let her children go. The mother 'couldn't cope at all'[46] when the daughter decided to stay on in the north of England after her marriage rather then returning to London, where her parents lived.

The effect of parental overprotectiveness and fearfulness on the children was often to induce similar fears in them. They might find difficulty in achieving autonomy as adults. One woman felt herself obliged to turn down the opportunity of studying with her contemporaries in the United States because she could not bring herself to leave her parents. She continued to live with them for the first year of her married life. Indeed, it was sometimes the children who as young adults were the more distressed by separation from their parents. If their parents moved away, adult children might feel bewildered, angry, or deserted even if they understood that such a move—perhaps a move to Israel on the parents' retirement—was in the parents' best interests.

For one woman born in 1951, the daughter of a survivor, it is difficult to distinguish 'what is attributable to being a Holocaust survivor, and what is attributable to the other family circumstances, such as the death of my father when I was 22 or 23 months old, and the various traumas that happened subsequent to that'.[47]

She identifies her feeling of difference at her Jewish school as arising not from her being the child of a survivor but from 'a much bigger point where I was different: . . . that I came from a one-parent family. I think that stood out much more, that I didn't have a father. I mean I was probably one of the very few children that didn't have a father.'[48] The resultant relative family poverty meant that she missed out on many opportunities available to her contemporaries. Nevertheless, she mentions certain features of her mother's behaviour which she attributes to her camp experiences: 'my mother always stockpiles food. There's always much more than she could ever cope with.' She also mentions her mother's need to remain in control: 'she doesn't like to lose control over anything now.'[49]

This theme of the need to retain control, often linked with battles over food, is a common one in these interviews. A number of young women developed eating disorders—anorexia nervosa (self-starvation), or bulimia nervosa (gorging). One interviewee interprets her middle sister's anorexia as an attempt to exert control over her survivor parents, who put intense pressure on all three of their daughters to succeed. In addition to her middle sister developing anorexia, she describes her own 'love–hate relationship' with food, and her younger sister's problem of having always been fat—this sister was regarded as a failure and was partially rejected by her parents when she persistently ran into difficulties at school.[50] The survivor mother of this interviewee had always refused to allow her daughters into the kitchen or to do housework 'as that was her domain and where she was in control'. As a young woman, her mother had been slim, but following her husband's retirement and their emigration to Israel, she now 'eats and eats and eats', and has become fat. Another interviewee, the younger of two sisters with two survivor parents, who was very conscious of having been pushed academically throughout her childhood, at the same time as being regarded as 'friendly and easy-going', unlike her 'clever but difficult' elder sister, tells how she developed anorexia and bulimia as a student at Oxford University.[51]

One only child whose mother was a survivor of the Riga ghetto describes her mother as conveying complicated contradictory messages about food. Her refusal of food as a very young child was explicitly linked by her mother with her own experience of starvation. Later she insisted on elaborate food prohibitions for her daughter, ostensibly to 'help' her not to become fat. This daughter, who became a psychology student, thought that the battle over food represented her mother's way of withholding pleasure from her, and of projecting her survivor guilt on to her with the food she offered.[52]

Problems relating to food seem to have been transmitted exclusively between mothers and daughters. There are references among these interviews by sons to their mother's abnormal attitudes to food but no instances of their developing such attitudes themselves. And although there are references to family eating habits being 'different' to others in families where both parents were survivors, there are no specific references to fathers' attitudes to food deriving from their experiences of starvation in the ghetto, in camps, or during the turmoil of the immediate post-liberation period.

The ability of survivors to function effectively as parents depended not only on their own adjustment to the past but on their present circumstances and the resources available to them. For some, their own lack of parenting experiences and of relatives to whom they could turn for support was a constant problem. Mothers were especially likely to suffer from the absence of their own mothers when they gave birth. One survivor says, for example: 'and when I had the baby I felt very . . . really strongly, how lacking I was in a mother and in somebody to talk to and relate to.'[53]

When both parents had lost most or all of their families, they sometimes had little idea of the needs of growing children, especially as they themselves had no experience of ordinary childhood. Some-times unconscious envy of their children appears to have interfered with their appreciation of their children's achievements. An elder daughter describes how, throughout her childhood, she was under constant pressure to succeed at school, but was never praised or encouraged, and was for years prevented from learning to play the piano, which was her dearest wish. She and her two sisters also suffered from her mother's occasional outbursts of irrational anger, when she would even beat them 'with iron bars'.[54]

Children seem often to have gained a sympathetic understanding of their parents' unresolved anger from the past at an early age, perhaps by talking about the behaviour to their siblings. But they themselves were likely to be afflicted later in life by the consequences; lack of confidence in themselves, low self-esteem, and often recurrent depression or despair.

The repeated observation of irrational anger and violence in some survivors has led to the psychoanalytically inspired concept of 'identification with the aggressor'. A distortion of the concept brings us to the notion sometimes bandied about that there is no difference between oppressor and victim. Primo Levi refutes this way of understanding the matter:

I do not know, and it does not much interest me to know, whether in my depths there lurks a murderer, but I do know that I was a guiltless victim and I was not a murderer. I know that the murderers existed, not only in Germany, and still exist, retired or on active duty, and that to confuse them with their victims is a moral disease or an aesthetic affectation or a sinister sign of complicity; above all, it is a precious service rendered (intentionally or not) to the negators of truth.[55]

The sense of duty among the second generation to bear witness, as a way of helping not only to redeem the sufferings of their parents but to perpetuate the memory of genocide, is widespread. Second-generation groups seem to have become more popular in Britain in recent years. Among our interviewees, some were enthusiastic about such groups: others were adamant that they wished to have nothing to do with them. In addition to providing a sense of 'belonging', which many of the second generation have felt to be lacking in their lives, such groups may have a therapeutic function. However, a tendency to perpetuate the 'heroic view' of the Holocaust, by which every victim/survivor must be seen as a hero, aroused strong feelings of distaste in some of those interviewed, who nevertheless expressed their own commitment to 'passing down the memory' to their children.[56]

The story of the transmission of the Holocaust experience to the second generation is still unfolding. Even fifty years on, some survivors are only now beginning to be able to speak for the first time, and the children continue to reflect on and re-evaluate the legacy, not least in pondering how to pass down the memory to their own children. Not only the survival itself, but the achievements of the second generation and of their descendants, like those of their survivor parents, help to testify to the ultimate failure of the Nazi policy, which proposed the subhumanness of the Jewish people, to crush their spirit and drive them from the face of the earth.

Notes

My thanks to all those interviewees who have contributed to the archive. I would especially like to acknowledge those who required great courage to risk reawakening their pain in order to give their testimony.

Thanks also to Bill Williams, Jennifer Wingate, and Paul Thompson for their help and support in this work. Also to Bob Wilkins, Selma Leydesdorff, and above all to Shamai Davidson, whom I miss, but whose wisdom and compassionate understanding of Holocaust survivors and their families remains an enduring example.

1. See e.g. Stuart Lieberman, *Transgenerational Family Therapy* (London, 1979); John Byng-Hall, 'Family Myths in Family Therapy', *British Journal of Medical Psychology*, 46 (1973), 239–49; 'The Power of Family Myths', John Byng-Hall interviewed by Paul Thompson, in Raphael Samuel and Paul Thompson (eds.), *The Myths We Live By* (London, 1990), 216–24; Moshe Almagor and Gloria R. Leon, 'Trans-generational Effects of the Concentration Camp Experience', in Paul Marcus and Alan Rosenberg (eds.), *Healing Their Wounds* (New York, 1989), 183–5.

2. See e.g. Helen Epstein, *Children of the Holocaust* (New York, 1979; repr. London, 1988; Aaron Hass, *In the Shadow of the Holocaust* (London, 1991); Harvey Barocas and Carol Barocas, 'Wounds of the Fathers: The Next Generation of Holocaust Victims', *International Review of Psychoanalysis* (1979), 331–40; Dina Wardi, *Memorial Candles: Children of the Holocaust*, London, 1992. See also, Shamai Davidson, 'Transgenerational Transmission in the Families of Holocaust Survivors', *International Journal of Family Psychiatry*, 1 (1980), 95–112.

3. H. Klein, 'Families' of Holocaust Survivors in the Kibbutz', in H. Krystal and W. G. Nederland (eds.), *Psychic Traumatization* (Boston, 1970).

4. An oral-history project initiated by women who were themselves daughters of survivors resulted in a publication: Jewish Women in London Group, *Generations of Memories: Voices of Jewish Women* (London, 1989). This work is principally concerned with exploring the intergenerational continuity of Jewish women's identity rather than with issues related to the Holocaust and its aftermath.

5. Some of the survivor parents had already been interviewed for the 'Living Memory of the Jewish Community' project, part of the National Life Story Collection (NLSC), British Library, London. The choice of second-generation interviewees depended on personal contacts as well as suggestions by survivors, most of whom had themselves volunteered to be interviewed following the 'Remembering for the Future' meeting of survivors held in London in July 1988.

6. NLSC interview—not yet catalogued.

7. Ibid.

8. Ibid.

9. Ibid.

10. NLSC interview C410/115.

11. Ibid.

12. Ibid.

13. Ibid.
14. Ibid.
15. See e.g. Anton Gill, *The Journey Back from Hell* (London, 1989).
16. Primo Levi, *The Drowned and the Saved* (London, 1988), 70–3.
17. NLSC interview C410/115.
18. NLSC interview C410/117.
19. Selma Leydesdorff, personal communication.
20. See e.g. Ben Hilfgot: amateur video made by student group on a visit with him to Poland in 1985. His son Maurice Hilfgot was interviewed for the present project.
21. NLSC interview C1960.
22. Ibid.
23. NLSC interview C410/111.
24. NLSC interview C410/129.
25. It is sometimes proposed that Anglo-Jewry experienced 'collective guilt' because of not having suffered the Holocaust directly; but, given the general level of unawareness in Britain, it seems more likely that there was collective ignorance—perhaps coupled with resistance to knowing. In spite of the Nuremberg trials, and some knowledge in Britain of conditions in Dachau and Belsen in the immediate post-war period, it was not until the time of the Eichmann trial in the 1960s that awareness of conditions in Auschwitz and the scale of the horror began to reach popular consciousness.
26. NLSC interview C410/020/06.
27. See e.g. Leo Eitinger, *Concentration Camp Survivors in Norway and Israel* (London, 1964).
28. e.g. Rosalind Ramsay, 'Post-Traumatic Stress Disorder: A New Clinical Entity?', *Journal of Psychosomatic Research*, 34 (1990) 355–65; S. W. Turner *et al.*, 'Psychological Sequelae of Torture', in J. Wilson and B. Raphael (eds.), *International Handbook of Traumatic Stress Syndromes* (New York, 1992); Leonore C. Terr, 'Childhood Traumas: An Outline and Overview', *Americal Journal of Psychiatry*, 148 (1991) 10–19.
29. NLSC interview C410/129.
30. NLSC interview C410/015.
31. NLSC interview C410/129.
32. NLSC interview C410/114.
33. NLSC interview C410/126.
34. NLSC interview C410/123.
35. NLSC interview C410/102.
36. NLSC interview C410/113.
37. NLSC interview C410/004.
38. e.g. NLSC interview C410/117.
39. NLSC interview C410/112.
40. Ibid.
41. Ibid.
42. Ibid.
43. But this cannot be the only, or even the most important, explanation. The same mutual attraction and recognition by children of survivors has been repeatedly commented on in Israel and the United States. Even more remarkable, perhaps, is the same phenomenon noted in Hungary among those who had grown up without knowledge of their Jewish identity. See e.g. Jerenc Eros, András Kovács and Katalin Lévai, 'Comment j'en suis arrivé à apprendre que j'étais juif?', *Actes de la Recherche en Science Sociale*, 56 (1985), 63–8.
44. NLSC interview C1960.
45. Ibid.

46. NLSC interview C410/114.
47. NLSC interview C410/115.
48. Ibid.
49. Ibid.
50. NLSC interview—not yet catalogued.
51. NLSC interview C410/114.
52. NLSC interview C410/123.
53. NLSC interview C410/008.
54. NLSC interview—not yet catalogued.
55. Levi, *The Drowned and the Saved*, 32–3.
56. NLSC interview C410/126.

9

Grandmothers, Mothers, and Daughters

Intergenerational Transmission in Displaced Families in Three Jewish Communities

LENA INOWLOCKI

What happens when generations in a family cannot talk to one another about what was most important for their lives? Those who experienced Nazi persecution, the loss of their family, and the destruction of their community have since been preoccupied by these events. But, at the same time, because of the intensity of the trauma, they have not been able to talk about this period in their lives. In contrast to other groups who also suffered during the war and who have now begun to talk about their experiences of hardship, especially to their grandchildren, such an intergenerational narrative has remained impossible in most Jewish families. For them, the only stories that can be told are those of resistance or escape. But the heart of their experience cannot be turned into a story for the grandchildren, who must be protected from knowing about the pain and absolute despair, from the complete absence of meaning of the individual, and the collective, suffering.

Case studies of the consequences and effects on survivors and their family members of not being able to talk about what happened have focused on individuals and families so severely affected by the trauma that it dominated every aspect of their life. But this is not true for all families. While it can be said that the persecution of the older generation always figures as a central existential condition for themselves and their family members, many make conscious efforts to find ways of living their lives, and sometimes even to create especially meaningful areas of life.

The family members' lives have been affected not only by the trauma of the persecution itself but also by the post-war social consequences, especially the years of displacement before finding a place to settle down 'for the time being', and failed attempts at migration overseas. Both are typical for Jewish survivors from eastern Europe who have settled in western Europe. How are these experiences represented in family communication?

We may also wonder how traditional practices are transmitted in these families. Living 'in the traditional way' requires a lot of practical knowledge. Such knowledge is not handed down by formal explanation but is imbibed through a shared cultural environment.[1] With displacement, and the disruption of family rootedness and continuous social connections, one might have expected traditional ways of life to disappear within a generation or two. Why was this not so?

In attempting to understand transmission between the generations in these families, I carried out interviews with three generations of women from three different Jewish communities: in Amsterdam, Antwerp, and Astadt.[2] These three Jewish communities share a background of persecution and displacement, but each has a distinctive history, and characteristics which are theirs alone. In Amsterdam, it is rare to find three-generational Jewish families who came from eastern Europe. Before the war, few eastern European Jews had migrated there; and after the war only a very small group of displaced persons who came to The Netherlands remained, usually because they had relatives there. Most went on to emigrate. Unlike the Jews of Antwerp and Astadt, the majority of Amsterdam Jews have a definite local affiliation which leads them to consider themselves as Dutch Jews. The Polish Jews who arrived after the war were made to feel they should not speak Yiddish, at least not in public: it sounded too much 'like German'. Speaking Polish was discouraged as well, as it sounded 'too harsh'. There was considerable pressure, and a strong wish, 'to be Dutch'. A woman of the middle generation describes how her father's greatest desire had been to be chosen as one of those citizens to receive a ribbon from the Queen, as is the custom each year. This would have been for him the ultimate recognition both of his appreciation of, and his integration into, Dutch society.

The post-war Jewish community in Astadt was established mainly by surviving Polish Jews, and by a smaller group of former German Jews who came to the city from different 'Displaced Persons' camps in the Allied zone. Most of the survivors who had made their way to the Allied zone after liberation had planned to emigrate to North or Latin America or to Palestine; but this proved impossible because of visa restrictions. An established Jewish community took shape only slowly, and with some reluctance. The more religious Jews did not remain in

Germany, and there has been no Orthodox revival there, as in Antwerp and Amsterdam. The Jewish community in Astadt is the least enclosed of the three communities studied, in the first place on account of the school situation. The Jewish elementary school also admits non-Jewish children, and there is no Jewish high school, unlike in both Antwerp and Amsterdam.

In contrast, going to Antwerp seems like entering a time warp. The journey begins the moment you leave Antwerp station. Next to Moroccan groceries, Flemish beer cafés, and Indian novelty stores, in a dozen narrow streets, there are kosher butchers, restaurants, and bakeries; and shops for religious books and supplies, for children's clothes, fabrics, and diamonds, as well as synagogues, schools, and social and cultural organizations for the Jewish community. There are old and young men wearing caftans; women with their hair covered by *sheitels* (wigs), pushing prams with a baby at one end and a toddler at the other and another three or four children following; young people speaking to one another in Yiddish. Only in Brooklyn, Jerusalem, or London, communities founded by immigrants from eastern Europe over a hundred years ago, can a similar reproduction of a traditional lifestyle be found.

Although the three families described here vary in their degree of observance, in this they are typical of the variation in their respective communities, as they are typical also in respect of the varying degree to which they participate actively in their own local communities. They are also typical in that their children attend Jewish schools, indicating some degree of traditional orientation.

The interviews took as their focus the communication process between the generations concerning the persecution, on the one hand, and the continuity of traditionality on the other. Traditionality can include the keeping of religious traditions, but is meant more generally as an orientation towards traditional beliefs, norms, values, and practices. This broader concept is more adequate since the women I interviewed did not explain their practice of observancy in terms of religious belief. Whether they were more or less observant, or not at all, their deliberations on how they lived and acted were not connected to religious rules, but to whether they continued to follow a particular ethic and ritual practice that they had known from home. Older women, for example, compared how they lived now to how their family had lived before the war, maintaining similarities in attitude and in principles in spite of all the differences; similarly, mothers expressed the expectation that their daughters would continue to live in the way they had brought them up.

The similarities and differences between the generations were of particular interest to the women of the middle generation, some of whom found themselves pulled in both directions. For some, their interest was expressed during the interview in a concern to protect and also to control their daughter, or daughters, and they insisted that the interview should take place in their presence. Some women of the middle generation also came to the interviews with their mothers. In addition to the protective intention, there was also a more or less direct interest in hearing their mothers' life stories. For the analysis of the interviews, the unexpected presence and participation of the middle generation fortunately provided many interesting insights into intergenerational communication.

The topic of continuity and change from one generation to another proved a relevant and not too threatening focus for the interviews; a topic which could be elaborated in different ways. To ask directly about the experience of persecution and its consequences for the family would have been too stressful. Several women of the older generation specifically insisted before agreeing to be interviewed that they would not be questioned about it. Others, however, spontaneously chose to take the traumas they had undergone as the central theme in their life story.

Among the women of the older generation, who had all been raised in observant homes, those who recalled their experiences of persecution described losing their religious faith, and giving up being observant. In contrast, those who referred only briefly to such experiences, or said explicitly that they would not talk about them, were observant. Family allegiance to observancy also precluded the middle and the younger generations from speaking about the persecution.

In the middle and the older generation, the Amsterdam family is somewhat less 'Dutch' in its identification than others in the sample. The children had grown up in Amsterdam; their mother Mrs Neumann came to Amsterdam when she married. She grew up in an observant home, her parents having come from Hungary to western Europe as survivors. She did not go to university because this would have risked bringing her into too great contact with non-Jewish peers. When her two daughters were born, close together soon after her marriage, she gave up the artistic career which she had only just begun.

Her priorities were the traditional ones—first, to take care of her husband; then, her children; and lastly, herself. One of the main influences in the family's decision to remain in Amsterdam had been the availability of an Orthodox Jewish education for their children.

Mrs Weiner, Mrs Neumann's mother, was a widow who spent a lot of time with her daughter's family. In her interview she speaks about how the upbringing of her granddaughters has followed the same traditional lines as her own, but how they know so much more than she did by reason of their religious education. She praises one of her granddaughters for being the epitome of gentleness, beauty, and attentiveness; and the other for her energy. But she describes both as studious. She refers briefly to her own survival, mentioning the constant fear that her 'Aryan' disguise would be unmasked, but she does not elaborate. In this family, talking 'too much' about the persecution is frowned upon. Mrs Neumann and her daughters repeatedly refer disapprovingly to an older woman relative who does so. Mrs Neumann mentions that her husband had himself been in a concentration camp as a child, and adds, 'Thank God, we never talk about that.'

How can the deliberate avoidance of this topic within the family be understood? On the face of it, trauma theory suggests that suffering is intensified, for the younger generations too, when the experience of persecution is unmentionable. But perhaps we should follow Howard Becker when he points out that research should be not so much about people's problems as about the solutions they have found.[3] What researchers may find problematic as solutions, for instance 'Thank God, we never talk about that', should not obscure what are actually creative attempts to live with an unbearable past.

When the daughters Daphne and Nurith were interviewed, they called in their mother to help explain why they had separate lessons from boys in their school—not because the reasons were not obvious to them, but because they needed her help in communicating with me who, though Jewish, seemed ignorant in these matters. A long conversation followed, which allowed Mrs Neumann to explain her own attitude to the observance of traditions. She argued against a departure from the traditional rules such as not lighting fires on the Sabbath, even though lighting fires could no longer be considered to be work:

but if one does not hold firm to this essential, this essence of Jewishness, and grinds everything down, nothing at all remains of it. Nothing more. Only persecution in the war, because one remains a Jew whether one keeps it or not. The Liberals were persecuted, just like the Orthodox. It did not help them at all. So one might as well maintain Jewishness in its original form and with its roots—keep it that way. And especially if you understand, given that girls now have the same opportunity as boys to learn everything just as well—then they do it not only automatically like my mother did it, but also out of conviction, and with comprehension, and they know at least why you do it; and when they don't understand something, they have learned at least where to look it up, and they can also read it in the original language.

Mrs Neumann refers to her daughters' generation as the first in which girls have had the opportunity to study the religious books. Before the war, girls had learned about Jewish life, keeping a kosher home, and carrying out religious duties almost exclusively within their mothers' households. 'Learning' itself, the study of the codifications and the interpretations of the religious laws, was restricted to boys and men. Girls did not even learn Hebrew, the language reserved for the study of the books. They were able to follow the prayer book because the letters were the same as in Yiddish, the common vernacular; but they had no understanding of what they were reading. Mrs Neumann interprets the new possibility in terms of an obligation on the younger generation to take the rules even more seriously. Furthermore, she argues, it has been proven by the persecution that the only positive Jewish identity is the traditionally observant one. Because of the persecution, traditions must be more strictly observed than ever before.

As for the daughters knowing about the persecution, Mrs Neumann remarks drily later on, 'for them it is history, just like where Napoleon died; if you have heard it once, there is no more interest in details'. Daphne quietly contradicts her mother, saying that she chose to study the persecution for her finals. 'All right,' her mother responds, 'you may know about it as history, but not what your grandparents' part in it was.'

Mrs Neumann's priority is to give her children a stable and balanced home. The impressive effort in this family to constitute a positive sense of being Jewish through the strict maintenance of traditional practices is linked to reducing the preoccupation with the persecution. The social consequences of following this path for the younger generation are to confine them to a restricted group within the Amsterdam community. There are also clear expectations: study and work are only permissible to the extent that neither interferes with an early, preferably arranged, marriage, and the bringing up of a family. The daughters' ambitions may have been raised by their extensive studies: conflict might arise in the future. But for the time being, interestingly, it is the daughters who defend their strictly observant school education when Mrs Neumann characterizes it as 'brainwashing'.

Mrs Neumann is not the only respondent to disparage her daughters' education while at the same time considering it absolutely necessary. The teaching of observancy in school is more formal, more rule-orientated, and more explicitly verbalized than the indirect and implicit instruction which the middle generation themselves received. There is also a certain tension for the middle generation between what they hold to be 'right' and their actual life experience: for example, Mrs Neumann insists that women must continue to be excluded from religious community functions; but at the same time she displays in the course of her argument an increasing scepticism about the reasons for their exclusion, attributing it to men's fears of women. As she becomes more agitated, her older daughter admonishes her to be calmer— more, one might say, like a Dutch Jew. Daphne also uses her formally acquired knowledge to argue for women's exclusion, on the basis of the normative expectations of 'modesty', knowing that her mother cannot but agree.

We can understand the constructive efforts as 'generational work', as activities of younger and older generations in a family— grandmothers, mothers, and daughters—to redefine their identity.[4] Given the events of the persecution, and the communicative crisis constituted by the unspeakable memory, there is no generational narrative to which each can relate. In the encounters sought by mothers and daughters in the interviews, the contours of differences and similarities between them are drawn.

The generational work in this interview consists of the mother and the daughters describing and discussing their knowledge and practice of traditional observance, thus actively supplanting the destruction of the old life world. They show that leading their lives by prescription is not easy, but neither is it limiting; and it is certainly not enforced: observance can be enjoyed when performed according to the rules. 'The rules' are a matter of lively debate, their essential meaning worked out and understood on the assumption that carrying them out is a duty which they can rely on one another to perform. The grandmother, however, remains outside this construction of family belief, as if her contribution might interfere with the process by introducing too much lived history. She tries to ally herself with the others by talking in her interview mostly about her granddaughters, rather than about herself or her earlier life.

In the Astadt family the underlying theme in the interviews is the conflicts and opportunities which had arisen as a result of moving outside a given traditional community order. Maya, a 15-year-old, expressed her intention to 'live as a hippie' in different parts of the world; to become a model, or film star, and to avoid anything which might tie her to a desk. She also says how much the persecution of the Jews, and of her grandparents in particular, preoccupies her, and how impossible she has found it to communicate about this past with her classmates in high school, although she can talk about it to her old friends from the Jewish elementary school. She suspects older Germans of having been, or even still being, Nazis—she describes an incident when she had been persuaded to give up her seat on the bus to an old man only to notice a swastika on his lapel. She enjoys the social aspects of living in Astadt and having different groups of friends, but thinks it likely that renewed anti-Semitism may mean that she will have to become a fugitive one day. She emphasizes how she would marry for love regardless of nationality, be he French, Italian, or German—well, not necessarily German. But even then her mother would help her out, wouldn't she? Her mother, Mrs Goldfarb, to whom she addresses this appeal, does not respond during this interview itself. But in her own interview she talks about her fears that her daughter will move too far outside the Jewish community, thus breaking the tenuous links that still connect her. This was what she herself had done, or almost done, in her own youth.

Before her own interview, Mrs Goldfarb joined her mother in her interview. When she arrived, Mrs Weiss was just describing how she had managed to save her nieces in Nazi-occupied Poland. To her daughter she remarks: 'But this must bore you.' 'No,' her daughter replies reluctantly, 'we have to listen to this now.' 'My husband and I never talked about this in front of the children,' Mrs Weiss told me. Mrs Goldfarb contradicts her mother: 'You were always talking about it.' It seems that both mother and daughter are indeed referring to the same kind of 'talking', expressing Mrs Weiss's simultaneous pre-occupation with what had happened and her avoidance of talking about it except by allusions, which in her daughter's perception occurred constantly.

Mrs Weiss went on to talk about how she had got by with 'Aryan' papers because of her looks, and her perfect Polish, and how that had enabled her to save other family members from being deported to the camps from the ghetto. But she had not been able to save her own parents, even though her presence of mind had prevented their deportation a few times. She sums up the futility of her efforts by concluding mournfully, 'one saved the father, one did not save him'. During the interview, the hopelessness and powerlessness brought about by the persecution becomes more and more pervasive. Overcome by sadness, and worried about Mrs Weiss's frail health, I was about to bring the session to an end. But Mrs Goldfarb took the initiative, asking her mother why, given her traditional upbringing, she had not been observant herself—half-jokingly challenging her with the thought that even if the war had not intervened, she would not have agreed to a traditionally arranged marriage. Earlier Mrs Weiss had described the traditional life of her parents and extended family with sad longing. Now, in answer to her daughter's question, she remembers, in a lighter tone, how even as a young girl she had been different from others, more independent, and attracted to the Polish, non-Jewish society; and also more accepted than usual for Jews. She wouldn't even have minded not being Jewish, except that she had already been born that way: 'Should I have converted? But that would have killed my family.' But her parents had not worried about her. Within the large family there had been space for difference.

Mrs Weiss's wish to mix with a different social group without having to leave her own community was not uncommon in pre-war Poland. But what is unusual about it is that she can remember and express how she felt at that time. The German occupation made it absolutely necessary for her to change sides, to become so Polish that she forgot her upbringing. In contrasting herself with others who had passed themselves off as Christians but who had secretly continued to observe Jewish prayer times and holidays, Mrs Weiss says that she forgot completely about such religious obligations: her unresolved ambivalence and her moral dilemma result from her having been able to accomplish completely, and relatively successfully, what had seemed to her before the war to be desirable. But having been forced to obliterate her Jewish upbringing and sense of belonging made it seem to her that she had abandoned her family.

Mrs Weiss asked me whether her granddaughter cared about what had happened during the war, saying that Maya never called on her to ask her about what she had lived through. Maya had explained to me in

her interview that she preferred to listen to her paternal grandmother
about how she had managed to survive, rather than to her maternal
grandmother. Her paternal grandmother had recently returned to
Auschwitz equipped with a video camera, and could tell a story of
survival, as well as document it, in an acceptable format. One could say
that she had turned the endless exposure to suffering into a narrative—
a story that could be told—by reschematizing it as purposeful survival.
This grandmother held strong religious beliefs, and she and her
husband celebrated the holidays in a lively way. In contrast to Mrs
Weiss, the traditional context seemed to be a way of giving meaning to
survival rather than becoming overwhelmed by desolate and painful
thoughts.

During Mrs Goldfarb's interview, Mrs Weiss remained in the room,
seemingly absorbed in her own thoughts, though occasionally commenting unexpectedly on her daughter's story. Mrs Goldfarb's life
story highlights her childhood, marked by the emotional consequences
of the persecution for her parents, as well as by her own experience of
displacement and failed attempts at migration. She describes her
friendships with non-Jewish Germans today, and the communication
gaps between herself and them: unlike her friends, she cannot tell
coffee-table anecdotes about her grandmother. She also describes,
somewhat faster and in a low voice, but still with her mother present,
how she almost broke off contact with her parents and with the Jewish
community. Now she greatly fears similar developments with her own
daughter who might not be able to find her way back as she had.

In this family, the persecution is a preoccupation about which they
do not talk to each other. Rather, each generation attempts to live with
the knowledge without letting it become overwhelming. What can be
talked about more easily are the conflicts in each of their lives which
arise as a result of the expectations of remaining within certain
traditional boundaries. Marrying a non-Jewish partner inflicts deep
pain and loss against the background of the persecution. While in this
community it is relatively common and acceptable for Jewish men to
marry non-Jewish women who convert, it is Jewish women who are
held more responsible for maintaining the traditional culture, especially
through their choice of partner.

Reassurance is sought by Maya from her mother, and by Mrs
Goldfarb from Mrs Weiss, that there is a possibility of universal values
and freedom of action, even though they know the limitations. Their
generational work consists of appeals to one another to recognize that

they have all faced similar situations of conflicting pressures on them. They seek each other's reassurance that they will continue to find supportive understanding when needed.

Close contacts with non-Jews often engender different ways of interpreting past and present experience. Whether such contacts are perceived as harmonious or conflict-ridden, they create a general need to reflect on these relationships against the background of the war and the persecution; for the Jews of the three generations in Astadt, the mere fact of living in Germany demands explanation.

In Antwerp, by contrast, members of the large Orthodox part of the Jewish community need no such explanations, and expectations of their life course are defined much more clearly. For boys, general studies will gradually give way to exclusively Jewish learning in school, and after some years of advanced religious studies they may qualify for one of the professions in teaching and observance; or they may follow their fathers into a career in the diamond trade or industry—work which can be combined with the necessary interruptions for praying and keeping the holidays. For girls, school consists of more general subjects: they learn, for example, more foreign languages than boys. After school, they spend a year in a Jewish seminary, which entitles them to teach at the elementary level. But few young women pursue a career straight after school: mostly they marry before the age of 20, and marriage at 16 or 17 is not uncommon among the Orthodox youth. Work is only taken up some twenty years later when the children have grown up. The sexes are separated from the time of going to school; boys and girls grow up segregated from one another. From the perspective of outsiders we might ask: how is it that they expect their parents, with the advice and help of other relatives and matchmakers, to find partners for them? And as for the women, how is it that they will grow up to feel that having many children is more valuable than pursuing work interests or a career?

We can try to understand how such traditional expectations of a Jewish woman's biography have become accepted. In a similar way to the cultural microcosm of the Amsterdam family, but on a larger scale, there is no place for recalling the persecution within the new orthodoxy. This partly seems to be because, within religious reasoning, the persecution becomes merely an instance in the everlasting plight and rescue of the Jews. As lived history it is not important. Furthermore, since the Antwerp community seems to represent a successful revival of how things used to be, and can continue to be, to remember the loss and destruction of the old life world would be out of place and anachronistic.

Antwerp is the only one of these three communities where there are relatively extended families; the older generation had usually immigrated with their siblings before the war, and the more observant of the middle generation have a large number of children, ten being no exception. When interviewing members of an extended family, I often met nieces, cousins, and grandmothers at each others' houses. The older generation in the other two communities lacked this *shtetl*-like custom of frequently visiting one another.

Two women of the older generation talked in very different ways about their wartime experience. Mrs Edel described what had happened after her deportation. Her sadness and longing for those she had lost brought the events vividly into the interview situation. She interrupted her narrative when her granddaughter dropped in for a visit, resuming it after her departure. She told me that she never talked about what she had been through to her granddaughter. The break between past and present is reflected in her switching from French, which she talks with her granddaugher, back to German and Yiddish, the languages of her youth, as she resumes her story: 'J'étais tellement—verzweifelt' ('I was so—desperate'). She hardly ever talks at all about the past nowadays; people have other interests. Mrs Edel was not observant, and said that she had lost her faith. In contrast, Mrs Nacht, an in-law, lives observantly. She combines her interview with a visit to her granddaughter. Even when alone, she explicitly says that she will not talk about what had happened during the war: in fact, she says she refuses ever to talk about it to anyone, even to her sister who had endured the persecution with her, though they recognize the signs of each other's suffering and nightmares. She talks about positive aspects of her life—how she had chosen modern furniture after the war, and how she liked to dress her children well. Her memories of her own childhood in Poland are of discrimination and the beginnings of persecution. What she experiences as crises in her family now—only alluded to with sighs, the details being filled out by other family members—makes her doubt that she ought to have survived Auschwitz. After her interview, her granddaughter lovingly accompanies her back to her house.

Mrs Fayn, from the middle generation, talked in great detail about the developments and expectations in her life. She chose a situation when she could be alone with me. She had not grown up in Antwerp, and did not identify with the new orthodoxy. In order to spare her daughter the conflicts that she had experienced of being different within a largely homogeneous community, she had enrolled her in a strictly Orthodox school.

Tania, her 14-year-old daughter, understood the interview in a similar way to her mother, namely as an opportunity to reflect on her own life. She took me into her room, and then, with the ethnographical eye of the native who feels different, she described the rigid expectations imposed on her, not so much by her parents but by her peer group within the community. Her mother, in fact, encourages her autonomy.

In their biographical reflections, neither Mrs Fayn nor Tania was preoccupied with the persecution, nor did they concern themselves with the demands of observing Orthodoxy, other than critically. As generational work, they did not have to involve themselves in the task of maintaining or reviving traditionality, as in the case of the Amsterdam family; or of preserving the memory of the destroyed way of life of the east, as in the Astadt family. Both these areas are embodied in what the Antwerp Jewish community has come to represent. Given this background, mother and daughter separately talked about their own life expectations as individuals, drawing attention to signs of autonomy in each other. The women of the older generation remain isolated with their memories, just as in the other communities; but in large families with many grandchildren comfort can be found.

Generally speaking the middle generation takes a special interest in the topic of the continuity and changes in traditionality within their families. This is reflected in the role of mediator, interpreter, and translator which they assume in the interviews. They had been directly affected by the disruption of the narrative, the total loss of all continuity in their parents' lives. At the same time, they feel responsible for how the younger generation would understand the significance they should attach to traditional orientations. During the course of the interviews with their mothers and daughters they drew out the connections with what they perceived as the positive aspects in continuity between the generations on the basis of their own life experience and expectations. These may be, as we have seen, a renewed observancy to stand in place of the memory of the destroyed traditional life; an affirmation of similarity in each generation's wish to belong and to be free; or, within a social network of established traditionalism and emotional support for the older generation, biographical expectations of autonomy. The connections are linked to what kind of community the women live in and in what ways the memory of history and the continuity of traditionality are part of a more general social construction.

The reconstruction of the constitutive aspects of transmission between the generations is possible through interpretive analysis.[5] By describing the communicative activities of the three generations—how they initiate, control, encourage, and protect the other generations in talking about the past and its meaning, we can understand how these activities give shape to the impact of the past. Such constitutive processes in family communication are especially significant when there is no narrative transmission. What cannot be told as the story of one's life experience, to make sense of the past to the younger generations, is nevertheless referred to, supplanted, or transformed in ways specific to each family. In these instances of generational work, we have seen how the meaning of the past and of traditionality is redefined by mothers and daughters to accommodate the changes.

Notes

I would like to thank the HOZV, University of Amsterdam, as well as the HSP II at the University of Kassel for supporting this research. I am grateful to Natasha Burchardt for her editorial advice. I would like to thank Fritz Schütze and Gerhard Riemann, as well as the other members of the research colloquium at Kassel University, for inspiring this analysis. Kathy Davis and Marek Czyzewski have also made significant contributions.

1. 'Practical knowledge' is understood here on the one hand in the sense meant by Alfred Schütz, *Collected Papers*, i. *The Problem of Social Reality* (The Hague, 1962), 13–14, to include 'ways of life, methods of coming to terms with the environment, efficient recipes for the use of typical means for bringing about typical ends in typical situations', in accordance with what is accepted as relevant within a group—here, the life world of the traditional eastern European Jews. On the other hand, 'practical knowledge' is also used more specifically to mean how women learned to transform everyday life tasks into 'domestic religion' (Barbara Myerhoff, *Number Our Days* (New York, 1978), 234–5).

2. The German city has been anonymized because of its relatively small Jewish community. The interviews were conducted between 1987 and 1990. The older women were mostly in their seventies—some younger—born between 1915 and 1930. They came from eastern Europe and they were persecuted during the Second World War. The women of the middle generation, born between 1944 and 1954, were in their mid-thirties to mid-forties at the time of the interviews. The majority of the younger generation were in their early to mid-teens, born in the early to mid-1970s; a few were older.

3. In commenting on a presentation of this three-generational interview at a workshop at the Helen Dowling Institute for Biopsychosocial Medicine, Rotterdam, 10 Feb. 1989.

4. This concept is analogous to that of 'biographical work', which represents a person's altered orientation to her changed personal and social identity through the course of life events. Such work consists of 'recalling, rehearsing, interpreting, and redefining, and this involves the communicative work of fellow interactants, especially significant others too' (Gerhard Riemann and Fritz Schütze, ' "Trajectory" as a Basic Theoretical Concept for Suffering and Disorderly Social Processes', in D. R. Maines (ed.), *Social Organization and Social Process: Essays in Honor of Anselm Strauss* (New York, 1991), 339).

5. The complexity of the intergenerational transmission of the family enterprise, led Daniel Bertaux and Isabelle Bertaux-Wiame to exclaim, with a certain exasperation, 'what if we had been interested in the transmission of values, of attitudes, of beliefs' ('Le patrimoine et sa lignée: Transmissions et mobilité sociale sur cinq générations', *Life Stories/Récits de vie*, 4 (1988), 22).

10

Memory of Slavery in Black Families of São Paulo, Brazil

MARIA DE LOURDES MONACO JANOTTI and
ZITA DE PAULA ROSA

The history of Brazil's slave past has been essentially reconstructed from the documentary sources left by the ruling classes. Recording the memory of slavery through the testimony of black men's families allows the historian to hear the evidence of those who until now have constituted the 'silent figures' of history. Since the hundredth anniversary of Slavery Emancipation in Brazil in 1988, a group of researchers from the University of São Paulo have been tape-recording the memories of black families of their captive past. So far 110 persons belonging to forty-five families living in the State of São Paulo, one of the twenty-six federal units of Brazil, have been interviewed.[1] Although up to now black families have been neglected as a possible source for Brazilian history, their oral reminiscences have shown how a collective memory of slavery does indeed persist.

We see memory as a dynamic and social process. When people who remember recall their past to a group which has shared their experiences, it can lend support to their act of remembering. In such collective and dynamic memory work, past and present values interact, breaking through a linear conception of historical time to a richer construction of reality.

The most solid and lasting social framework for the fostering of memory, especially oral memory, is the family. Reminiscences by familial groups can survive unbroken long after the disappearance of those who generated them. Family bonds are indeed so solid in Brazil that it is above all in this social context that personal reminiscences can turn into collective memory, making the voice of the few speak for the many.

The marks stamped by black slavery upon the various faces of Brazilian society and culture have been deep. The very concept of

Translator: Dulce Amarante da Silva Ramos

labour itself has been invested with a pejorative connotation: appreciation of idleness and contempt for unskilled labour, both always linked to the slave image, have become integrated into 'collective psychology as a deep and strongly rooted feature of the Brazilian character'.[2]

Emancipated from slavery, black freedmen, although they had acquired a new social and legal status, were in no condition to face the competition of immigrant wage workers in the process of industrial and farming expansion gathering way in the state of São Paulo. Consequently, with the stigma of their previous bondage against them, and the indelible stamp of their race and colour, they have come to form a mass which is today the main constituent of the poorest stratum of Brazilian society.

Under the colonial system, which in Brazil continued up to 1822, coercive toil was imperative for slaveholders to get a fast return on the capital they had put into the slave. To facilitate coercion, they sought to nullify the slave's individuality, reducing him to the condition of a mere machine, utterly deprived of free will. However, the myth of black men's docility has been disputed by recent studies of their extensive rebellions and resistance, 'forms of struggle were not sporadic, but they continued as long as the institution lasted'.[3]

Nothing at all is head of black slaves during the first three centuries of colonization in the state of São Paulo. Their numbers only rose to a significant level from the late eighteenth century onward, when the region became integrated into an export economy based on the traditional trinomial: monoculture, great landed estates, and black slavery. From then on, as coffee cultivation intensified, there was a large influx of black people: by 1871 there were 173,267 slaves counted in São Paulo, mainly in coffee-producing areas. Even though they arrived later than in other regions of Brazil, their fate was typical enough. In the second half of the nineteenth century violence against slaves intensified as the slavery system crumbled before the advances of free labour capitalism. The resulting tensions, which hindered the consolidation of black families, are also reflected in the typically fragmented form taken by memory of the slave past.

The testimonies we have used here come from groups of adults who each belong to the same family, representing three successive generations within it: usually grandparent, parent, and child. The recordings come from black families living in the areas where the coffee economy, and thus a great mass of slaves and their descendants, have been concentrated: Vale do Paraíba (Paraíba do Sul River Valley) and Centro-Oeste Paulista (the central and western regions of the state of São Paulo). Other interviews were also recorded with families in the city of São Paulo, which because of its rapid industrialization and urbanization drew in large numbers of black people, attracted both by job opportunities and also by the city's lack of direct links to their former life condition. These testimonies record a history of Brazilian society which rarely portrays famous public events, but rather the slow course of continuity and change: a history of daily life and the culture of ordinary men and women.

Within the life stories collected we have detected two types of narrative structures: stories about everyday social life, and especially the world of labour; and stories about family life, which stress courting and coupling, births, losses, separations, changes of domicile, festivities and parties, and the changing roles taken up inside the family by its members. These narrative structures also reveal certain guiding themes: satisfaction at the fulfilment of one's life project or sorrow at its failure; pride in one's race or a sense of inferiority, either apparent from, or masked under, remembrance or pseudo-forgetfulness of a mythical captive past; and, at the same time, the mechanisms by which such remembrances are transmitted powerfully, in unspoken terms between its generations.

While many historians may admit an identification with their subject, the very separation in time from the past usually allows the research object a certain independence. A written document, even if once oral, is artificially mummified, cut off from the course of life. The coldness of the printed word somehow shields the researcher from emotion. The historian who fails to provide a good interpretation of a testimony from the nineteenth century may possibly be criticized by another scholar. Yet, how different is our relationship to our contemporaries! Some notes taken down by one of our researchers, a woman who had just recorded the testimony of a young black woman—from the third generation of black people born after Slavery Emancipation—read as follows:

She is deeply concerned about the present situation of black people, and said it was most important that someone should do something for the benefit of her race. The interviewee, whose name is Cleide, hoped there would be something in return from our project, because she believes these tapes ought not to be merely transcribed and filed, but also listened to and discussed. At that very moment I felt that a great responsibility was being transferred to me. . . . The weight of this responsibility came from the interviewed girl's hopes, and I would like not to cause her to be disappointed.

Most people in telling their life story and giving their opinions present their individual role within a social whole. To start with, reference almost always takes place to their ancestors' full names, indicating these witnesses' strong concern to root their own identity, searching for their origin, demonstrating a knowledge of their forefathers. In some cases pride in racial purity and a captive past is evident, but more often they point to cross-breeding with white men or Indians.

Felipe Miguel, born in 1892—thus from the first generation of the post-Emancipation era—begins his account:

My father's name was Paulino Miguel Pereira, and my mother was Teodora. Her father was Lino. He was the son of an Indian. I think his name was Marino Barbosa. My mother, I believe, was Teodora Barbosa.[4]

Alfredo Antônio tells us about his slave grandmother, mentioning she was of the 'Mozambique race'. He attributed his sister's being named after the main female character of a famous Brazilian novel, *Isaura*, to her similar physical attributes, for she was white-skinned and 'not of the slave race'.[5] While white men speak of black people as 'Negroes' in a homogenizing term, the blacks themselves make their own fine distinctions through many differing expressions, like 'Mozambique race', 'slave race', 'African race'.

There were other witnesses who referred with much more reluctance to the black race, and thus to the captive past of their ancestors. Some even denied having any memories of their slave ancestry. Thus Benedita Loureiro, born in 1907, instead emphasizes her life of toil, and the sacrifices she made to raise her children. Encouraged to speak about her parents, she states that:

Neither mother nor father were slaves. How did things use to be in those days? A baby who was born *ventre-livre*,[6] because of already being inside its mother's belly, was that baby not to be a slave? On that matter, about those things, I don't know anything at all. I'm not from the slavery days.[7]

So this witness fails to elaborate the fragments of remembrance that were transmitted to her, even denying she knows anything about them.

Most immigrant and Brazilian white families have some knowledge of their origins. But this is not the case for black families, among whom there are those who do know—roughly one in every four families—and the others, who do not know. Appreciation of origin is the starting-point for identity, and Maria de Lourdes knows that very well:

I tell my girls there are people of our colour who don't know even where they come from. But not us. The African, in our family, he stands close.[8]

Black family history is structured above all by the turning-points in a struggle for survival which because of their marginal condition was often violent, even insane. These witnesses scarcely refer to political events in their country's history. For them, dates seem irrelevant; and the only epochs are childhood, youth, and old age. Their testimonies move around events and conjunctures which they themselves select.

Very often, images of death and abandonment surface in evocations of childhood. Recollection of that period is commonly marked by mention of the loss of father or mother, and of being brought up by relatives or acquaintances: not unexpected in view of the notorious instability of most poor families. Often the whole memory of childhood is globalizing, brief, and painful:

On my life as a little girl, what I can tell is that I lost my father too early, at 10 years old; so my grandmother joined us. My mother needed to work to raise us, so that she would not be forced to 'give' any of us to anybody else.[9]

After the death of a father or mother, it was usual for a reorganization of the family to follow in which relatives took on new roles so that the original nucleus would not fall apart completely.

In representations of childhood, almost always the presence and authority of one among the family is symbolically consolidated, in terms of his or her personal features or behaviour towards the child. A powerful grandmother, an angry mother, an unaffectionate father are all characters typical from these three generations of witnesses, reflections of the violence permeating relationships under slavery. Thus Benedito Guido Evangelista tells us:

Very little dialogue with my father indeed. It was better with my mother. My father didn't beat me. But my mother . . .—always. And that often for trifles. She used to take whatever was close to hand and strike my face; blood flew from my nose . . . But she was an excellent person.[10]

In much the same way, for Felipe Miguel of the Pereira family an angry mother character permeates childhood

Once, mother thrashed me with a leather strap, leaving me all covered with blood. If it had happened here [in São Paulo], she would have been arrested. She did it because I had been fighting with another boy. She used to drink. She used to beat my father: such tremendous thrashings!

Yet their very lack of strong affective ties, the irregular composition of their familial nucleus, the absence of marriage as a lawful juridical institution, and the ceaseless struggle for survival caused the witnesses to appreciate even a precarious security provided by adults, and so almost to tolerate the violence they had suffered from them.

The role of the grandmothers emphasizes how the family was often dominated by a woman; generally either an abandoned or a widowed mother. Justina, from the Ayres family, says:

My grandmother was very fierce. She was good, though. When some little thing happened and mother arrived from the factory, she didn't need to beat us again, because our grandmother had already done it. We liked our grandmother because she used to tell us stories at night.

Among these families it is unusual to come upon memories of slavery transmitted through these moments of contact across the generations. Direct personal memories are often embedded within the myths of folk narrative and fables about black people and their image: tales which cannot be found in children's books.

Memories of school are brief, for most black country children rarely attended more than three years, and they include glaring experiences of prejudice. José Benedito Ferreira from Sorocaba told us how his father was 'expelled from the school by its head' after a 'fight over some snacks' which were stolen: he was suspected, because they knew he was too poor to bring his own. As for José himself:

On my first year at school I did well. But the second left a deep mark on me. My teacher—I don't know what she had against our race—she used to injure me. But she went at it thoroughly. No matter what I might have done when I was playing, she came and censured me—'The little Nego has got a frog face!' This made a big impression on me, you know! It's something I still think about over and over again, right up till now. But I've never opened my heart to anyone. I've never talked about this. Not even at home.[11]

In these memories, childhood ends abruptly with the start of work, whether paid or not. Often school attendance ended early. Glória Pereira, born in 1923, explains why she could only reach the second grade of elementary school:

I started work when I was five—I looked after another child. My sister started work at 7. Poor child, she needed to climb on a stool to get the kitchen done.

Glória believes that in the past children were more responsible, more like little adults:

When we were 5 years old, we were responsible. A child of 5 isn't like that today. We had some sense. We'd learned more, suffered more. We went to school and when we got back home again, we had to work.[12]

Felipe Miguel, Glória's father, also tells how he left his home when he was 12:

I set out like a good walker, straight on to the road, taking my hat. I had no proper clothes. But there was that straw hat, and two trousers made out of flour sacks—two trousers and two shirts. All I had. I was very poor. Then I found a man picking coffee beside the road, and I asked him: 'Do you know whether your master needs farmhands?' . . . I knew he used to because I had an uncle who had gone and worked there. So Mr Luís told me: 'He does. When someone shows up, he gets him to pick coffee.' Then he says, 'But who are you?' I say, 'It's me.' I was 12. He says: 'Ah, but he doesn't take children. He takes young men, 15–18-year-olds . . . upward.'

Black family memory of childhood has no place for the mythologized happy and smiling times common in bourgeois reminiscences. It is this contrast which gives such a poignant meaning to the sheer brevity of Edna Aparecida's testimony:

My childhood, I can't even remember it. I hardly had a childhood. . . . We were too poor.[13]

The historian Tania Regina de Luca has pointed out how in the first decades after Emancipation, black people could not effectively face the competition of immigrants or of native white men, so that their work 'often carried the mark of servility, favouring the preservation of the old dependency ties'. For the second generation, by contrast, a more effective entry into the labour market from the 1950s brought changes in attitudes.

Labour comes then to be considered as something that redeems, able to turn an individual into someone respected. The sacrifice brings its rewards, realized in the acquisition of one's own home or car, and through one's children's education. Productive activity and saving come to be seen as edifying and go together with values such as honesty, probity, and responsibility.[14]

The marks of servility surface in the testimony of Maria Francisca Bueno. Born in 1882, she was brought to her master's home at the age of 7, against her own will, to work as a domestic servant; and she was only able to leave when she married:

My life has been one of suffering. I was struck with anything. Such as a round ferule, an instrument with a long handle and five holes, which as it hit sucked the skin off my hands. When the beating was over, I was made to wash my hands in salt water. When I was a young woman, my mistress gave it to me the same way. She beat me with anything: stick, slipper, rod. I was beaten right up till I got married. I was a housemaid, just like a real slave, with no earnings at all. Only got something to eat and drink, and shreds to dress in. When I got married, they didn't give me anything! Nothing, nothing, nothing! . . . My mistress had been the owner of my grandma. My mom was the daughter and she was my mistress's maid, but she was freed in the captivity days. She worked for that same mistress who raised me.[15]

Maria Francisca has broken this black family tradition of generations of service to the same white family. She refused to give one of her own children to serve in the house of her old mistress's daughter.

The family narratives of Maria Francisca are also an illustration of how memory can leap-frog across the generations. Her daughter, Maria Aparecida de Andrade, retains only vague stories about captivity and says little about them. But her granddaughter Maura Aparecida, born in 1948, held on to her grandmother's memories, and eventually made herself the accepted authority on the family's stories. Her own testimony describes the mechanism for transmission explicitly:

I was raised by my grandma rather than my mother. Grandma is now 107 years old. When I was a child, she used to tell her own mother's stories over and over. Today she doesn't want to tell no more. Sometimes, my daughters ask her to tell but she doesn't.[16]

There appear to be some consistent patterns in the mechanism of transmission of memory. The main memorialist chooses the ideal listener among those with whom he or she lives; there are no kinship rules whatever for making this choice. It is also noticeable that the stories are repeated again and again, always very emotionally. The narrative unfolds following a sequence drawn either from the father's or the mother's family stems; it is very rare for both sides of the family to be equally represented. Different generations living together in the same domestic space, the simplicity of social life, limited leisure opportunities, and the carrying out of domestic tasks together all help to bring family members close, and to encourage transmission.

Because of their greater contact with institutionalized knowledge, for example through schooling, some of the youngest generation contest their parents' and grandparents' attitudes to their slave past. The older generation invariably present the Emancipation from

Slavery, proclaimed on 13 May 1888 by Princess Regent Isabel, in a wholly positive light. The testimony of Hermelinda da Silva Leite, born in 1903, is typical:

The 13th of May was a good thing because in the old days black men were dominated and had no freedom. My mom used to give many examples. Black men were not permitted to go out; were kept confined in the *senzala* [slave quarters in the plantations], all of them together. She said they ate from the trough all together. I think that now is better.[17]

But to a young anonymous witness, the change now seems much less:

There's always been bondage. Even now, there are people who are like slaves because of their poverty, because they lack the means of making a living. Now, it would be a good thing if another Princess Isabel could come along to protect these people and give them liberty. Slavery doesn't seem to be over. It's over in the law, but not in the way of life. It's still master and slave today.

And indeed, the historian Suely Robles Reis de Queiroz would confirm that, 'as a matter of fact, the 13th of May did not mean an immediate disappearance of slavery practices': black people joined the 'free' labour market with too many disadvantages still to overcome.[18]

The Fabiano family, of Sorocaba, hold on strongly to their reminiscences of their slave forefathers. The transmission of these stories through their family members is remarkable. One story exerts a special fascination on them all. The fullest version is told by Thereza Henriqueta Marciano:

My mother's father was sure a slave—one of those who got themselves punished. . . . His master fell in love with my granny. She was black and very beautiful, very beautiful indeed. He pursued her but she didn't want him. So instead, her master forced her to marry my grandfather, who was much older than her. She was almost a girl and he was an old, old man. Imagine! So grandfather refused to get married to a girl! My father told me that grandfather has tried to commit suicide: he slashed his belly and threw himself into a well, a well for leather tanning. Then his master, so my father told me in these very words, the master got grandfather fished out from there, got him out of water, got him sewed up and married all the same. Granny had been a child in master's household, but grandfather worked on the land.

Less openly this story also appears in other testimonies from this family. Thereza's mother, Isabel Fabiano André, daughter of these grandparents, does not speak explicitly about their marriage, but she points out how forced unions were one of slavery's great evils:

And then, they forced women to marry anyone. I think this was what my aunt used to talk about . . . how painful marriage was.

It is significant how she cites as her source for this image of slavery a relative now passed away, thus lending authority to her account. Thereza's daughter Cleide, by contrast, when telling this same story, only alters some aspects of the narrative from the full version which her mother has told her:

Ever since I was a little girl I feel such a revulsion . . . These things from slavery days, they do hurt.[19]

This family story also has a mythical dimension. In fact, stories of forced marriages between an old black man and a seductive young woman were also told by some other families, with minimal differences only in the details. And such stories undoubtedly helped to build a slavery imagery—the cruel and lustful white man, contrasted with his beautiful, pure prey, a black woman; and the virtuous, good-hearted old black man, who does not hesitate to take his own life rather than be made the tool of such villainy. Interestingly, at the time the white masters ascribed to black people precisely the lust and cruelty which in these retrospective stories appear in reverse. In nineteenth-century moralistic speeches, young black women were often singled out as corruptors of their masters, using their physical attributes to take advantage of them. Conversely, in Umbanda, the Afro-Christian religion practised in Brazil, old black men are the characters who are supposed by devotees of the religion to be invested with superior virtues and wisdom, to fulfil requests from the faithful.

Perhaps reflecting the desire to alter their social situation, the theme of a young black woman resisting her master's approaches also occurs in many other accounts, in which other aspects of her physical appearance are stressed. She is described as of mixed race, almost white-skinned, or almost black-skinned, with blue or green eyes, wavy or straight hair, well educated, with fine feelings and gestures, holding herself high, and so on: in short, close to the idealized heroine also cultivated by the ruling classes.[20]

Such mythical elements come together in the legend of Anastácia, the slave of noble African origin, priestess and healer who died under torture inflicted by her master, a man who could not resist her charms. Yet even so, in her final moments, Anastácia saves the life of the master's sick son. This very widespread legend is found not only in families but in literature and the media. For black people, Anastácia's superior and suffering character is linked to their own roots in African culture, and some today pray to her for help, and proclaim they have received her graces. Tinged with violence, such stories and legends appeal especially to the younger generations, who are rebelling against the discrimination and oppression they suffer today. As part of family history they play important, complex roles, very much like those of the myths that explain the origin of social groups, peoples, and nations.

Yet such traditions are not handed down unchanged: they are transmitted through a creative narrative combining both continuity and enrichment as each listener in turn becomes a teller. In this view, narrator and listener both participate in a common narrative flow, in which the story remains open to new proposals, to the addition of new details which draw on and disclose the unlimited dynamics of memory.

Perhaps no testimony expresses more vividly the meaning that telling a life story can have for the narrator than that of Benedita de Jesus, who describes it as a form of personal redemption:

I think it's very good to be interviewed. It's something that marks one's life. I'll be able to say to other people: 'Look here, this is what my life was like.' Because to the world I was dead. I don't know what was happening to me because I didn't remember anything. Now it's different. I will have something and I'm gonna read. I'll say, you know: 'Oh, I was all this much!'[21]

Other witnesses emphasize the importance of family stories for the whole group. Thus Ediana Maria says:

My grandfather says his grandfather had come from the Congo, Africa. He tells about the time when they were slaves. Sometimes, he himself mixes everything up. These are stories that we, in reality, have to assemble, piece by piece, to build a complete story.[22]

The fragmentation of memories in former slave families resembles the fragmentation of every other historical source the historian makes use of in order to build a narrative. The younger generation of black families here acknowledges the need for a collective effort to build an acceptable history, which may help them to find, through their origins in the past, a sense of their social selves. This collective effort to transmit family history involves grandfathers and grandsons, but more usually, because grandfathers are more often out working, grandmothers and granddaughters, together attempting to breathe lasting life into memories, always under threat of erasure through the fragility of the family's own ties.

Faced with such fragility, the historian too has a social task, to rescue the memories of black people, who, if now free, still remain marginal. The witnesses in their turn demand—and receive—the researchers' involvement. As Cleide Aparecida Marciano put it:

There's a lot of time we wanna tell someone about how we feel, but no one never showed up. Sooner or later, our day will come for us to open our hearts and speak out things we feel: that May 13's Emancipation Day has happened only that very day! Though our fetters are gone, got nobody to hit us and nobody to watch us no more, there's always someone pointing at us: 'That's a negro! That's a negro and a negro is no good!' There'll come a time someday for us to speak. I've enjoyed it [giving testimony]. Though I don't know how to express a lot of what I'm feeling, feel real glad; now I can lay my head on my pillow and sleep easy. One day someone's gonna read and feel what we feel.'[23]

Notes

1. This project has been co-ordinated by Maria de Lourdes Monaco Janotti and Suely Robles Reis de Queiroz, and supervised by Tania Regina de Luca and Zita de Paula Rosa. Its documentary collection at present includes 150 audio-tapes and their respective transcripts, photographs, copyright authorizations, and researchers' field notebooks. All these originals are now kept in CAPH (Centro de Apoio à Pesquisa Histórica) of the History Department of the University of São Paulo, their duplicates being kept at CEDIC (Central de Documentação e Informação Científica) of PUC/SP (Pontifical Catholic University of São Paulo).
2. Caio Prado Júnior, *Formação do Brasil Contemporâneo* (São Paulo, 1957), 347.
3. Suely Robles Reis de Queiroz, *Escravidão Negra em São Paulo: um estudo das tensoes provocadas pela escravidão no século XIX* (Rio de Janeiro, 1977), 201.
4. Pereira family (São Paulo): Felipe Miguel Pereira, born 1892.
5. Moraes family (from the town of Cunha): Alfredo Antônio des Moraes, born 1914. *Isaura*: see n. 20 below.
6. The Free-Womb Act (*Lei do Ventre-Livre*) theoretically emancipated all children born of slave mothers after 1871. In reality, their parents' owner had to raise these youngsters till 21 years of age, when they were expected, by making themselves useful to their 'would-be' owner, to compensate for their non-productive childhood years.
7. Ayres family (Sorocaba): Bendita Loureiro Ayres, born 1907.
8. Atanazio family (São Paulo): Maria de Lourdes Ferreira, born 1941.
9. Ayres family (Sorocaba): Justina Ferreira, born 1928, daughter of Benedita Loureiro Ayres.
10. Moraes family (Cunha): Benedito Guido Evangelista, born 1940, son of Alfredo Antônio de Moraes.
11. Ferreira family (Sorocaba): José Benedito Ferreira, born 1927.
12. Pereira family (São Paulo): Glória Pereira Paraná, daughter of Felipe Miguel Pereira, born 1923.
13. Alves family (from the town of Maristela): Edna Aparecida Alves de Lima, born 1955.
14. Tania Regina de Luca 'O trabalho e suas Representações', in *D. O. Leitura* (São Paulo), 7:77, (Oct. 1988).
15. Bueno family (Rio Claro): Maria Francisca Bueno, born 1881.

16. Bueno family (Rio Claro): Maura Aparecida Almeida de Oliveira, daughter of Maria Aparecida de Andraede, born 1927, and granddaughter of Maria Francisca Bueno.
17. Silva Leite family (Piracicaba): Hermelinda da Silva Leite, born 1903.
18. Suely Robles Reis de Queiroz, 'Lembranças do passado cativo', *Ciência Hoje*, Special Insert, 8:48 (Nov. 1988).
19. Fabiano André family (Sorocaba): Cleide Aparecida Marciano, born 1957, granddaughter of Isabel Fabiano André, born 1894, and daughter of Thereza Henriqueta Marciano, born 1932.
20. A Brazilian novel in which that mythical stance has been elaborated is Bernardo Guimarães, *A Escrava Isaura*, first published in 1875.
21. Atanásio family (São Paulo): Benedita de Jesus Atanásio, born 1911, aunt of Maria de Lourdes Ferreira.
22. Ferraz family (Piracicaba): Ediana Maria de Arruda, born 1969, granddaughter of Antônio Carlos Ferraz, born 1915.
23. Fabiano André family (Sorocaba): Cleide Aparecida Marciano, born 1957.

11

Spoken and Unspoken Words in the Life of a Cypriot Woman

A Life Story by her Granddaughter

ELENA GEORGIOU

> I speak of this journey as leading to my grandmother's house even though our grandfather lived there too. In our young minds houses belonged to women, were their special domain, not as property, but as places where all that truly mattered in life took place—the warmth and comfort of shelter, the feeding of our bodies, the nurturing of our souls. There we learned dignity; integrity of being; and there we learned to have faith.
>
> (bell hooks, *Yearning*)

I am a Cypriot woman. I was born and raised in England and have an English history spanning thirty years. However, my Cypriot past goes back for generations; through parents, grandparents, great-grandparents, and so on.

Four years ago I left London to study in New York. The separation from family and community was the impetus I needed to begin a journey of exploring the women of my culture. Through my studies I discovered oral history and made it the vehicle to carry me through the venture of recording the life stories of the women from the community to which I belong.

For this article I chose to work specifically with my grandmother because, initially, I felt we had the common ground of both having left the places of our birth as adults; she from Cyprus to England and I from England to New York. My aim was to weave a portrait of the female fabric of a Cypriot woman as seen through my eyes, as felt through my experience, and as known through my ancestry. As is the nature of work and life, however, the study took on a personality of its own. For the purposes of this article I am focusing on the struggle to get the testimony I desired from my grandmother and the relationship between her life, what she felt, and what she could actually tell me.

It had been a year since I had last seen my family, who in the mean time had returned after thirty-five years in London to live again in Cyprus. And I was now taking a break from my studies in America to join them in Cyprus for a short vacation. At Larnaca airport taxi drivers were their customary aggressive selves. One grabbed my suitcase and I had to grab it back and tell him I didn't need a ride. Then I saw the familiar figures of my grandmother, dad, mum, sister, niece, aunt, and uncle: all engrossed in conversation. I walked up behind my grandmother and gave her the first hug.

'What were you all doing? You weren't even waiting for me?' I joked. 'Oh, we've been waiting for hours,' my mum replied, 'But then your plane was delayed.'

'You haven't got an American accent yet,' my uncle said. 'How are you?' they all asked at the same time.

My grandmother and her two children, my mum and my uncle, squashed themselves into the back of the car. My father and I were in the front. We all looked like characters from a Woody Allen movie. Bouncing along a gravel road in the dry, midday heat, I immediately jumped in at the deep end: 'Yiayia,' I asked (that's grandmother in Greek), 'Yiayia, I want to write your story for school. Is that all right?' 'OK,' she responded.[1]

Well, OK translated into reality meant not OK. Absolutely not OK at all! A couple of days after my arrival I asked her if she could set some time aside for us to get started, and she asked me if we could wait to start next week. I said yes, even though I did not think it was a good idea. I wanted detail. I wanted depth. I wanted to get as much information as I could get to do her justice. But, if she needed to wait, then that was the way it was going to be.

The following week came and she asked me if we could postpone it for another couple of days. I was getting worried. My holiday was for only two weeks, and one of those had already gone! I waited for those days to pass with bated breath, in the hope that she would change her mind, and come to me. But in vain, and by her body language I could sense that talking about her life was the last thing she wanted to do. I was disappointed. I had really wanted her to want this as much as I wanted it. However, I understood, and made a decision to forget about the whole idea. I wanted to be respectful of her feelings.

My uncle and my mother, on the other hand, would not let her forget. 'When are you going to sit down with your granddaughter? When are you going to tell her your story? You can't change your mind. She has to do it for school.' They went on and on. Their insensitivity made me feel awkward. Yiayia was backed into a corner, and I felt as though I were responsible for that. The whole event became so public that neither one of us was allowed to forget. I felt lik a voyeur. I had asked Yiayia to give me an account of a life that, she obviously felt, was too painful to remember, let alone talk about. With unspoken words we agreed there was no turning back. She allowed me to interview her the day before I left.

Yiayia had stayed overnight at our house. We sat outside on the veranda still in our nightgowns. My mum promised me that she would stay upstairs and not disturb us, and my dad was out at work.

Putting the basic black metal tape recorder on the white formica table I wondered whether she had ever seen anyone have their voice taped. Rather than ask her, which I felt would have added to the awkwardness of the situation, I chose to deal with it by pretending it wasn't really there. She did the same. Knowing my grandmother's silent strength and her general reluctance towards the whole procedure I made the decision that the best way to begin the interview would be to start by talking about someone else's life rather than hers. When she picked up her crochet needle and continued work on her latest bedspread I knew she was ready to start.

THE TESTIMONY

Tell me first about your mother and father.[2]

My grandmother was a widow with two daughters; life was difficult. Her sister became ill. She got an illness called tuberculosis. People didn't get better from this illness. They had to take her out of town, and then she died.

My mother got engaged at 17 without a dowry because her fiancé was very dark-skinned. She would cry because she didn't want someone so dark-skinned. Eventually, she was able to end the relationship for this reason and very soon after that she was introduced to my father. He was from a village. He was a builder. They got engaged. He was a good man. His family didn't care that my mother didn't have a dowry. They had some land. He only had one sister and she wasn't very responsible.

My grandmother bought land for them and my father built his own two rooms and a stable. One room was for my parents, another for the children, and a stable for the animals. My father was diligent in his work. He would let the animals into the backyard every day. We even had horses. He wouldn't let us clean anything—he did it all himself. We were scared of the horses so we stayed away. My mother wasn't frightened of anything.

Was your mother 17 when she got married?

My mother was engaged at 17 and married at 18. She had seventeen children, but they didn't all survive. Some died before they reached forty days. Only six of my mother's children survived; four girls and two boys.

My father built us each a house, yes every one of us, even if it was just two rooms without much furniture. He wanted to build us all a house because he had to get married without one, and this made life very difficult for him. He never went to the coffee-shops like other men; he would finish his work and come straight home. We would eat together around a big table, and we always had to eat before it got dark so that we didn't have to light lamps; to save fuel. That's how life was.

When we were small, my mother would buy one pair of sheets at a time, and then save them for us. She started collecting for our dowries when we were very young. All my sisters got the same amount as I did. We all had to get everything the same. My father was very strict, very strict. We couldn't have many clothes. He didn't want us going out for walks. Yes, life was so different, so different, that sometimes it does seem like a lie.

It was only when I got engaged that I was allowed to go out for the day to the sea, and that I found out that there was a cinema in my town. My oldest sister didn't even do that. She wasn't allowed to go anywhere; her husband was too jealous. That's what was good about my husband; I was free to wear what I wanted and to take my children and go out. He would even take us out. He took us to the cinema, and on little walks. His problem was that he always spent everything he had today, and then we had nothing for tomorrow.

How old were you when you got married?

I got engaged at 17 and married at 20. We spent three years engaged, waiting for the house to be built. You didn't get married without a house. We had a bit of furniture. We had cast-iron beds—the most expensive—my mother bought them, and I had lace curtains. I had a dinner service and silverware for twelve. Everything was counted. We weren't allowed to have one glass more than our sisters.

I wasn't allowed to go out to work when I got married. Where would I go? Work in the orange groves? No, no—I wasn't allowed to work. I washed and starched clothes at home for a local hotel. We had big sinks for our washing. We didn't have washing machines like nowadays. All day Friday and Saturday we would wash, my mother would help, and we would dry. Life has changed so much. We were strong then; a strong, healthy family.

All the generations down to my children were strong. Andy, your uncle, is strong, but Loulla, your mother, she has been weak ever since she was a child. But my children turned out to be good people; good people considering, as a family, we went to live in England with four pounds in our pockets.

Andy and I went to England first. On Saturday we arrived in London and by Tuesday I found work! I found a job sewing skirts and jackets in a factory owned by Jewish people in Goodge Street.

We stayed with a Cypriot woman for a week, and then she helped us find a room to move into. Her family helped me. They advised me to continue sewing, and for Andy to stay as a waiter. Andy began by washing saucepans in a large restaurant. He would come home and say, 'Mama, I can't do this any more, the place smells so bad.' But that was the only work that they would give him because he did not have his work papers yet. Little by little, and then he joined me in the factory when he became legal.

There were other Cypriot women there, 'Yialousitises' (from the name of a large village in Cyprus). They were from villages. They would talk while working, and when they ate their food they would drop it on themselves. I would watch them and be ashamed. I was very uncomfortable around these women. In the end I stayed home and did my work. Then Andy found another factory for me to work in, with him, in Aldgate. I used to take two trains to get there. Imagine, being able to travel; take two trains and I still didn't know any English! I could make out a few English letters. I travelled from Finsbury Park to Moorgate, and from Moorgate to Aldgate. I was there for five years, and the people that owned this factory were Jewish too. Both my bosses were good to me, and cared about me.

Four months after Andy and I first came to London, my husband, and my two other children—Loulla, 15 years and George, 4 years old—joined us. We all lived in one room for a while. We had to move three times before we found a house to live in. Andy and I saved money. We got £110 to put a deposit down on a house in Finsbury Park. But we still needed another £25. The house couldn't be put in Andy's name because he wasn't quite 21, and they couldn't put it in my name without my husband's name too. There was no way I wanted that. But the man selling the house kept it for us until we got the £25 and until Andy reached 21.

If I had put the house in my husband's name I wouldn't have felt safe. He would have sold it. I had a home in Cyprus. I went back to sell it twice but I couldn't. I rented my house in Cyprus and then I gave it to my daughter; she paid what was left on it. The only reason we owed money was that my husband took a mortgage on it to buy a taxi-cab, but he just ate up all the profits. He was the one that left us owing money on the house. He would go out at night and not come home. Whatever money he had—he spent.

Whatever he gave me I tried to manage with. I didn't want to see my children starve. I managed to dress the children and myself by crocheting bedspreads and selling them. When I came to England I just crocheted bedspreads for the members of my family. I could turn my hand to many things. I crocheted, I embroidered, I starched clothes, I did clothing repairs, and I got decent money.

Everyone thought that it was my husband that gave me money for clothes. I

Elena Georgiou

dressed well. As I said, he was not a jealous man. I could visit my friends when I wanted. But I was a quiet person from a quiet family. Work always came first.

Did you have an arranged marriage?

My marriage wasn't arranged. I felt an affection for my husband. He was from a good family. His father was a policeman, and he sent him to English schools. No, no—his family were good people. It was my husband that ran away from home, and worked in a mill. He would follow me around. I told him it wasn't right, and that he should come to my house and ask if he could visit me. So he came to my house. He was unkempt. He didn't have anyone to take care of him. He already had a girlfriend—I heard about it. Yes, we knew about it. But it seemed to us that he wanted to be a husband and a father.

Did he ever work in England?

Yes, he worked on the trains. He would wash the silverware—but he didn't stay there either. Then he got a job in a bottle factory—but he would always say he was sick. When I worked he wanted me to give him my money to go food-shopping so that he could buy a few things and keep the rest for himself. I would get angry because money was tight. We had bills and rent to pay. I suffered.

Then I got sick. I had pneumonia. I was in Archway Hospital for six weeks. One week before I came out of hospital they took my daughter into hospital with tuberculosis. She was there for a year! So many things happened to us. We weren't used to the climate, and we didn't have the money to eat properly. When they let me out of hospital they told your grandfather that I had to stay home till the health visitor said it was all right for me to go back to work. But I had to go back straight away. Who was going to feed us?

My boss said, 'Clea, are you all right?' I told him yes. He was worried because I came back six days after having had pneumonia—but we needed the money. I was given sickness benefit—but your grandfather wasn't working. When the health visitor came to our home and found out that I wasn't there, she had words with him because he had let me go back to work. We couldn't live off sickness benefit. Your mother had been working but now she was in hospital too. She was in hospital for a whole year! Your grandfather would go to the hospital to visit her, but really it was to get her signature so that he could claim her sickness benefit and spend it on himself.

The house we were living in at the time was damp, and when the people that we rented from found out that your mother had gone into hospital with tuberculosis they threw us out. They were scared. We had to try and find somewhere new to live.

At that point my mother came out on to the veranda. 'I'm not going to disturb you,' she said. 'I just wanted you to know that I'm going out and that you have the house to yourselves.' As soon as my mother was out of the door my grandmother went into the kitchen, and started filling a bucket with water. 'What are you doing?' I asked. 'Washing the veranda,' she answered. 'But I did that yesterday.' 'You have to do it every day!' she pronounced. I couldn't just sit there and watch while she mopped. 'Here, let me do it,' I said, taking the mop from her and hoping that I could continue with the interview while I mopped and she crocheted.

'OK, you do that and I'll go upstairs and get dressed,' she said avoiding my gaze. I quickly realized that this was her way of telling me that she didn't want to talk any more. I felt a sudden drop in my stomach. I had mistakenly thought she had felt comfortable with the situation, but I had been wrong.

When my mother came back I told her that we had finished, so that no one would continue to harass Yiayia into doing things she did not want to do. I had learned many things from her testimony, the one important lesson being that she had had a lifetime of doing what was for the best rather than what she wanted. I did not want to add to that.

The end to the morning's work left me with contrary feelings. On the one hand, as a family member I was pleased that the work which my grandmother had found painful had come to an end. But on the other hand, I was still not quite ready to let the work rest. I was aware that the stores of my memory contradicted parts of my grandmother's testimony. I hypothesized that either Yiayia had simply not chosen to remember them as meaningful parts of her life or that she had chosen to leave out what seemed to her to be either shameful or painful details. I decided my mother would be a good person to ask for verification. So, I waited for her to return and with tape recorder in hand I went to her bedroom with two specific questions that would give important and final details.

Mum, do you remember that you told me that Yiayia used to take in washing? When was that?
When I was very young.
How young?
For me not to remember, I must have been quite young—8 or 9.
Who did she used to wash for?
We used to call them 'Artistes'. Ladies that go out with men privately—not in a house, a special house.
Prostitutes?
Yes, but they used to be in a hotel all by themselves. Every one on her own. So they were private. They didn't have a Madam. They called them 'Artistes'. Your Yiayia used to do their clothes because they needed special care. They

had beautiful clothes. In those days they used to wear satin petticoats and satin panties. Only prostitutes and rich women had satin underwear at that time; only they had the money.

Do you know what year Yiayia went to England?

1951.

And why did she go at that time?

Because your grandfather wasn't looking after us. He mortgaged the house to buy a car. He didn't pay for it. He had other debts and they were going to take the house away from us. A relative of your father's came to Cyprus and at that time you needed something like a sponsor. In those days when someone came from England even if you didn't know them you still went to visit them. Your Yiayia went and talked to them and she asked the people if they would send her 'the invitation' so that she could come to England. So they did.

For your Yiayia to feel that she had to go to England your grandfather had brought her to an unbearable point. When he had his last girlfriend for good.

What do you mean for good?

She was a steady one. Your Yiayia's sister found out and came and told her. Your Yiayia's sister used to clean people's houses and she would see him come out of the hotel with her. Yiayia confronted him and they had a big fight and then she decided to go. She wasn't going to take him to England but she decided to give him another chance. But he was just the same. When they got to England he didn't have girlfriends but he just stopped working. They fought in England worse than they did in Cyprus—much worse. That was the time I was ill—very ill—with TB—he came to kill her with a knife.

Bappou?! [Grandfather] Why?!

They were fighting. I had TB. She had pneumonia and bronchitis. Your Uncle George was a baby with no one to look after him. And your grandfather spent his days in coffee-houses.

At this point I felt the interviewing had come to an appropriate end. Yiayia and I never mentioned the interview for the rest of my stay (or, for that matter, since then). I caught the plane back to America breathing an ambivalent sigh of relief.

One of the reasons I had wanted to interview my grandmother was that I remembered her as a good, interesting, and detailed story-teller. She was an elder in my community and an elder in my family, a highly respected woman within her own world. Consequently, I felt privileged to have her as both a relative and an interviewee. However, in hindsight, having asked her to accompany me on this reluctant journey, I am now able to consider and see things from what I imagine to be her perspective, also.

When I first posed the question to my grandmother she heard her college-educated grandchild asking her to relate the story of a life full of hardship and struggle that she had hoped she would never have to mention again. When I came back to America to write up the testimony I began to have recollections of instances, family occasions, when her children would relate a negative story concerning my grandfather's past and she would quietly say that they should not speak ill of the dead; that they should let him rest in peace.

Also, with hindsight, I was able to reflect on Yiayia's 'talent' for story-telling. I recently had a conversation with my sister, who is a hairdresser. She sets my grandmother's hair once a week, and knew of the struggle I had had with the interview. My sister said, 'You should hear the stories Yiayia tells me!' Obviously I became insanely jealous for a minute and then logically concluded that Yiayia's stories only came to her when she felt relaxed and when she was using them as a tool to connect a hopeful future with a bearable past. In my enthusiasm (arrogance?), and good intentions as an oral historian I did not have the foresight to pause and question myself as to whether this story would dredge up the pain Yiayia had put to rest when she buried my grandfather. And Yiayia, knowing nothing of the world of 'academia' (and probably not caring either), only saw a clumsy grandchild, coercive children, and a black tape recorder sitting on a white table capturing words that had the capability of bringing back disturbing memories.

Yiayia's silence surrounding this story was not incongruent with her personality in general. Before embarking on this oral history, the stories concerning my grandparents' marriage and my grandfather's irresponsible behaviour were not related to me by her, but rather by my mother and my uncles. As her grandchild I watched Yiayia's minimal interaction with my grandfather; I watched her silent protests against his disrespect, but I never heard her say anything negative about him, or their marriage, in front of me. In asking Yiayia to tell me her life story I was asking her to talk in the most complete way she could imagine, which would have meant talking to her grandchild in a manner she had never done before. By asking for this information I was aware that I was changing my relationship to her, but I was naïve not to consider that it was also changing her relationship to me. I imagine Yiayia probably did not feel the trials of her marriage appropriate subject-matter to be related to her grandchild and, furthermore, knowing Yiayia's personality, a painful past was very likely something that she would not have chosen to discuss with anyone.

Embarking on this work, I expected a voyage that would enable me to explore the bearing my Yiayia's past and present life has had on my past and present life. However, along with all the preconceived ideas that I had, the project itself seemed to appropriately acquire a life of its own. Silence became the inaudible, intangible, and uneasily communicated focus. While thinking that this work was probably going to be a more traditional generational study in which I would attempt to document an elder of my community, I was forced into the discovery that this form only seemed to add to the voyeurism that I was already feeling as a result of my grandmother's reticence towards the whole process. In addition to this, I also began to feel the inappropriateness of the more linear perspective of traditional ethnographic work; that is, the power of the interviewer over the interviewee. Instead, being able to write this as a work that deals with my feelings, as well as my grandmother's, has allowed a more circular and reciprocal process to be revealed. By placing myself in the picture I feel that I have reduced the feeling of voyeurism and am, consequently, less troubled with my relationship to the work. The edge between 'researcher' and 'informant' has been rounded, which makes me feel I am achieving a presentation that would not only have been more acceptable to my grandmother but which is also more acceptable to me.

Thus, it is not through objectivity that this oral history finds its value, but through a relationship in which both 'interviewer' and 'interviewee' are involved together both as family and as participants in an academic project. As researcher my goal has been to document the life of a woman to whom I am bound by culture and a common heritage. And as family, my goal has been a testimony of the life of a woman to whom I am also bound by blood, love, and silence.

Notes

1. All my conversations with Yiayia take place in Greek with English words sprinkled in sparingly.
2. For the purpose of this article, I have cut much of the earlier testimony to concentrate on her memories of her life as an adult and, more specifically, her life in marriage.

Bibliography

Anthias, Floya, 'Women and the Nation in Cyprus', Institute of Commonwealth Studies, London, Postgraduate Seminar 'Women, Colonialism and Commonwealth'.

Blum, R. H., and Blum, E., *Health and Healing in Rural Greece* (Stanford, Calif., 1965).

Campbell, J. K., *Honor, Family and Patronage: A Study of Institutions and Moral Values in a Greek Mountain Community* (Oxford, 1974).

Dubisch, Jill *Gender and Power in Rural Greece*, Princeton, NJ, 1986.

Fernea, Elizabeth Warnock, *Women and Family in the Middle East: New Voices of Change* (Austin, Tex., 1985).

Friedl, Ernestine, *Vasilika: A Village in Modern Greece* (New York, 1962).

Gadant, Monique (ed.), *Women of the Mediterranean* (London, 1986).

Home, Gordon, *Cyprus Then and Now* (London, 1960).

hooks, bell, *Yearning: Race, Gender and Cultural Politics* (Boston, 1990).

Meyerhoff, Barbara G., *Number Our Days* (New York, 1979).

Okin, Susan Moller, *Justice, Gender, and the Family* (Princeton, NJ, 1989).

Personal Narratives Group, *Interpreting Women's Lives: Feminist Theory and Personal Narratives* (Bloomington, Ind., 1989).

Psycho-Sociological Research Group, *The Cypriot Woman* (Nicosia, 1982).

12

Kichuk Paris

A Bulgarian Family Story

VALENTINA STOEV

We seem to be carrying with us a load of knowledge and ideas, a
capital of images, observations, and so on, which are not of our
making. It is as if, having come to this world, someone has given
us a bag full of our fathers' and forefathers' investments, and we
just have to put our hands inside it.

(Peyo Yavorov, in Mihail Arnaoudov, *Individual-psychological
Interviews with Yavorov*, 1911).

I was brought up as a well-behaved child of Communist Bulgaria. But
from childhood, I always knew from within my own family that there
were other ways of understanding life. When I was a small girl, my
grandmother first took me to church, and showed me how to make the
sign of the cross. Secretly: because my father was director of the public
radio and television station in Plovdiv.

For five hundred years under Turkish rule, Plovdiv, my home town,
the ancient Thracian Puldin and later Philoppolis, was the commercial
and administrative capital of Bulgaria. Kichuk Paris—little Paris—is
one of Plovdiv's poorest working-class neighbourhoods. As a child I
often got lost in 'the Ear', the part of Kichuk where the streets
resembled the folds of a human ear. It was easy to get lost in this
labyrinth of tumbledown, ramshackle houses. Heavy pots of bright-red
geraniums miraculously balanced on the window-ledges. Every yard
had a vine-covered trellis under which the men gathered over a glass of
brandy in the evenings.

My father's kin lived in Kichuk Paris. In fact our family originally
came from the heart of the Rhodopes, the mountains to the south, on
the border with Greece. But in the wake of the First World War they
had moved to Plovdiv. We lived there in a corner house together with
my grandma and the family of my aunt—my father's sister. We grew

hollyhocks and raspberries in the garden, and an almond and morello cherry trees in the front yard.

In the next street my great-grandmother lived with her two sons and their families. When my great-grandmother Elena died in 1974 she did not know her age; but in the family we believed she was 108, the oldest woman in Plovdiv. She had witnessed the end of Turkish domination in 1878, both world wars, and the beginning of Communism: all the turning-points in the making of contemporary Bulgaria.

She had a special liking for small flat loaves. She consumed them with her usual breakfast of wine-sops, her lunch of milk-sops with a drop of brandy, and her supper of wine-sops again. By mere chance, my mother's name was also Elena, and both women liked each other very much. Every day my mother bought a small flat loaf and dropped in at great grandma's. She also bought her a bottle of brandy every month. Till her last day Grandma Elena had a clear and quick mind. She hated medicines and mistrusted doctors. She drank a little wine and brandy, but for her health only. She hated regular drinkers. Her husband, Grandpa Lambri, who died before I was born, had been a heavy drinker. When I was a child, Great-Grandma Elena insisted that I should take a spoonful of dry red homemade wine before lunch. In winter I always did so.

Elena's daughter was my Grandma Gina. When my younger sister, also Gina, was born in 1964, my mother set about 'salting' her. Many people believe that if babies are salted within ten days of their birth, they will never sweat when grown-up. After being salted, the baby should be wrapped in diapers for a while and then rinsed with walnut-leaf water. My Grandma Gina opposed my sister's being salted. She had the right to do so as the baby was named after her. She thought that the salt could kill a baby. Mother insisted that I had been salted too and there was nothing wrong with me so far. In the heat of the quarrel, Great-Grandma Elena came into the room bearing a gift for the baby. She was almost 100, but she immediately grasped the situation. Silencing Grandma Gina with a wave, she pointed her walking-stick encouragingly at Mum, thus settling the dispute in her favour. Mother immediately started the procedure. She put on too much salt, and my baby sister got red, but uttered not a sound: she blissfully smiled as mother put her into the water. Unable to stand the sight any longer, Grandma Gina left the room slamming the door behind her.

On Saturday afternoons, like many children in the neighbourbood, I remained locked in at home. Our parents worked till midday, and after work the men hurried to the nearest pub to get drunk. Across the street was the house of Lyubo Koshtito. It was a two-storey house, the biggest in the neighbourhood, dubbed 'the Castle of Sighs'. Its sitting-room boasted a big crystal mirror with a hoof—for luck. When he came home on Saturday as drunk as a fish, Lyubo Koshtito took a coal-burning stove and a big hammer out into his yard. He also took out the dinner plates and glasses and began smashing them with the hammer. On the next day there were pieces of china and glass all over his yard.

Like the other grandmothers, Grandma Gina did not want us children to witness such drunken stupidities. That was why we were kept locked in. Yet we were smart enough to watch everything from behind the curtains. Grandma went mad when she caught us red-handed. Another day, when he had no more dishes or glasses to smash, Lyubo took out a big aluminium wash-basin. He put it on the stove and began hitting it. The stove broke but the basin remained intact. He got very angry and threw it away without looking where. The basin flew across the street and landed in Bozhana's yard. I could not see it land, but that evening my cousins told me every detail of the story. But we children discussed the Saturday outrages under our breath. It was an unwritten rule never to comment in public on what happened in the neighbourhood. By contrast, Sundays were dull. Men suffered from their hangovers and women noiselessly tidied up their houses. And on Monday life returned to normal.

I would often sit on the couch next to my Grandma Gina, and soon she would tell me different stories from her life. I was so enchanted that I did not notice the hours fly by. Usually Grandma began with the story about Grandpa Vlas. She believed that God created people in pairs. That was why, she insisted, happiness was so hard to find: most of the people could not find their mates.

Grandma Gina believed she had been unusually lucky. Brought up in the mountains, as a girl, she liked riding. She was long-haired, and a bold rider on her white horse: she could ride standing. One day a travelling salesman from Plovidiv was passing through the village and saw her on the horse. It was Grandpa Vlas.

He could not take his eyes off her. He was on his way back to Plovdiv with two friends, but he refused to go on with them. He said he could not budge without this girl. His friends saw that he was desperate and decided to help him. They asked around and found where the girl lived. Then, they made a plan with Grandpa Vlas. As night fell, they kidnapped Gina together. They threw her on a horse and made off for Plovdiv. The girl fought all the way: she kicked and pushed Vlas, but he did not react. He was a tough man of Rhodope ancestry too.

They reached Plovdiv at dawn, and his small, poor house in Kichuk Paris. There Vlas asked Gina to marry him. She refused to marry a perfect stranger, and said she would escape from him. He locked the door and nailed the windows. She told him that she would climb up the chimney, if need be, rather than stay with him. For hours, right into the night, they argued about his marriage proposal. But then, as they talked, little by little she became convinced that, after all, he was a nice and kind man. 'He would not hurt a fly,' she used to say.

The contrast between his physical strength and his kind nature seemed to attract Grandma to him. It was 1920. At that time if a girl spent the night at a man's house she either had to marry him or be disgraced.

The next day Gina's parents Lambri and Great-Grandma Elena arrived in Kichuk Paris. They were furious with Vlas. Who was this man who had dared to carry their daughter away? They both urged Gina to come back with them. They preferred her to be disgraced than to marry a man whom nobody knew. Vlas invited them into his house, but they refused to come in. Then Gina appeared at the window and told them to go. She had already made her choice. She never regretted it. Grandpa Vlas was the kindest man she had ever met. 'He never touched spirits.' She warned me: 'Keep your eyes open when you choose your husband! And if he drinks, run away from him!'

Great-Grandma Elena and her husband Lambri moved from the Rhodopes to Kichuk Paris after Gina married Vlas. Elena had a big icon of the Virgin Mary over her bed. It was one metre high and half a metre wide—the biggest icon in the neighbourhood. Its lamp was always burning. Once a year Mother would buy a bottle of burning gas for the icon lamp. Mother was not a believer; she did this out of love. When I was born in 1954, my two grandmas Elena and Gina secretly arranged for me to be baptized. Only afterwards did they announce to my parents that, like all Christians, their daughter too had been baptized in church.

Elena believed that her miraculous icon had saved her life more than once. A rope hung in front of it, holding a discoloured curtain. This curtain was almost never used, although it was meant to hide the icon from the eyes of intruders who might report its existence to the Communist authorities. Elena was not afraid of the official authorities. She was neither a Communist Party member who could be expelled from the party, nor a worker anywhere who could be sacked. The worst thing that could happen to her was to have her icon taken away, but nothing of the kind had ever happened in our neighbourhood. There was an icon in every house and the authorities were well aware of it. The problem was that Elena lived with her grandchildren and great-grandchildren. Anyone who attended church services was expelled from the Young Communist League (Komsomol) or fired from work. Like all high-school students in Communist Bulgaria, I joined the Komsomol at the age of 14. Expulsion from the Komsomol meant expulsion from school, and no chance of any higher education.

The whole neighbourhood knew of our icon. It was one of our common secrets. Nobody would betray Great-Grandma Elena, just as nobody would tell an outsider about Lyubo Koshtito and his wash-basin, or about the red Easter Eggs which our mothers made, even though at school we were taught that Easter and Easter eggs were a nonsense. Anyone who could not keep his or her mouth shut about what happened in the neighbourhood would be ostracized.

Elena hated both Turks and Communists. Under Turkish rule Christian churches had to be built deep in the ground, as they were prohibited from exceeding the mosques in height. The Communists, for their part, simply banned religion altogether.

One of our family stories was that of Great-Grandma Elena's false death in 1930. It was in the midsummer, and Elena was drawing water from the well in her yard. She dropped the bucket into the well and lost consciousness. A passer-by saw her, took out the bucket, and poured water over her. She did not budge. The whole neighbourhood was in turmoil. Elena lay on the ground motionless and pale. Everybody thought she had died of sunstroke. Usually the dead were left unburied for twenty-four hours, while the funeral was prepared. Elena had not been unwell and nothing had been prepared for her death, but by the next day everything was ready. But just as the coffin arrived and she was about to be put inside it, her son Todor noticed her momentarily stir. Nobody else saw the movement. Todor stopped the ceremony. Everybody felt sorry for him, believing that he had gone crazy from grief. Ordering them to wait and not move his mother, Todor went out of the house and after some time returned with a doctor. Great-Grandma Elena still lay unconscious under the old icon. The doctor put a small mirror in front of her lips, and the mirror went misty.

That is how I learned that a mirror can tell if a person is dead or not. In this way, thanks to the icon, the mirror, and my grandpa Todor, Elena lived another forty-four years. She did not like to speak about this experience. Time and again I asked her to describe death to me. I wanted to know if God really existed, and if there was life after death. She was maddened by my questions, which obviously showed the influence of my teachers and my atheistic education. Elena claimed that there was an after life, and that she had seen God while she was dead. That was all she would ever say.

When I asked these questions, Elena waved her stick at me: 'Those who have crammed this nonsense down your throat will go to hell.' By 'those' she meant Communists, but she could never use this word. Her grandson, my father's brother Dinko, was a guerrilla fighter. He fled to the Rhodope mountains in 1943, at the age of 17. Elena never identified Dinko with the Communists.

As children, my cousins and I sometimes were taken by Grandma Gina for a day at the Bachkovo monastery in the same mountains. She used to show us the frescos painted there by Zahari Zograph, and tell us that had Zahari Zograph known about Communists, he would surely have painted them together with the adulteresses and rich women on the path to hell. 'They'll turn in their graves one day.'

Grandma Gina hated the Communists for two reasons: my grandpa's early death, and religion.

In late August 1943 Dinko, my father's brother, left for the mountains to become a guerrilla fighter in the Anton Ivanov detachment. It numbered 180, and Dinko joined the 'subversion band' of some thirty young men who knew the Rhodope mountains well. Their task was to provide cover for the detachment which was to spend the winter dug in till the spring of 1944, when full battle was to be resumed. The subversion band took the biggest risks of all, luring the enemy into fights. Nevertheless, late in January 1944 the police discovered the detachment: 150 guerrillas against 15,000 police and army troops. Only thirty guerrillas survived. The subversion band which operated in the Rhodopes was luckier: it lost only six men. My uncle used to say that in this life luck was quite important.

After joining the guerrillas, Dinko was sentenced to death in his absence. In the autumn of 1943 his parents Gina and Vlas and his 9-year-old sister were arrested by the police. My father managed to escape to Krichim. Gina, Vlas, and my aunt spent about twenty days at the police station in Kichuk Paris. In all probability they would have been shot without a trial or a sentence had it not been for Gina's brother Todor once again. He bribed a police-officer with money and soap. Todor had a soap factory and soap was scarce at the time.

They were moved to the State Security prison, where they spent another forty terrible days of beatings and torture. Grandma Gina never wanted to talk about it. Vlas and Gina were then sent to Zlatograd, and their young daughter had to go home. She made for Kichuk Paris all alone and barefoot in the severe winter cold. She had nowhere else to go but to old Elena. She threw herself into her arms and lost consciousness. After the hunger, beatings, and torture she fell ill, and ever since has suffered heart problems.

Vlas and Gina spent six months in Zlatograd, deprived of any visits and letters. They heard rumours that the Anton Ivanov detachment had been defeated and all the guerrillas killed. Gina all but lost her mind thinking of her children's fate. Only after the Communist victory on 9 September 1944 was she released to find her three children alive and well. But, in the mean time Vlas had caught tuberculosis. He died on 31 October 1944. Gina remained a widow for forty-two years.

She believed that had her son not joined the guerrillas, her later life might have been altogether different.

Soon after the Communist victory Uncle Dinko lost his illusions. He said that power had been seized by criminals who were launching a campaign against the real Communists. Some of Dinko's closest friends and fellow-partisans were interned on changes of 'anti-party activities'. If a person declared himself against the authorities and revealed their crimes, he was stigmatized as an enemy of the people. After 9 September 1944, the new rulers founded a special Sixth Department, which according to my uncle was aimed at fighting those who believed in Communism. 'When I went to the mountains, I had no idea that such things could happen.'

Because he was honest, Dinko continued to fight against the ruling mafia's crimes. Eventually he was expelled from the Communist Party in 1969 and lost his job. In 1978 the threat of internment loomed large over him. His was a life of continual threats. A high-ranking friend of his finally managed to save him from being interned.

At home, conversations with Uncle Dinko were mostly about 'those criminals' who had come to power. Mother would close the windows and pull the curtains down. She was scared stiff lest someone would overhear us. She often warned me not to tell anyone of our talks at home. She and Dad were certain that they were being followed, that their letters were read, and that the telephone was bugged. Thanks to the widespread network of informers, the entire Bulgarian people suffered from paranoia. Nevertheless, Uncle Dinko was restored to Communist Party membership in 1980.

My father, aunt, and uncle had all believed that as Communists they were building a better society. My father also gave his working life as a journalist and television director to this cause. They could never understand how the realities of Communist rule could differ so much from their ideals. Their generation will always carry this ideal in their hearts. This is the tragedy of their lives. They remain certain that the dictators created the conditions for the betrayal of Communism, and not the Communists themselves.

Gina had none of these doubts. She hated both Communists and the rulers of the so-called Communist regime. 'Politics is a dirty job. If you have a profession, don't mess with politics. It is for those who are good for nothing.'

The battle of ideas between them framed my childhood. I learnt as much, perhaps more, for my future from my grandmothers as from my parents.

As everywhere in Bulgaria, in Kichuk Paris hundreds of small private pubs have mushroomed since the 1989 changes. One hot July afternoon last summer I was walking around my old neighbourhood, and once again I got lost in the Ear: and this time I got scared. I was dying for a drink, and I opened the door of a pub, but did not dare go in. It was full of men only! They stared at me. I asked them if the pub was for men only, but they just went on staring. So I said, 'I would rather die than bring dishonour on my name by entering a pub meant only for men. For I am the grandaughter of Gina, the daughter of Elena who died at the age of 108.' Then the men all stood up, and began treating me to drinks and a song from the guitarist. I recognized my old neighbour Lyubo Koshtito. New to me was Skamnyara: an actor, singer, and shoemaker at the same time. He kept drinking brandy, repeating all the time: 'you have forgotten Kichuk Paris, haven't you?'

Grandma Gina died in 1986. Even now, six years after her death, I can still feel her beauty. She wanted two things: to be buried in Grandpa Vlas's grave and to have a church funeral service performed. 'If anyone is too afraid to enter a church, they had better not come to the funeral,' she said. The funeral service was held in the church where she had taken me for the first time as a child.

My sister and many of my cousins are scattered round the world from Canada to Australia. But I know that their children, like mine, will be told many of these same family stories. They too can feel, deep inside them, the wind blowing from the mountains.

REVIEW ARTICLES

Family Memory:

A Review of French Works on the Subject

Anne Muxel

The subject of family memory[1] is one that evokes a wealth of images
and sentiments that are intrinsically familiar to everyone. In the field of
sociology of the family any study that focuses on the phenomenon of
intergenerational transmission and, in a broader sense, any biographical analyses of family histories, or works that piece together and
interpret individual and collective life stories, will eventually touch
upon the question of memory. An omnipresent subject whose
illustrative qualities are made use of without measure, family memory,
from a sociological point of view, remains nevertheless difficult to
analyse and interpret. Memories, because of their almost indiscernible
boundaries and countless possible interpretations, pose particularly
complex questions for sociologists. Should we interest ourselves in
analysing the mechanisms that create memories for an individual or in
those that create collective memories for a familial group? Since they
cannot be disassociated, how are these two kinds of mechanisms
reconciled to engender a memory that can only be the result of a
compromise between personal and collective norms and whose very
formation implies a re-evaluation of the past in the eyes of the present?
Memory is always expressed in these two interactions. Therefore any
sociologial study of family memory must necessarily begin with a
comprehensive reading of the forces that give rise to these interactions.

A review of French works on this subject would allow us to delineate
the boundaries of a research topic which, despite appearances, is little
developed in France. Despite appearances, because even though
numerous studies and investigations exist in which family memories
are used illustratively or anecdotally, or even instrumentally, as a
storehouse of information about the past, these resulting interpretations

often resemble the contents of the memories themselves: a fragmented material composed of recollections that are themselves difficult to interpret and interrelate.

We must also note that memory is a multifaceted concept that is often interchanged with other similar concepts: history, transmission, heritage, tradition, identity—to cite only the most obvious. There are, in fact, very few works that are explicitly centred on family memory as such. Even when family memories are at the heart of other subjects of investigation they themselves only rarely become the object of a constructed theoretical or problematic approach.

Maurice Halbwachs, a French sociologist and student of Émile Durkheim, was the first sociologist to propose a framework for the interpretation of memory. His work, *Les cadres sociaux de la mémoire*, published in 1925,[2] and a few years later his book, *La mémoire collective*[3], changed the focus of the debate that was then raging between spiritual and materialist philosophers for whom memories were first and foremost the product of an individual's experience and personality. Going against the philosopher Henri Bergson's dominant theory of the time,[4] Halbwachs introduced an entirely new way of looking at memories. Rather than being shaped by the life of the individual, memories are shaped by society. An individual's memories are produced in a series of social and collective interrelations, without which the memories would neither exist nor be expressed.

How then should one view the collective memories of a familial group? How does each individual in his or her own manner recall a common past? In his studies Maurice Halbwachs furnished numerous guidelines for a comprehensive and analytic interpretation of the mechanisms of this collective memory. We will list here three of the most important.

First, each individual memory is a perspective within the collective memory of the familial group. It moves with the individual's changing position in the life cycle, as well as in the wider society.

Secondly, as a consequence, the collective memory of the family is not at all homogeneous. It is the result of a series of compromises and re-evaluations constantly affected by circumstances that exist within the group. It is a process of piecing together the past from the present.

Thirdly, memory manifests itself in two forms: one that Maurice Halbwachs places within the framework of an individual's personality or personal life, and the other, more impersonal, concerning recollections having to do primarily with the group. In sociological studies memories of the first kind, except for their illustrative function, are often ignored, but more often find a place only in the fields of literature and psychoanalysis, which are concerned with emotions and images through which memories find expression. Sociologists work mostly with family memory of the second kind: the collective memory of a group. This type of memory is considered to be the expression of a common family identity, transmitted from one generation to the next, acting as an anchoring-point for traditions and the maintenance of family characteristics.

An exhaustive list of studies that have touched upon memory either centrally or tangentially would of course be impossible in this article. We will, however, present a smaller list of studies that can be taken as an overview of recent French investigations of this subject.[5]

For a recent and analytic interpretation of Halbwachs's theories of memory, one can first refer to Gérard Namer's book *Mémoire et société*.[6] Although theoretical works on this question are in general absent from modern-day sociological studies, we do find traces in recent works on philosophy (Paul Ricœur), history (Pierre Nora), and even psychoanalysis (Serge Tisseron).[7] Given sociology's infatuation with the study of biographical and autobiographical materials in which the question of memory is obvious, this situation seems paradoxical. Recent works in French sociology have been characterized by an enormous interest in all facets of private life and most notably the family. This would lead one to believe that a subject like family memory would have a wealth of theoretical research devoted all to itself.

On the other hand, a significant number of works have touched upon family memory as a side issue by approaching subjects in which memory is intrinsic. Studies of the phenomenon of intergenerational transmission, especially of social status, material property, and symbolic property, deal with memory as an instrument of socialization. Family memory is first and foremost a factor of social and cultural identity. Functioning as a living link between generations, to use the words of Maurice Halbwachs, it is with and through memories that the identity of a social subject pieces itself together. As Françoise Zonabend writes: 'This perpetually recreated family experience introduces man to his social role.'[8]

In recent years this function of memory has been particularly noted in works trying to specify the differences between certain social groups. No single study with a comparative focus exists in France that compares the ways in which members of different social classes express and use family memories. Several case studies and investigations, however, have been published that focus on the treatment of family memory by one particular social group.

Family memory occupies a central place in the lives of the aristocracy and the high bourgeoisie. Éric Mension-Rigau, in his study of aristocratic families,[9] illustrates the numerous material manifestations of memory: the château, affirming the family's historical link to their property and region, the heirlooms within (furnishing, art, etc), and, in the titled families, the coat of arms and the family's genealogy, as well as the numerous written historical accounts. Driven by the same imperative for continuity, the intergenerational memory of families in upper bourgeoisie is generally extensive and very precise; each generation is charged with keeping the memories and passing them on. Beatrix Le Wita, in her study, identifies certain mediators that help fulfil this responsibility.[10] First of all there is the family's genealogy, if not accompanied by a portrait gallery as in aristocratic homes then at least by a family photo album. Each family also tends to have a member who becomes particularly responsible for the updating and the passing on of the family history. Lastly, as a more diffuse but certainly effective method, family members are instilled with the distinctive characteristics that have distinguished their family from generation to generation such as a good education or simply good taste.

Among the middle classes, family memory is much more sparse and much less affirmed by such mediating objects. Above all, their memories centre on the story of their daily experiences. As Beatrix Le Wita observes: 'Lower managers, white-collar employees, and workers all tell their family history not as a search for personal social identification through genealogy, but as a simple history, even common history.'[11] In his meticulous recounting of the life of Suzanne Mazé, Maurizio Catani compiled and interpreted what is probably a life's worth of memories.[12] They confirm such observations on family memory.

In a peasant's family, by contrast, genealogical memories are very important and generally linked to the possession of their land. It is often the elderly, the grandmothers and grandfathers, who pass along the knowledge and anecdotes that are associated with their property. Françoise Zonabend shows in her study how these memories serve a double function: they legitimize the family's sense of belonging in the village by specifying family relations, and at the same time in each branch of the family they reinforce its role and uniqueness. These memories are in fact not impartial. One often observes discrepancies in the recollection and importance given to these memories between the two branches (the mother's side and the father's side) of the family. As she remarks: 'The memory of each branch of the family tree is proportional to the value accorded to it.'[13]

The diversity in the types of family memory, which is linked to the scope of genealogical knowledge and the narrative method used to recount them, is thus a product of the cultural identity and socioeconomic status of the family groups studied.[14]

Family memory is also expressed differently according to sexual identity. These differences have become the subject of another field of research. In the life stories collected by Isabelle Bertaux-Wiame, work is an ever-present reference for men while for women family life is given priority.[15] This differentiation has a social and not a biological basis. Anne-Marie Devreux also shows how gender-specific memory is not just a product of the cleavage between masculine and feminine identity but also of the role played by the subject's fathers and mothers in their lives.[16] Lastly, François de Singly and Gilda Charrier, in their investigation of a couple's individual memories, show that women hold the larger share of the conjugal memories, which may imply a stronger emotional attachment to their partner in women than in men.[17]

It would be impossible to conclude this all too brief review of French research without briefly mentioning memory's obvious complement: forgetting. The interpretation of gaps in one's memory is at the very foundation of psychoanalytic work. Even so, recent works have also illustrated the interest that this type of study presents for the social sciences: they permit the updating of certain mechanisms used to plot social trajectories and certain kinds of material and/or symbolic transmissions within the family. All those who have collected family histories using stories that span several generations and branches of the family are aware of the variations among the testimonials of the different members: the presence or the absence of certain elements in the story, or their exaggeration or obscuring. The intricate web of what is said and not said reveals the different appropriations of the family group's collective memory by each member according to individual experiences. We must note the work of Philippe Lejeune who analysed, in his own family history and great-grandfather's autobiography, the distortion and obscuring of certain family memories, finding that occasionally family secrets had been repressed from generation to generation.[18]

While certain gaps in the family histories can be linked to internal secrets and taboo subjects, others owe their existence to events in history whose influence reaches beyond the individual to touch an entire generation. Nicole Lapierre's attempt to uncover the story of survivors of the Jewish ghettos in Plock (Poland) revealed the enormous difficulties that people faced in trying to explain to their children what had happened. For the next generation, this painful past was buried in silence, making any attempt at passing the story on as difficult as trying to understand the events themselves.[19]

The very diversity of French research which relates to the subject of family memory would make a fully exhaustive review impossible. I have here therefore concentrated on describing the approaches which are being most explored in France today, and which will be needed to carry our understanding further.

Notes

1. For this article 'family memory' is used to represent an individual's memories of his family. 'Collective memory' is used to represent each individual's memories of a group activity.
2. Maurice Halbwachs, *Les cadres sociaux de la mémoire* (Paris, 1925).
3. Maurice Halbwachs, *La mémoire collective* (Paris, 1950).
4. Henri Bergson, *Matière et mémoire* (Paris, 1896). One can also refer to the little book *Mémoire et vie, Textes choisis* (Paris, 1976).
5. For a more extended treatment see Anne Muxel, 'La mémoire familiale', in François de Singly (ed.), *La famille. L'état des savoirs* (Paris, 1991).
6. Gérard Namer, *Mémoire et société* (Paris, 1990).
7. Paul Ricœur, *Temps et récit*, (Paris, 1983); Pierre Nora, *Les lieux de mémoire* (Paris, 1984), 1986; Serge Tisseron, *Tintin et les secrets de famille* (Paris, 1990).
8. Françoise Zonabend, *La mémoire longue. Temps et histoire au village* (Paris, 1980).
9. Éric Mension-Rigau, *L'enfance au château* (Paris, 1990).
10. Beatrix Le Wita, *Ni vue ni connue: Approche ethnographique de la culture bourgeoise* (Paris, 1988).
11. Beatrix Le Wita, 'La mémoire familiale des parisiens appartenant aux classes moyennes,' *Ethnologie française*, 16 (1984), 57–66.
12. Maurizio Catani and Suzanne Mazé, *Tante Suzanne: Une histoire de vie sociale* (Paris, 1982).
13. Zonabend, *Mémoire longue*.
14. Anne Muxel, 'Chronique familiale de deux héritages politiques et religieux,' *Cahiers Internationaux de sociologie* 71 (1986), 255–280; Anne Muxel and Annick Percheron, 'Histoires politiques de famille: Premières illustrations,' *Life Stories/Récits de vie*, 4 (1988), 59–72.
15. Isabelle Bertaux-Wiame, 'Mémoire et récits de vie, *Pénélope*, 12 (1985), 62–9.
16. Anne-Marie Devreux, 'La mémoire n'a pas de sexe', *Pénélope*, 12 (1985), 55–62.

17. François de Singly and Gilda Charrier, 'Vie commune et pensée célibataire', *Dialogue*, 102 (1988), 44–54.
18. Xavier-Édouard Lejeune, *Calicot* (Paris, 1984).
19. Nicole Lapierre, *Le silence de la mémoire* (Paris, 1989).

Transmitting History and Making It

Elizabeth Tonkin

Paul Connerton, *How Societies Remember* (Cambridge: Cambridge University Press, 1989).
Robert Borofsky, *Making History; Pukapukan and Anthropological Constructions of Knowledge* (Cambridge: Cambridge University Press, 1987).

My mother was the eldest of five and sixteen years older than her youngest brother, who is fifteen years older than I am. This is a very 'mild' discrepancy between generation and relative age, yet in a short time span the effects of even a small discrepancy soon widen: I am of a different social generation from my youngest first cousin, although—as the kinship term 'first cousin' proclaims—he is of the same genealogical generation.

Anthropologists have noted that, in different societies, kinship terms classify relationships according to different principles, but generation and sex are regular bases of category distinction. Sometimes, they serve to enforce rules of distinction that are not otherwise visible— such as when people of the same age are of different generations. In talking of transmission of information between generations, then, we cannot take for granted that the social and the genealogical generation coincide. Connerton follows Marc Bloch and others in stating that 'in ancient rural societies ... the education of the youngest living generation was generally undertaken by the oldest living generation'. Here, relative age rather than generation seems to be the point and, although he refers to a widespread literature in which the grandmother is stereotyped as teacher, there must always have been periods in the life cycle of any domestic group in which grandmother is not an old lady.

Learning is a complex business, too; and there are a great variety of communities, which seem alike only in their having small-scale and relatively informal 'occasions' of different kinds, where it is clear that children are omnipresent, looking, listening, and cumulatively picking up what is going on. That means they can pick up representations of past history as well as contemporary understanding in public, and not only in the small families (not necessarily private domestic units) long characteristic in western Europe. The image of the wise granny (or grandpa) may be accurate for some kinds of informal 'intergenerational' transmission, but it is obviously not the only one.

Unfortunately anthropologists have as yet hardly extended their very considerable understanding of how differently forms of social organization are constituted to the study of what effects these differences may have on transmission. Borofsky is an anthropologist who has given us some very enlightening, and perhaps surprising, information. Pukapuka is a small Polynesian atoll (population 785 in 1976) which has been unusually comprehensively described by a number of outsiders and insiders, from anthropologists to administrators. The Borofskys arrived in the midst of a cultural revival, only to find that although islanders insisted they were reviving an older form of social organization, it was a form that none of these commentators had mentioned.

To solve this puzzle, Borofsky looked very carefully at how knowledge was transmitted. Learning by watching others is common, with practice more important than precept. 'People are doing you a favour by answering your questions.' This is partly because Pukapukans are egalitarian but also (as Polynesians have often been described) very status-conscious. Any comment is evaluated in this light, so that a public account is also a means of sparring and competition. What appears to be friendly discussion challenges all participants and individuals may avoid criticism by avoiding an opinion, or by altering their own version to agree with a more accepted authority. If asked directly—for instance by a visiting anthropologist—they also have to demonstrate that they are knowledgeable too.

The sequence of skilled observations of Pukapuka makes it clear that what look like fundamental features (such as inheritance) have changed rapidly and frequently. The patterns of status claim mean that adults 'do not always find out exactly what they want to know. They have to infer for themselves the meaning of someone's comment or where its significance lies. The fact that Pukapukan status rivalries pervade public discussions means that no real group consensus may develop on matters of tradition.' It is in such circumstances (carefully set out by Borofsky) that what would appear to be an obvious piece of intergenerational transmission starts to waver, without any implications of bad faith by his informants.

Borofsky's book is relevant to all students of oral history, since it shows how significant social conditions are for the ways that knowledge is gained, and how these conditions can be more labile and flexible than informants report and generalizing analysts record. It is tempting to assume that where numbers are small and everyone knows everybody else, every adult's knowledge will be the same. Borofsky shows how and why people differed all the time, particularly in their accounts of the past. By contrast, Connerton, arguing about the nature of social memory, assumes that there will be mutual gossip in a village setting and that this will ensure that 'a village informally constructs a continuous communal history of itself'.

While both the authors under discussion are interested in how knowledge is transmitted, intergenerational transmission is not the focus of either, so I must not review Connerton, in particular, from a perspective he did not intend. However, the comments I have cited here are symptomatic of an approach which I found ultimately unsatisfying. I found his initial answers to the question 'how is the memory of groups conveyed and sustained?' extremely sensible, clear, and usefully referenced. His subsequent elaborations, which select commemorative rituals, and then the significance of bodily practice in social (re)constitution, are likewise unexceptionable. But how significant are these formal rituals in contemporary British society, for instance? Does TV mediate participation in new ways, while bodily practices (on which Connerton actually says very little) transmit society informally? Unfortunately, there is no analysis which lets us apply and question Connerton's points in such ways.

The German Working Class and National Socialism: Two Reviews

Lutz Niethammer (ed.), *'Die Jahre weiss man nicht, wo man die heute hinsetzen soll': Faschismuserfahrungen im Ruhrgebiet* (The Years When No One Knew Where They Would Be from One Day to Another: Telling about Fascism in the Ruhr) (Berlin/Bonn: J. H. W. Dietz Verlag, 1983).

Lutz Niethammer (ed.), *'Hinterher weiss man, dass es richtig war, dass es schief gegangen ist': Nachkriegserfahrungen im Ruhrgebiet* (Afterwards We Knew that it was True, that it had Gone off the Rails: Post-War Testimony in the Ruhr District) (Berlin/Bonn: J. H. W. Dietz Verlag, 1983).

Lutz Niethammer and Alexander von Plato (eds.), *'Wir kriegen jetzt andere Zeiten': Auf der Suche nach der Erfahrung des Volkes in nachfaschistichen Ländern* (Now We'll Get to Other Times: The Search for Popular Testimony in Post-Fascist Regions) (Berlin/Bonn: J. H. W. Dietz Verlag, 1985).

It is impossible in a brief review to do justice to the first three volumes which are the outcome of the research, led by Lutz Niethammer and Alexander von Plato, on German working-class life during National Socialism and through to the first fifteen post-war years. Their original project was based on two hundred interviews carried out in the Ruhr in 1980–2 and the first two volumes are a rigorous analysis of this material. The third volume draws in other authors and widens the perspective to the whole of Germany and also to other countries which experienced fascism, like Italy and Austria.

The hypothesis with which they began is summed up in the poem they cite at the outset, written by Bertholdt Brecht:

> New times don't loom up out of the blue.
> My grandfather already lived in the new era,
> My grandson will probably live in the old one.
> New meat is cut with ancient cutlery.
> New methods spread old nonsense.
> Wisdom was passed on from mouth to mouth.

In short, one cannot understand the Federal Republic by cutting it off from the preceding age. The same nation experienced the totalitarian system as the founding of democracy. To emphasize the break between past and present, the advent of a new era, is to misunderstand the expectations of the German people at the founding of the Federal Republic. And their subjective evidence does indeed reveal the continuities in political culture. There was no 'zero hour' in the Ruhr coalfield after the war; for both Hitler and Adenauer won their support through promises of more welfare and a better standard of life.

This is research carried out on the basis of an exacting epistemological reflection as well as the highest methodological standards. The limitations of contemporary testimony are recognized: for example, the absence of any voice from the militant Communist trade unionists, because all of them were hunted down and 'eliminated'. The interviewing was based on open questions in order to encourage their informants to structure their own accounts and choose the themes themselves.

Most accounts of the German working class under National Socialism have taken one of two dichotomous perspectives. One is that the fascists succeeded in rallying the working class through mass psychology. The other is that the working class as a whole can be represented through the heroic but limited resistance of its leaders. Neither view leaves much space for the practical, ambivalent experiences of everyday life under fascism. The Ruhr project dispels such Manicheistic simplicities.

The analysis of the life stories helps us to understand the adaptations and compromises through which workers had to survive. These are vividly illustrated in a recollection of a conversation between one informant's grandfather and mother as the French were crossing the Rhine. The grandfather told her to destroy their Nazi insignia: 'If anyone asks, we are, and always have been, Social Democrats.' When the mother protested that this was a 'disgusting' thing to do, he simply answered: 'But times have changed, and we have to adapt to them.'

It was for just this reason that many Germans decided at the end of the war that they must keep their distance from politics. And this decision also shapes their memories. They may condemn the war and the Nazi regime as a crazy venture, but they do not connect this with the politics of their own life experience. Those who fought in the war describe it in terms of a personal story of fighting and often of adventure, without placing it within the political context of mass mobilization. Those who were already in middle life under National

Socialism also often describe how they tried to keep their distance from the Nazis. Certainly they made no determined stand against the more subtle mechanisms through which German society was being remoulded, although the theory that this reflected the acceptance of fascism for its material benefits by a silent majority in the working class rests on a weak basis, for the active opponents of racism simply have not survived to add their witness.

In the same spirit, the 'good' and 'bad' years which present informants remember reflect the phases of economic boom and unemployment. They denounce the demagoguery, the terror, and the oppression imposed by the Nazis; but they also applaud some of their social measures and attitudes. They assert that 'workers enjoyed esteem in these days'. Those who were young under the Nazis remain approving of the new leisure activities they encouraged, which often enabled young men and especially young women to get away from the authoritarian control of their families. For them especially, the turning-point was when the war carried on, and many of them were sent to the firing-line. They returned, personally shattered, to try to recover a place in a society for which all that they had fought for was now deemed useless.

These authors do not offer us easy answers. They do not deny that the working class resisted fascism, but they refuse to delude us into believing that a majority of Germans fought against it. Instead they have put at the centre those who committed themselves neither to the prevailing order nor to the resistance. They confront us with the ambiguities of the silent majority.

At the beginning of this research they had hoped that it would help the discovery of a democratic alternative between fascism and consumerism. They had also believed that they shared important values with the old Ruhr working class. Nor were they totally disappointed. Nevertheless, they show a special honesty in revealing how the experience of the interviews also brought home the gulf between them and their informants. It has left them 'rather confused' ever since. We can only admire such a study, which leads its protagonists to admit that such encounters may cause deep 'wounds'. They are inflicted by ruptures in our belief in a common human sense of compassion (*Mitmenschlichkeit*); ruptures also in our belief that knowledge necessarily has a civilizing (*aufklärerisch*) mission.

Freddy Raphaël

Lutz Niethammer, Alexander von Plato, and Dorothee Wierling, *Die volkseigene Erfahrung: Eine Archäologie des Lebens in der Industrieprovinz der DDR* (The Workers' Own Experience: An Archaeology of Life in the Industrial Provinces of the DDR) (Berlin, Rowohlt, 1991).

The title of this massive, 640-page, attractively printed book made me immediately curious. For West Germans, the DDR seems part of an even less well-known 'wild east'. But the life stories within it helped to change my views. They bring home to us that several generations in both East and West Germany share a common past, above all in the period of National Socialism.

The life stories presented here come from the so-called *Aufbaugeneration*, the founding generation born between 1906 and 1929. They were chosen to present 'continuities and discontinuities of individual life experiences before and after 1945' in the DDR. As a social scientist, I was also interested in the evidence which they could offer on the forming of generations and transmission between them in the DDR. In relation to similar studies of the same age group in West Germany, this evidence might help to answer some crucial questions which had been raised: in what ways did these generations, who have a great deal of German history in common, deal with their past in the context of the different political systems after 1945? What are the similarities and differences in the ways in which these historical and biographical experiences have been transmitted from generation to generation in East and West Germany?

The authors do not consider these analytical questions, nor do they present their methodological background and concrete procedure in analysing their empirical material. The reader finds only tentative hypotheses formulated in the first part of the book, which is in the form of a report about the project: during the post-war period the *Aufbaugeneration*, especially the male skilled workers, had the chance to move to higher social positions as a result of the changes in the élite in administration. As a result of the same process women had the chance to take the place of men as skilled workers in industry. The consequent high social mobility guaranteed a high social integration in society. The positive experiences, especially of this generation, were not connected to the political system or the ideological programme and were not repeatable for the following generations. So the 'old' integrated generation held positions of power, and in so doing represented values which were not an intrinsic part of the system but rather developed within the historical situation of post-war East Germany. It was not possible to transfer these values to succeeding generations, and furthermore they prevented these younger generations from finding their orientation within the existing political system. As a result a break between generations and within the culture could be predicted for the future.

Niethammer formulated this hypothesis about the 'post revolutionary *Aufsteigergesellschaft* of the GDR' in 1988, one year after doing the field research. As a political diagnosis with sociological explanation it was quite a precise prognosis. In this sense it offers another perspective (experiences of generations), which allows more differentiated insights into the DDR society than the current predominating party and political history in this field. It is not quite clear, however, if this hypothesis is the result of a systematic analysis of the life stories presented in the book.

In the presentations of the thirty stories, chosen from nearly 150 interviews with single people or with couples, we do not find a discussion of this assumption in the individual life stories. Without doubt there are interesting observations about the general structure of life stories and several attempts at explanation. For example Dorothee Wierling shows how Wolfgang Gröner achieved stability in living through such contradictory political systems as National Socialism and the system of the DDR by concentrating on his work, especially on the social context of the plant. 'The factory as a refuge' makes it possible to achieve continuity in life. In the discussion of this case it remains unclear if this orientation determined his life history—the lived-through life—or if it is a strategy in his narrated present in order to repair something in the past.

Furthermore the observation that Gröner was structuring his life in 'four time-phases' is of analytical interest. But what function does this life-organization have for the actual self-presentation and how is it connected to the experienced life in the past? Apart from a few brief comments on the remarkable structures in the stories, the interpretations are, for the main part, mere reiterations of the life stories from the interviews. From the point of view of a biographical researcher, there is a lack of systematic distinction between the two time levels in the case studies of this book: the experienced past and the reinterpretation of the past by the autobiographer in the present.

Finally there is no comparison of the individual case studies, which could lead to theoretically generalized statements deduced from the case studies. So the biographies remain 'individual', as Niethammer himself remarks. The 'general' of the past as it appears in the life stories is not systematically worked out and formulated.

The authors obviously assume the life stories and histories as particular to the individuals. The next book is planned as a comparison of stories about certain events (collective myths), apparent to all cases, with the aim of reaching more generalized conclusions. In my opinion this would ignore the opportunity to compare the case stories in their overall form (*Gesamtgestalt*), and so reach theoretical generalizations. Although the organization of the stories in three chapters with the titles 'Erbe und Tradition' (Heritage and tradition), 'Niemandszeit' (No man's time), 'Aufbau und Stillstand' (From building to standstill) allow us to sense the authors' thoughts in this direction, it is a pity that they are not made explicit.

Roswitha Breckner

BOOK REVIEWS

Lissie Aström, *I Kvinnoled: Om kvinnors liv genom tre generationer* (In the Female Line: Women's Lives through Three Generations). (Lund: Diss. Liber Förlag, 1986.)

In her dissertation *I Kvinnoled* the Lund ethnologist Lissie Aström uses life-history interviews with women from nine three-generation chains to show, in her own words, 'how women receive, use, and transmit a cultural heritage. The time is our own century, and the emphasis is on the spheres of home and family.' Culture, gender, and class are keywords.

It is assumed from the start that dominance/subordination structures the relationship between women and men as well as between working-class and middle-class women. Another important dichotomy is centripetal/centrifugal. The circular, centripetal movement strives inwards, towards care and self-sacrifice; the centrifugal force outwards, towards self-assertion and socio-economic success.

Through the life histories of mainly middle-class women, Aström shows how the restricted, family-centred, female role became an offensive, career-*and*-family lifestyle in the course of the twentieth century. The apparently contradictory, socializing values—subordinated/centripetal as women; dominant/centrifugal as class—have developed into a strength, not least through the high premium set by the middle class on intellectual knowledge and education for both girls and boys.

Among the working class, according to Aström, the centripetal forces—the caring and lack of power—were more equally distributed among women and men. Working-class experience has, in her view, been lacking in centrifugal force. Both sexes have directed their efforts inwards, towards the family, in ways which have contributed towards the preservation of traditional gender roles.

Nevertheless, by way of conclusion, Aström sees a tendency among women, irrespective of class, to develop a common female perspective, as one of the changes which has taken place during the twentieth century. It consists of 'a striving to use one's entire human potential'; a lifestyle where the centrifugal disposition, the potential for power, is not allowed to outweigh the centripetal forces, the transmission of female values.

The strengths of Lissie Aström's study are many. Her research is well documented, structured, and written. Most of her informants are middle-class women and she writes about their everyday life, its frustrations and rewards, with great insight and understanding. She is one of them, as she tells the reader, and her own life as a middle-class, educated housewife becomes part of her sources. Through the life histories and her own private insights, she throws light on the strengths and strategies of ostensibly self-effacing and subordinated lives. It is a history which needs and deserves to be written.

At the same time, Aström's personal involvement in the theme of her research is responsible for some of the weaknesses of the book. She aspires to a comparative class perspective. But it would have been more fair if she had openly declared that her comparative class perspective is very unevenly balanced, so that her statements about the lives of working-class women are made on the basis of very few interviews. Her comparative gender perspective is even more biased, as no men's life histories are included. Aström can, however, be said to have made up for the last defect through a recent book: *Fäder och söner: Bland svenska män i tre generationer* (Fathers and Sons: Among Swedish Men in Three Generations), Stockholm: Carlssons, 1990. Unfortunately for the non-Swedish reader, the English summary is less than one page.

In spite of these criticisms, Lissie Aström's study is an important contribution to the understanding of change and continuity in the lives of middle-class women during the twentieth century. Its strength lies in the accounts of the world the author knows best.

Birgitta Skarin Frykman

John Egerton, *Generations: An American Family* (Lexington: University Press of Kentucky, 1983).

Pre-literate societies are held out, and rightly so, as communities in which story-tellers hold an honoured place. Their memories become windows on the past and they the preservers of history. Without question, they accept that it is their duty to pass the history on to the succeeding generation so it will know whence it came.

As is true with all modern societies, the United States is a literate nation and as such does not feel compelled to venerate elders who are the bearers of history. From our youngest years we are taught that if we want to know the past, we can look it up in the volumes that stack the shelves of the libraries which dot our land from coast to coast. As a result, we seem not to understand or care that our unwillingness (maybe it is inability) to listen to the past denies to each of us the opportunity to know the history that is carried in the minds and hearts of the elders.

What they bear is not the formal history of a nation, but the history of the family; of friendships; of shared experiences; of daily toil. It is the remembrance of celebration; of struggle; of joy; of death; and, most of all, a remembrance of constant renewal. This history is not recorded in dusty volumes because the people who carry it seldom have an opportunity to give life to the past of their ancestry.

Although the book that is being reviewed is now ten years old, it is timeless and thus this review is still timely. It is the history of a nation seen through the eyes and carried in the minds and hearts of two ordinary individuals. John Egerton, understanding that shared memories allow us to travel through the past in a way no other form of history provides, set out to find a family who would 'be a prism through which the shape and texture and resonance of American life could be transmitted' (p. 15). He found his family in the small town of Lancaster, in Garrand County, Kentucky. When he came upon Burnam and Addie Ledford in 1978, he knew that his search was ended. For the next five years Egerton mined the history that was being preserved in the minds of 102-year-old Burnam and his 93-year-old wife of seventy-five years. Over the years his involvement with Burnam and Addie, and to a lesser degree with their rather large and far-flung family, was more than a professional relationship. It became, although Egerton does not admit it, a personal, caring, and loving relationship.

Burnam and Addie were children of the frontier who had learned from their elders the history of their heritage. Daily they preserved this common history and to it added their own personal story. Through the memories of their elders they had been transported back to a time before they were and the nation was. They came to know and honour the journey that their forebears had taken as they opened up the frontiers of colonies on the verge of becoming a nation.

With a clear mind and lack of self-importance, they take their listeners (that is what readers of this book are) on an unforgettable journey, a journey that I would not have missed. Nor should anyone else, for this is what oral history is supposed to be.

The book is not without faults. Most importantly, the author has not indicated who has been interviewed or where the interviews and related materials are archived and whether they are available to scholars and researchers. As has been said by others, it is time for authors to realize that the interviews that they generate are primary source material and should be available in the same way as manuscripts are. A less serious shortcoming is the lack of an index. There are so many names and facts interwoven within the narration that sometimes there is need or desire to go back and refamiliarize. Without an index there is no simple way to do this.

Regardless, this book is a celebration of the life of the ordinary people and for this reason it is truly people's history.

John J. Fox

Renate Siebert, *'È femmina però è bella': Tre generazioni di donne al Sud* ('It's a Girl but She's Beautiful': Three Generations of Women in the South) (Turin: Rosenberg & Sellier, 1991).

This book about 'three generations of women in the South' is original and fascinating for many reasons. The most important is its historical and biographical depth. The three generations of women cover a range of time which goes from the beginning of the century to 1985. In the passages of these lives, we are able to perceive waves of change in southern culture and lifestyles which are extremely important in approaching an understanding of the history of the Mezzogiorno and of Italy as a whole. The three generations are linked to one another in family groups, as mothers, daughters, grandmothers. The initial nucleus is composed of young university students, who are closest to the author's professional work as a professor of sociology at the University of Calabria. Starting with these young women, the author has proceeded to their mothers and grandmothers, all living in Calabria. The research thus consists of the reconstruction of fifteen female genealogies (fifteen 'threesomes') told in long life histories, and of the author's interpretation and organization by themes (the body, work, marriage) and subjects (the generation of daughters, mothers, grandmothers).

The originality conveyed by the biographical depth must be underlined for several reasons. In Italian social history and sociology there is no comparable research with a similar genealogical structure, much less so concerning southern women. The presence of the first generation is the element which most starkly illuminates the biographical depth. The older women, the grandmothers, born between 1900 and 1921, belong to the rural environment, have a background of farmwork, and are still rooted in rural contexts. The story of the hardships of a very recent way of life, and the evocation of a cruelly suppressed female sexuality, rivet the reader's attention with all the power of a nucleus of solid, unrecognizable difference which yet concerns us. The frozen, 'imploded' sexuality, as the author writes, is evoked in brief, stark passages: 'When they closed the door behind me,' says one narrator about her wedding night, 'I froze and I got up frozen and I am frozen to this day.' These stories are impressive autobiographical *tours de force*, which generate almost paralysing emotions: we gaze motionless into a near past inhabited by rules and gestures so rigid that they seem deceptively distant.

The genealogies also illuminate the formidable social mobility which has taken place in the Italian South over the last fifty years. This change has proceeded, as was to be expected, from the agricultural to the service sector, through the painful experience of the transoceanic, European, national emigration of the heads of the families. We listen to farmworker grandmothers, shopkeeper mothers (or homemakers to non-farming husbands), and student daughters. The apex of this ascending mobility is still uncertain, because occupational outlets for an educated female labour force are the least available on the labour market in the South. Yet the university is the symbol of the new generation's further advance: the descendants of illiterate grandmothers can now call themselves 'university students'. Cultural mobility is also evidenced by the language used in the life histories. The reader travels from sheer dialect to the mothers' hybrid language (with occasional grammatical lapses and backsliding to dialect), and finally to the plain, average, correct, media-shaped Italian of the students. Social mobility, language, emigration, education, and, finally, the changes in the institution of marriage: these are the coordinates of change illuminated by the research.

Once again, the older generation suggests the subtlest insights. New feelings emerge in the midst of the arranged marriages of women subjected to familial authority, tiny germs of romantic love, early signs of a way of feeling which preludes the formation of a different type of couple. One of the keenest insights concerns the parable of the power relationship between husband and wife through the life cycle. In the beginning, it is always an almost suffocating domination of the man over the woman's field of action. With the passing years, the male's tyranny decreases and the relationship is reversed: the woman survives births and children, goes through extreme existential hardship, and keeps the family together through daily life and financial problems, while the man loses his aggressiveness, weakens his tyranny, perhaps becomes an invalid, and, condemned to dependence, is no longer to be feared.

Permanences, however, are no less eloquent than changes. A particularly striking one concerns the total censorship in mother–daughter communication of all that concerns female sexuality, from menstruation to intercourse to birth control. This lack of communication generates dramatic consequences; the women speak about it with boundless anger, but they keep transmitting it to their daughters today.

Some critical remarks might be advanced on the third section of the book, dedicated to 'the women's South'. The author here discusses the South's wide imbalance between the huge private sphere and the limited, almost barren public sphere. All public institutions, from public parks to social activities, from schools to services and the electoral system, seem to be weak, erratic, ridden and dominated by patronage. The lack of an accepted public role and of a public dimension in expectations for women outside the family has hindered their civil and political emancipation. Though this is true, the author makes less persuasive claims upon it: that southern women are not as caught in the web of patronage as the men are; that they keep healthily outside the perverse mechanism of the local power system; and that this estrangement is accompanied by a potential for innovation, capable of regenerating collective action and change. The author takes it for granted that 'dissatisfaction' can 'objectively' generate protest, and lists the complaints on which sooner or later southern women are bound to act. For an author so attuned to the category of 'subjectivity' as the hinge of a woman-orientated analysis, Siebert uses with surprising frequency the term 'objectivity' or 'objectively'. Indeed, in the whole corpus of research on the 'subjectivity' of southern women, there is not much ground for believing them to be uncontaminated by the vices of the southern public system or seeing them as protagonists of a movement for radical change.

The second remark concerns the relationship to oral history. This book is the result of an encounter between sociology and oral history, and my impression is that this has resulted in both enriching and impoverishing interpretation. One is unconvinced at the overinterpretation, the textual expansion, the cultural overdetermination of each single word. On the one hand, this is precisely what Luisa Passerini praises in her introduction: 'no detail is so trivial that it does not call upon the highest theory in order to claim the meaning towards which it strives.' On the other hand, however, this approach remains unconvincing: the material collected by the research is so rich that it does not need such an exercise, at least not to this extent. Occasionally the author treats the life stories as texts, rather than problematic and multidimensional self-representations. The minute analysis of speech, the in-depth exploration of individual expression is typical of certain uses of interviews in oral history. This, however, directs attention away from fully exploring certain precious insights which the book does perceive: for instance, the author evokes the concept of emancipation and its applicability to the reality of southern women, but does not ultimately deal with its most intricate, problematic aspects.

Simonetta Picone Stella
Translator: *Sandro Portelli*

Sherna Gluck and Daphne Patai (eds.), *Women's Words: The Feminist Practice of Oral History* (London and New York: Routledge, 1991).

Women's Words is a valuable collection of essays for oral historians who have grappled with issues of interpretive authority, exploitation, and responsibility to a community of narrators. It contains several marvellous essays that should generate discussions about the ethics of fieldwork, and the practice of feminist scholarship in situations of cultural conflicts, opposing agendas, and very real power imbalances. This would be an excellent book for graduate and advanced undergraduate classes on methods.

Gluck and Patai have divided the book into four parts. In the first, 'Language and Communication', Kathryn Anderson and Dana C. Jack warn that conventions of social discourse often prevent interviewers from hearing what narrators are saying—and not saying. They urge interviewers to learn to listen to both narrators and to themselves as participants in a communicative process. In an essay redolent of the romanticism of cultural feminism, Kristina Minister argues for a 'feminist frame' for oral-history interviews based on an understanding of the workings of a 'general female sociocommunication subculture' (p. 28). Gwendolyn Etter-Lewis asserts that black women's life stories, while demonstrating a general female tendency to understate or downplay achievements, also show a culturally specific attachment to family and to the larger community or to the race.

In Part Two, 'Authority and Interpretation', Katherine Borland, Marie-Françoise Chanfrault-Duchet, and Claudia Salazar offer interesting examples of interpretive conflicts based on diverging methods of enquiry. Their essays underscore a theme that also pervades the first section, and the entire collection: the need for a close attention to the *context* of the speaker's life and to the act of story-telling itself. A subliminal thread emerges here and is amplified in Part Three: the feminist assumption of equivalence, of our-essential-commonality-as-women, is inappropriate to many kinds of cross-cultural research. The Other is always the Other, and her interests and agendas are *not* always similar to ours. Only a close attention to the narrator's definition of the situation will allow us to discern the function that the interview has for her, and how she views her own life experiences as part of history.

Part Three, 'Dilemmas and Contradictions,' contains several splendid essays. Judith Stacey's 'Can There Be a Feminist Ethnography?' questions the ways in which feminists do the 'passionate scholarship' aimed at social change. Stacey found herself confronting situations of 'inauthenticity, dissimilitude, and, . . . betrayal . . . that are inherent in fieldwork research' (p. 113). On several occasions her role as a researcher conflicted with relationships of mutuality and trust that she had developed as a 'participant' in her host community: her closeness to several narrators gave her access to family tragedies and difficulties that strengthened her research, but generated serious ethical conflicts. Similarly, Daphne Patai asks, 'Is Ethical Research Possible?' between US academics and Third World women. Patai notes the imbalance between the power and resources of US researchers who study impoverished women in other cultures. She also presents a tough-minded critique of therapeutic views of reminiscence and life-story-telling, and offers an acerbic dismissal of the 'mystifying chumminess' of the 'situated' interviewer who believes that the divulging of her class, racial, political, and/or sexual identities dissolves her obligation to confront issues of power and authority in her own research (p. 149). Sondra Hale offers a confessional account of the limitations of feminist assumptions of similarity and advocacy research in her essay on a frustrating encounter with a Sudanese leader who quite clearly possessed her *own* agenda for Hale's research.

Part Four, 'Community and Advocacy', which concludes the volume, offers interesting, if largely descriptive, perspectives on the elusive and contradictory relationships between 'empowerment', life histories, and 'community'. Rina Benmayor describes the mutually supportive agendas of an adult-education project and oral history programme in a Puerto Rican neighbourhood in New York City. Linda Shopes and Karen Olson also discuss the relations that both built and maintained with working-class women and men in areas near Baltimore, Maryland. Sherna Berger Gluck relates the travails of advocacy oral history among Palestinian women in resistance to the Israeli occupation. Laurie Mercier and Mary Murphy describe a collaborative project from hell that became mired in a 'tyranny of structurelessness' that was compounded by chronic shortages of time and money.

While these essays are somewhat uneven in intellectual range and challenge, all offer something to an oral historian, or to a practitioner of feminist, cross-cultural, or even post-structuralist research. The problems of this kind of work *are* real, and difficult.

Kim Lacy Rogers

Luisa Passerini, *Storie di donne e femministe* (Women's and Feminists' Histories) (Turin: Rosenberg & Sellier, 1991).

The book is composed of six essays on post-Second World War women's history and feminism. As in Passerini's earlier *Storia e soggettività* (1988), historical reconstruction is brilliantly interwoven with important theoretical insights. The first three chapters, which have already appeared in different form in Italian journals, include an essay on women's subjectivity in Italian oral history of the 1950s; a research project carried out with women political prisoners in Turin; and a survey of feminism in Emilia-Romagna. The other, previously unpublished chapters deal with the relationship between the student movements of the 1960s and the feminist movement; with neo-feminism; and with feminist methodology in social sciences. Beyond the thematic differences between chapters, the book reveals a consistent methodological approach, based—as Passerini's introduction explains—on the search for subjectivity both in the historical subject and in the interpreter, and in the dialectics of self-awareness and historicization.

A crucial question throughout the book, in fact, is the relationship between memory and history in women's movements. This concern emerges both in the discovery of a 'shared loss of memory' consequent upon women's withdrawal from public life after the Resistance, and in the complex interaction of personal memory and collective history in feminism. While memory has the power 'to enlighten something which history has not yet been able to thematize', in fact it may also blur into ideology and generate myths unrestrained by the checks of philology and documentation.

Passerini insists on the importance of subjectivity, on 'the inescapable value of individuality even in its constant tension and confrontation with shared identities and collective projects'. In continuity with such earlier work as *Torino operaia e fascismo*, Passerini presents women as historical subjects peculiarly endowed with the ability to mediate between public and private life, between different generations, between social environments and politics. Women's subjectivity is the centre of tension between determinism and freedom; the individual subject is more than the convergence of social factors, inasmuch as she retains the ability and the subjective initiative to project beyond the existing state of things. Subjectivity is not exempted from contradictions, between the old and the new, between a heritage of subordination and a yearning for future change; but the contradictions between behaviour and consciousness, Passerini explains, are a factor of strength in women's history: conscience may be seen as the sphere of women's freedom which existed even alongside unfree behaviour.

The book is explicitly concerned with cultural transmission ('Transmission and Freedom' is the title of the Introduction) and with pedagogic functions. The author justifies the 'unfinished' aspect of the final chapters precisely with the need to transmit a tradition and to work towards new conceptualizations of 'gender salience' and of the combination of gender with race and class, to redefine temporality and traditional chronologies and periodizations, and to integrate the history of non-political women with feminist thought. Passerini dwells at length on this last point: in order to face the ambivalent relationships with mothers and to recognize the continuity of our history with theirs, Passerini insists, it is necessary to search for 'each woman's specificity, and the recognition of the specificity of other women', which is also at stake in the delicate personal interchange taking place in interviews with women who are comrades or relevant figures in feminism.

Francisca Koch

ENDPIECE

We're All On Tape:

Voice Recording and the Electronic Afterlife

ALESSANDRO PORTELLI

I'll sing a song I composed myself. Don't tell anyone I'm a poet;
they might want me to write a book. Don't tell 'em I can sing, or
they'd want me to make records for that awful phonograph.

(L. Frank Baum, *The Patchwork Girl of Oz*)

How do you say I love you to an answering machine?

(The Replacements, from the album *Let It Be*)

'We're all on tape,' says a character in Don DeLillo's novel *Americana*:
'All on tape. All of us.' From time immemorial, images—paintings,
statues, and more recently photo or film—have been used as
replacements for the physical presence of the subject, a substitute in
the absence of the body. The recorded voice, however, has a more
problematic status. This is not due only to the fact that recording is a
much more recent technology than painting or drawing. It also
depends on the intrinsic link of voice, body, and movement. While the
image is by definition other than the body it represents, the voice, like
the shadow, is perceived as a product, an issue of the body itself,
inseparable from it even though it moves outward.

The different perception of image and recording is neatly summar-
ized by the British pop group Depeche Mode: 'the map represents you
and the tape is your voice' ('Protographic', from the album *Speak and
Spell*). In other words, while the relationship between the graphic sign
and the subject is metaphoric (based on analogy), that between the
voice and the subject is metonymic (the voice is part of the subject).
The graphic image retains the distancing implicit in the concept of
representation, whereas the recorded voice appears as the thing itself: a
recording is not a representation of the voice, but the voice itself.

Therefore, the presence of the voice leads to expect the presence of the body, of the speaking subject, a sensation reinforced by the fact that sound is deployed in time, and therefore evokes motion, action, presence—if only to remove it. Like the shadow (or the soul: 'spirit' is semantically linked to 'breath') detached from physical bodies, recorded voices can evoke a sense of unreality; although recording is by now a taken-for-granted aspect of our technological soundscape (and the intrinsic tool of oral historians), yet the bodiless voices it conveys retain uncanny potential undertones.

Being on tape as metaphor of the unreality of contemporary life is a frequent motif among modern and especially post-modern authors. Pedro Pietri, one of the most outstanding poetic voices of the New York Puerto Rican diaspora, uses the recorded voice constantly as a metaphor of non-life. In one of his poems ('Do Not Observe the Non-Smoking Sign'), a recorded message unanswerably repeats contradictory, double-binding orders, representing both the schizophrenic condition of immigrants and aliens, and the poet's obsessive need to re-establish communication with the lost, the departed, the dead. At the other end of New York's ethnic range, the minimalist writer David Leavitt (in a story called 'Spouse Evening') describes a dog sitting by a radio 'surrounded by a comforting wave of half-human noise' (his master's voice?) near a hospital bed in which a woman lies voiceless. On the night table is a tape recorder with a note: 'Hello, I'm Claire'— as if the machine had vampirized her name, as well as her voice— 'Please turn over the tape in my tape deck.'

Examples could multiply. From a regional and feminist viewpoint, the Kentucky poet George Ella Lyon compares the vivid reality of local voices based on experience with the artificiality of televised voices ('Walter Cronkite's accent') and the arid lifelessness of impersonal, subjectless discourse metaphorically identified with recordings: 'We might as well seek truth from the telephone computer which tells us "the number is . . ." or expect welcome from the Atlanta airport simulated guide, "You are entering the People mover. There will be no food or drink beyond this point" '—as if the recorded voice were ushering travellers into the world of the dead.

The answering machine is a peculiarly disturbing object in this paradigm. While the telephone always conveys voices away from the physical presence of the speaker, yet the wires ensure a physical, almost tangible connection. Most of all, precisely because it conveys only voices, the telephone is an intrinsically dialogic means of communication. The answering machine, however, while imperiously commanding one to speak, does not listen. It is, in this sense, the epitome of the unidirectional quality of electronic media; 'the common trait of these mediatic voices', Paul Zumthor writes, 'is that they do not admit of an answer.' In the novel *The Death of Jim Loney*, by the Native American author James Welch, the hero tries to connect with his sister, calling her long-distance. First he gets an operator, but then his sister's voice comes on: 'This is Katherine Loney. I will be out of town until Friday the twenty-third of December.' He tries to speak to her ('And Loney said, "Kate?" ') but all he gets is a continuation of the message, until the operator tells him 'I'm afraid she's not in . . . That was a recording.'

The separation of voice and body represented by recordings can be viewed, however, in more than one way. After all, the separation of soul/shadow and body indicates death, but also eternal life. This ambivalence can be detected, for instance, in the works of the Canadian author Margaret Atwood. In *Cat's Cradle*, for instance, when a character's call is answered by the 'disembodied voice' of a machine, the narrator goes on to comment: '[It was] an angel voice wafting through the air. If I died this minute it would go on like that, placid and helpful, like an electronic afterlife.' Perhaps the machine is so indifferent to death because it was never alive to begin with (it is a secretary's voice, a metaphor of the alienation of women's work in this society); perhaps, on the other hand, it represents the voice's and the soul's ability to overcome death. In another Atwood novel, *The Handmaid's Tale*, the heroine who vanishes from a male chauvinist dystopia leaves behind—for historians to find generations later—not the proverbial manuscript, but a set of cassette tapes. In this case, the heroine's voice, taped and transcribed to become the novel's fictional source, represents the fact that—beyond oppression, exclusion (even from the written record), and even beyond death,—the voice lives on to tell the tale. The tapes are a metaphor of women's memory, and perhaps of the memory of the oppressed in general, which lives on even after both they and their oppressors have vanished. Thus, the non-life of the monologic answering machine is balanced by the eternal life of recordings as metaphors of memory.

This is implicit in the wonderful metaphor chosen by Philippe Joutard as the title of his book on oral history, *Ces voix qui nous viennent du passé*, these voices which reach us out of the past. It is a very disturbing metaphor if one looks at it twice, because until sound recording came along the only voices that could reach us out of the past were those of ghosts. Several novels, indeed, do make the connection between ghosts and recordings. In Lee Smith's aptly titled *Oral History*, the young heroine is working on a paper for her oral history class, and tries to tape the voices of dead ancestors who are said to be still audible at times in the haunted family house in the Appalachian mountains. Inasmuch as it contains voices from the past, every oral history archive is a haunted house.

Another metaphor, even more intriguing, is found in a book by Ann Rice, which I happened to pick up during an oral history conference in Baltimore, because I was attracted by its title: *Interview with the Vampire*. I had often been bothered by the sense that, in fieldwork, I was somehow vampirizing my sources, sucking the voice, pouring it into my tape, storing it in my cellar, appropriating it in many different ways. But it had never occurred to me to think of interviewees as vampires themselves, speaking through me, nesting within my own voice. None of these problems is present in Rice's book, which does, however, open with a typical interview setting: the student interviewer is checking the batteries, and the vampire Lestat asks him: 'How much tape did you bring? Enough for the story of a life?' A very good question: for one thing, a vampire's life is very, very long (in this case, it begins in 1780); for another, is it life? Can we correctly speak of 'life history' in this case?

Unfortunately, Rice does not develop the possibilities of her wonderful idea at all. After the first two pages, the interviewer disappears, and the story is just a first-person monologic narrative. We never hear the interviewer asking questions; we don't even see him as he sits there listening or interrupts the vampire to change the batteries or turn the tape. Taping turns out to be just a modernized version of dictation, and Rice misses the opportunity to connect the vampire's undead existence after death with the metaphoric implications of the recorded voice.

Another image of survival after death—in the paradigm of Rice's vampire and Atwood's angel—is that of metempsychosis, which Alice Walker proceeds to connect to the recorded voice in *The Temple of My Familiar*. This very ambitious novel is about a woman who has been reincarnated continuously since the beginning of time, again a metaphor of women's power to survive and change. Again, when she disappears, she leaves behind a tape, from which her voice issues 'deeper and weaker, older than [the listener] remembered'. And the question she asks, and answers, is: 'What does not end? Only life itself, in my experience.'

The recorded voice, then, becomes an ambiguous gateway between life and death. While an image—a dead relative's photograph, for instance—evokes that person's memory, the recorded voice evokes the presence. The speaking person is both there and not there, both living and vanished, both physical vibrations of air waves, and ghost of absence and void. Nowhere is this ambivalence more perceptible than in the recording industry, with its contrast between instant consumption of ephemeral, quickly forgotten hits on the one hand and a technology of preservation and permanence of sounds and voices on the other.

The best example of this double play with recording and death is a recent hit by Natalie Cole, the daughter of the great pianist and singer Nat 'King' Cole. Natalie has recorded an album of her dead father's songs, a standard homage to the memory of an illustrious parent. However, because the songs had been recorded, Nat 'King' Cole's voice is not only remembered, but also physically and directly available. In one track of her album, thanks to advanced technology, Natalie manages therefore to sing a duet with her dead father: recording enables us not only to listen to the voices that reach us out of the past, but actually sing along with them. The song Natalie Cole selected for this uncanny revival is, aptly, 'Unforgettable'.

This article is partly based on sections of a book tentatively entitled *The Voice beneath the Text: Orality, Writing and Democracy in American Literature* (Colombia University Press, forthcoming).

Alessandro Portelli will be Special Editor of volume five of the *Yearbook*, on the theme of genre and narrative.

BOOKS FOR REVIEW and review correspondence should be sent to Selma Leydesdorff, Belle van Zuylen Ondersoeks Instituut, Rokin 84–90, 1012 KX Amsterdam, The Netherlands.

OFFERS OF PAPERS and editorial correspondence to Paul Thompson, 18 Lonsdale Road, Oxford OX2 7EW, England.

SUBSCRIPTION ENQUIRIES to Oxford University Press, Walton Street, Oxford OX2 6DP, England.

THEMES OF FUTURE VOLUMES: III, migration and identity; IV, gender, public and private memory; V, genre and narrative.